OH RIO!

WENSLEY CLARKSON

OH RIO!

THE BIOGRAPHY OF ENGLAND'S MASTER DEFENDER

JOHN BLAKE

Published by John Blake Publishing Ltd,
3, Bramber Court, 2 Bramber Road,
London W14 9PB, England

www.blake.co.uk

This edition first published in paperback in 2006

ISBN 1 84454 228 9

British Library Cataloguing-in-Publication Data:

A catalogue record for this book is available from the British Library.

Design by www.envydesign.co.uk

Printed in Great Britain by Bookmarque

1 3 5 7 9 10 8 6 4 2

Papers used by John Blake Publishing are natural, recyclable products made from
wood grown in sustainable forests. The manufacturing processes conform to the
environmental regulations of the country of origin.

Pictures reproduced by kind permission of Rex Features, Scope Features,
Empics, Cleva Media, Getty, News International, MSI.

Every attempt has been made to contact the relevant copyright holders, but some
were unobtainable. We would be grateful if the appropriate people could contact us.

The publishers wish to make clear that Rio Ferdinand has in no way
authorised the contents of this book.

CONTENTS

'Money, money, money, money, money; that's all I ever hear in this house. Manny, look at the pelican fly – come on, pelican.'

THE PSYCHOTIC TONY MONTANA, PLAYED BY AL PACINO IN SCARFACE (1983), RIO'S ALL-TIME FAVOURITE MOVIE

'When I'm 35, old and knackered, I hope I'll be able to hear someone say, "You see that kid there? He's going to be as good as Rio Ferdinand one day."'

RIO FERDINAND, 2002

'RIO' – THE WORLD CUP 2002 REMIX

During the 2002 World Cup, fans in Japan adapted the lyrics of Duran Duran's classic song 'Rio' to show their appreciation of the man's superb performances during the tournament.

Moving on the pitch now, babe, you're a legend in your time
In your England shirt, you're looking in your prime
With a step to your left and a flick to your right
You pass the ball to Becks
Sven knows you're something special, that's why
you're playing with the best.

CHORUS
His name is Rio and he dances on the pitch
When his name's called the opposition start to twitch
And when he plays he really gives it all he can
He's on the ball, his name is Rio Ferdinand.

I've seen you on the pitch and I've seen you on TV
Cost 18 million quid, you usually play for Leeds
On a Saturday and the midweek too
You're worth the dough because you know just what to do.

CHORUS
His name is Rio and he dances on the pitch
When his name's called the opposition start to twitch
And when he plays he really gives it all he can
He's on the ball, his name is Rio Ferdinand.

Hey now – wow – look at that
Did he nearly run you down?
At the end of the line, the goal's in sight
Line up the ball and score, and score, and score!
Just take your chance cause the nation's on your side
I'll tell you something, we think we can win it
The team's a sure thing, if Rio is in it.

CHORUS
His name is Rio and he dances on the pitch
When his name's called the opposition start to twitch
And when he plays he really gives it all he can
He's on the ball, his name is Rio Ferdinand.

INTRODUCTION

'Taking care of business' was the catchphrase used by many of the dodgier characters on the council estate where Rio Ferdinand was born and bred. The story of how he survived in that dangerous environment is as remarkable as his meteoric climb to the top of the football world.

For while this is primarily a book about one of the most exciting footballers on earth, I hope it also provides the reader with some answers about Rio's precarious existence before and since he made it. It may not reveal all of Rio's most secret or outrageous thoughts, but it is the first-ever account of his life and fantastic voyage from ghetto boy to World Cup hero.

Who is the man behind the public face? Whence comes his love of life's luxuries, his extraordinary ambition to succeed? How is it possible for someone from such humble beginnings to cope with superstardom while still in his teens?

I have spoken to many people in London and across England who know him well. One of his best friends, Leon Simms, summed him up: 'Rio's the coolest dude around. He knows how to make people laugh but there's a serious side to him. He gets what he wants.'

Rio's friends agreed to talk because they all respected and adored him. I spent many hours interviewing people from his childhood to find out the real truth about his impoverished background and his relationship with the two most influential people in his life – his mother and father. Many were convinced that Rio would appreciate my intentions in bringing this book to a wide audience. Their decision to sanction my efforts deserves my heartfelt thanks. I sincerely hope the book reflects the warm feelings for Rio that stretch from the world of football right into the mean streets of south-east London.

Another vital source was Rio's brilliant performances on football pitches across the globe. They tell us so much about his life that they provided the thread I needed to sew the narrative together. So here you have it: an extraordinary blend of two lives that collided to produce one of the most talented sportsmen of his generation.

Wensley Clarkson
April 2006

PROLOGUE

July 2002 and everyone was waiting with bated breath for the post-World Cup transfer bonanza. Surely this would be the moment when numerous new young stars of world football achieved their dream moves after performing in the ultimate shop window of Japan and Korea.

But in the weeks following the end of the tournament, and with the countdown to the new season already under way, the exact opposite trend began emerging – clubs throughout Europe had suddenly turned into the ultimate caution brokers.

Gone were the days of vast profits and healthy club bank balances. In their place came mounting debts, combined with inflated salaries. Even the most ambitious clubs were starting to feel the pinch, leaving fans across Europe frustrated by the lack of transfer activity.

In Italy, clubs were swamped with vast debts. In France,

respected giants such as Marseille and Nice were close to folding and even Paris Saint-Germain, bankrolled by media giants Canal Plus, were fighting to stay afloat. Germany's 36 professional clubs had been hit badly by a TV deal which collapsed. They were all being asked by their banks to provide guarantees to cover any projected future losses.

In Switzerland, three clubs were denied licences for the new season, while in Austria league champions FC Tirol were in the extraordinary position of having qualified for the Champions League while being relegated because they couldn't provide sufficient evidence of solvency.

The 72 Nationwide League clubs in England's lower divisions spent a total of around £3 million on transfers. In the summer of 2001 they'd splashed out £25 million. In the Premiership the figure dropped from more than £50 million in 2001 to £25 million during this close season.

And if there was little money going out, there was much less coming into the Football League via the transfer market. In the summer of 2001, clubs took in £47 million, mainly in the Premiership. This year the figure was under £20 million.

Gordon Taylor, chief executive of the Professional Footballers Association (PFA), said: 'The shame is that in quantity terms there has never been so much money in the game but the trouble is the distribution is so unequal. The top clubs say they can't give up any more money because they have to compete with the best in Europe. Many smaller clubs will be wondering if they can stay alive or will have to go part-time. But no club should spend money they don't have.'

The PFA covered wages for around 12 Football League clubs last season and Taylor believes the public are unaware of the plight of those players who are not household names. 'Nobody appreciates how vulnerable and insecure a footballer is on a 12-month contract at the lower end of the scale,' he said.

Into this uncertain future stepped Rio Ferdinand – football's £33-million wonderboy. Not even a catastrophic slump in the world's football marketplace could stop him becoming the most expensive defender on the globe.

But how did he get there?

Chapter 1

SOME MOTHERS DO 'AVE 'EM

St Luke's Church on the Friary Estate, in Peckham, south-east London. The rusting fridges and mangled bikes formed a line around both the front and back entrances. Muggings, burglaries and violence were a feature of daily life. People rarely ventured out at night because they were terrified they might encounter one of the many gangs of youths who patrolled the area. At the only shop on the estate the owner had metal shutters over the windows, but they were regularly prised open.

Peckham had been branded an inner-city ghetto for years. It was full of lock-ups and crack factories, of joyless estates where the police dared not tread, where milk was delivered from armoured floats and postmen did their rounds in pairs. The air was thick with the noise and smell of diesel-fuelled HGVs in the seemingly never-ending traffic jams on the A2, the main road from London through Kent to the Channel ports.

More than 70 per cent of the inhabitants of the Friary Estate were from ethnic minorities – West Indian, Vietnamese, Turkish, Somali, West African. Bizarrely, the entire place was connected to neighbouring estates by badly lit walkways. Anonymous passers-by wandered from one estate to the other, mugging, robbing, raping and vandalising as they went, then escaped by one of 49 access points. To an outsider, the estate was a total no-go zone. By day and night it remained largely deserted. Random aggression was rife and few would ever ask a stranger into their home. Only the very foolish were desperate enough to negotiate their way through the maze.

Pregnant teenager Janice Lavender knew within days of arriving on the Friary Estate that any son of hers would need constant supervision if he was going to stay out of trouble. All boys needed watching, cajoling and hauling into line. Only responsible, caring parents stood a chance of seeing their kids survive this environment.

Residents often found flick-knives on the tarmac, discarded during a fight the previous night, or empty wallets taken in random muggings. Low-rise blocks like the one Janice was about to make her home were drab and crumbling, creating a menacing sprawl as they merged into other estates. Although built just ten years earlier in 1968, the Friary Estate had rapidly decayed and was deemed by many to be *the* classic example of inner-city deprivation.

Children as young as eight were regularly hauled off local buses and trains for 'steaming' other passengers to steal their wallets. Some kids would press-gang weaker children into acts of spitefulness against even weaker children. Many of these kids were not yet 10 years old but boasted of carrying knives; others flashed their knuckledusters.

Janice Lavender moved into a block called Gisburn

House, a grim four storey, red brick council tenement building which overlooked some rusting cars and a couple of burned-out white Transit vans. Many of the occupants of Gisburn House were aimless young males, a large percentage of whom had fallen into a life of crime and drugs.

The flat on the estate which would become Rio Ferdinand's home for the first 18 years of his life was up four flights of narrow, dirty, urine-infested stairs. Its red-framed front door was secured behind black metal bars. The flat was small, with threadbare carpet, sparse furniture, scratched and battered, the walls badly in need of a new coat of paint. The cramped second bedroom contained just a bed. Lack of wardrobe space meant that clothes had to be hung from door frames. But for Rio it would become a place of comfort and safety, an escape from the fear that came with running the gauntlet through the estate.

But none of these conditions fazed Janice Lavender. She was one of 11 children whose Irish mother left home when she was young, and she was determined her own kids wouldn't suffer the same fate. 'My dad did a wonderful job in bringing us up but I can never remember being spoiled,' she recalled.

Janice left home at 15 and took a job at Top Shop in Oxford Street, in London's West End, to help pay the rent on her bedsit. When she was just 17 she got pregnant after starting a relationship with St Lucia-born Julian Ferdinand, whose family had arrived in Britain from the Caribbean in 1958. Julian's mother, Angelina, worked as a nurse at St Bart's Hospital in London. One day Janice met a girl at Top Shop who told her about a river in Jamaica called the Rio Grande, which means 'great river'. As Janice later explained: 'I knew immediately that was the name I wanted for my baby.'

November 1978 will be mainly remembered in history for

the mass suicide, or murder, of 913 people in Jonestown, Guyana. Since then there have been rumours of CIA involvement in the tragedy. Some even believe CIA agents posing as members of the People's Temple cult were gathering information in Guyana. But what is known for sure is that on 18 November cult leader Jim Jones ordered more than 900 of his followers to drink cyanide-poisoned punch. He then told guards to shoot anyone who refused or tried to escape. Among the dead were more than 270 children.

It was into this uncertain world that Janice's baby boy was born at King's College Hospital, Camberwell, south London, on 7 November 1978. He was almost named Gavin but his mother Janice and father Julian both preferred Rio, so Gavin became his middle name. The young parents never married, and for Janice: 'It was a big shock to come home with Rio. That tiny two-bedroom flat on the fourth floor was freezing. And back in those days it was quite a thing that Rio's dad was black and I was white.'

The racist bigots of the National Front were still active at that time and there was a lot of animosity shown to Janice and her tiny, milky-coffee-coloured baby. 'There was one particular person who would call us names – but as a woman with a baby, what do you do? There was me, this white woman, with a black child. I was so proud of him and I wanted him to look perfect every minute.'

Janice and her sister Carol adored walking around Peckham with Rio and Carol's son Ben in a double baby buggy. Janice explained: 'Ben is white with ginger hair – people's faces were a picture. Rio soon became a local celebrity even back then.'

The teenage mum was shown the ropes of estate life by single parents Sharon McEwan from Grenada and Dallas Gopie from Guyana. Janice remembered: 'At the end of a week when we didn't have much food or money left we'd pool together and feed the kids with something – rice, chicken, anything that was cheap.'

Janice and Dallas often took their sons Rio and Lawrence on outings to local parks and museums. 'You don't have to have money to support your children,' said Dallas. 'You just need to give them your time and your love, and Janice was very good at that.' And Janice was always saying to her friend, 'My Rio is going places. You mark my words.'

As soon as she could return to her job as a credit controller at Top Shop, Janice got little Rio into a nearby nursery school. She was determined to be a good role model to her son. 'I wanted my kids to know there's a big world out there with lots of things to do – but you have to work hard to get there. It was about Rio seeing that you have to work hard to make a better life for yourself.'

Janice eventually became a childminder so that she could keep earning a living but spend more time with Rio. Any spare cash soon went on sending her sports-mad son on after-school activities and even occasional holidays. There was a sports shop in Peckham called Mark One, where Janice would take Rio. 'The lady knew my situation and used to take us through to the cheap section we could afford. I always said to Rio, "It's not what you've got, it's what you do with it."' Rio's first holiday was when he was five and the family went to the Isle of Sheppey in Kent and stayed in a friend's chalet. 'We didn't have any money but still had lots of fun on the beach,' he recalled.

When Rio was about six years old, his mum Janice took him to see mighty Liverpool take on Millwall at the Den, just a few minutes away from the Friary Estate. 'It was the most wicked thing in my life,' is how Rio remembered it.

'The crowd was noisy. The players seemed like gods out there. I was drawn right into it.' Rio elevated Liverpool's John Barnes to the status of superhero as his goal helped the Reds scrape through 2–1.

That trip to the Den sparked Rio's obsession with football and he was soon kicking a ball around on the two concrete playgrounds at his junior school, Camelot Primary, in Peckham. There wasn't enough money available for a grass pitch. Rio's old headmistress, Joye Manyan, recalled: 'He was a tall lad and would play football whenever he was allowed to. He scored goals back then, too.' Keith Tewkesbury, facilities manager at Camelot Primary, had similar memories: 'Rio was always kicking a ball about and sometimes he would be out in the playground on his own just practising.'

In class, Rio proved to have a lively sense of humour and a good grasp of maths. 'I remember seeing him take care of a complicated question about fractions when he was just six. His mental arithmetic was good,' added Mrs Manyan, who described Rio's mum Janice as 'a very determined lady. She knew what she wanted for her children and didn't let anything get in her way. She could have made excuses, but she never did. She was a proud, decent woman.'

Most afternoons after school, Rio went for another kick-about with kids and their mums in the nearby park, just yards from a procession of drug dealers plying their goods to local youths. No one hung around in the evening because the area was renowned for street robberies.

Sometimes, if it was still light, Rio would turn a piece of balding grass in front of Gisburn House into his own imaginary Wembley Stadium. 'I'd charge around the place with an imaginary voice saying in my ear, "And it's another great pass from Ferdinand under the Twin Towers ..."'

When Rio was just seven years old he was transfixed by the England football team's progress in the 1986 World Cup in Mexico. And when it came to the side's controversial quarter-final clash with Argentina, he still rates Maradona's second goal after his 'Hand of God' effort as the best goal ever.

The Argentinian's jinking run past Peter Reid, Gary Stevens, Terry Butcher and Terry Fenwick, before slotting the ball behind Peter Shilton, made such an impression on the youngster that he went straight back outside to the playground with his pals and tried to recreate the same magic. 'That was the first World Cup I remember. You have got to admire Maradona's skill. I'd have liked to have played against him to see how good he was in the flesh, but you can't have everything.'

On the cracked and dirty concrete playground behind his home, Rio's obsession with Maradona often ended in disappointment. 'Most of my mates were older than me and used to get first pick of who they wanted to be in the playground so there were may times when I didn't get to be Maradona. I can remember being Craig Johnson of Liverpool – which was OK because he was a good player – and also Des Walker because people thought I looked like him, but not being Maradona really cheesed me off.'

It was around this time that Rio first started thinking seriously about being a professional footballer. Often he and his mates would sit down after a kick-around and talk about who they'd most like to be. 'We used to wish we could do the things they could and then try them out. I'd sit there daydreaming about it all.'

Rio formed a close attachment to his granny Angelina Ferdinand, who lived in a two-bedroomed terraced house just a few minutes' walk from the Friary Estate. She recalled:

'I made Rio Caribbean delicacies and told him stories about my childhood in St Lucia. Rio had a real sweet tooth and I loved making him biscuits as well.' He listened wide-eyed to his granny's stories, which included one tale about how a huge storm ripped the roof off her house in St Lucia when she was a little girl. Rio often kicked a football about on the green outside Angelina's home with her husband Raymond, and one time he narrowly missed thumping a ball through her front window.

But football wasn't so popular with Rio's dad, Julian, who, although he never married Janice, remained very close to his son and was a strong influence throughout his early childhood. (Rio's younger brother Anton was born when Rio was six.) Julian encouraged Rio to take up gymnastics at school. Julian also believed his son had great potential as an athlete. On 23 October 1987 Rio – then aged almost nine – was awarded a British Amateur Gymnastics Association Class Two certificate.

Rio also did ballet at school, but when he was nine and a half he and his dad were called in and told he would have to cut down on the dancing and gymnastics because he was growing so quickly some of his ligaments couldn't cope with the sort of movements required. 'If they tried to stretch him it would do him harm,' Julian explained, adding that Rio was heartbroken to have to quit gymnastics and was upset for weeks. 'So we took him out of ballet school and got him to do what he wanted because he was the kind of kid who could achieve what he wanted.' That meant playing even more football.

When Rio was at junior school, Janice was a very active parent and encouraged him to go and see his teacher whenever there were problems with classmates. Sometimes those insults had definite racial undertones, which seemed a sad reflection of the prejudices of the parents. But Rio rarely complained to his teacher. He was a smart, savvy, streetwise kid from an early age and had seen first hand what happened to kids who got lippy with other kids – they got a beating. He'd always walked away from confrontational situations without raising a fist, but that didn't mean he wasn't deeply offended by the bigoted attitudes of others.

Occasionally Rio would sit down with local white kids and try to change their racist views, but most of them simply looked blankly at him because they were too ignorant to know any better. Janice told him there was nothing wrong with being a different colour, a different religion. Rio knew his mum was right and he always kept her words of advice in the back of his mind.

But the driving force behind Rio's search for a better life went beyond adoring football. Now, looking back on those childhood days, he admits: 'I always wanted to be a footballer but, to be honest about it, I wanted to make big money – and, most of all, I wanted to be famous. I wanted to be a singer – still do – an actor, a dancer and a gymnast. Whatever, I wanted to be famous.'

However, after being advised to quit gymnastics to concentrate on football, Rio became even more focused. 'When I decided that was the thing to do, I became quite scared that I wouldn't make it. It was a pride thing. Even now, when everyone is telling me I've made it, I can't think of it like that.' So, initially, the young boy who was to go on to such dizzy heights was suffering from anxiety and a lack of self-confidence.

For the following couple of years, Rio played in the Blackheath and District Schools League. When he was 11 his skills were recognised by his uncle, Dave Raynor, who ran a Sunday-morning under-12s football team called Bloomfield Athletic, in Peckham. 'He was a natural,' Raynor said. 'I didn't even have to teach him football, I just guided him. He knew how to read the game.'

Rio also caught the attention of Dave Goodwin, who ran the Blackheath and District Schools League. Goodwin knew how valuable football was to the community because sports were one of the few activities that could keep youngsters away from bigger temptations like drugs and crime. He still believes: 'If you have something you want to do in life, if you have a goal, you can't afford to do silly things like go out late, smoking and drinking and doing drugs.'

Goodwin's reaction to young Rio's talents was instantaneous: 'I first saw Rio at 11 in a trial and already he looked like a seasoned pro. There were three main things that stuck out – his ability to pass the ball, the sheer vision he displayed and the way he organised a midfield.'

Naturally, Janice was there at most games to urge her son on. 'I knew all the rules because I'd been a Millwall supporter since I was a kid. My role was always shouting really loud from the sidelines. Lots of people came scouting and they all said what a great player Rio was – but I thought people would think I was biased if I agreed.'

Chapter 2

'REE-OOH! REE-OOH!'

Just before his twelfth birthday, Rio started attending Bluecoat Comprehensive School in Blackheath. Located just off a pokey backstreet and hidden behind a Shell petrol station, it was just two minutes up the road from unfashionable Charlton Athletic. Rio learned many of his basic soccer skills on the field next to the sadly neglected school sports hut.

That dilapidated hut, with its rusting radiators, crumbling, graffiti-covered walls and communal showers that were nearly always out of action, was where Rio and his teammates were expected to get changed for every home game. But they preferred to get changed at the school, and then walk 20 minutes through the south-east London streets to the playing field for a match.

Angela Rezki, Rio's sports tutor throughout much of his time at Bluecoat, remembers clearly: 'Rio was so talented and we all knew he would make it at football even though he was a bit of a Jack the Lad and fancied himself a bit.' She noticed that he knocked around with a group of rowdy older boys and for a while many people at the school feared that he could end up dealing drugs on the streets. 'He got into a bit of trouble, like all kids do, but his mum kept him on the straight and narrow. Rio did get a few severe tellings-off and got detention for forgetting to bring his kit. The rest of the kids took the mickey out of him, but he didn't like having to stay late after school, so he didn't make the same mistake again.'

At Bluecoat, Rio's amazing natural ball skills helped the U-12s side win the Metropolitan Police's five-a-side competition in 1989. Striker Yung Chu is in no doubt that 'Rio was always the star and the reason we had so much success'.

At that time the school team's other big 'talent' was Tony Russell, who went on to do youth training with Rio at West Ham, although he was eventually released. Rio and Tony stood out and would run rings round the opposition, according to their teammates.

PE teacher Matt Delaney, who ran the team, recalled: 'We didn't have a minibus, so everyone used to pile in the back of my VW camper for away games. Rio was a naturally gifted player, so he was a coach's dream and he was very serious about training.' Another Bluecoat teammate, Andrew Ashley, described Rio as 'a cool chap, a bit of a comedian. We always knew he was going to do well and I'm proud to have played alongside him.'

Soon Rio's performances at weekends for his uncle and Dave Goodwin's Blackheath and District Schools League were the talk of the area. Here was a tall, awkward midfielder capable of some fine trickery on the ball. Scouts

from some of the London clubs started turning up at
matches. Local coach and league organiser Dave Goodwin
encouraged Rio to talk to them all, but told him not to
jump at the first offer. 'Dave became the biggest influence
on my career. In terms of advice and encouragement, he
and his family were really good to me.'

Rio also played for a Sunday-morning outfit called Eltham
Town, whose coach Paul Caldwell explained: 'The thing
about Rio which was very unusual is that, apart from being
the best player by far, he also had the best attitude. Normally,
if you get the really skilful players, they can let it go to their
heads and they think they are God's gift at a young age –
that's when they fall down. But Rio was never like that and I
don't think he will ever become that way, either.'

Before long Rio noticed that although the teams he
played for were made up mainly of black kids, they nearly
always found themselves playing predominantly white
sides. A lot of the dads would come down from the pubs
after lunch to cheer on their kids, but the problem was that
many of them started talking about 'black this' and 'black
that'. Rio had heard all sorts of insults on the streets of
Peckham, but it seemed even more out of order to hear
them on a football pitch. He tried to blank out all the
insults and then say to himself, 'Yes, I'm black and proud of
it.' But there were certainly times when he was tempted to
lash out at the bigots.

Back at home, trouble was looming. Rio's mum Janice was
notorious on the Friary Estate for always having her finger
on the pulse. Every evening around 6.30 she'd walk out of
her front door, lean over the balcony and start hollering
across the estate: 'REE-OOH! REE-OOH!'

A brief period of silence would follow then Rio would tell

27

his mates he had to go. 'Come on, Rio,' one of them would often plead. Rio would then hesitate.

'REE-OOH! REE-OOH!'

By the time he'd heard Janice's voice for the fourth time, Rio knew he had no choice and would scarper off in her direction. But one evening he got a bit rebellious and didn't answer his mum's rallying call. 'Then my dad came for me. We could see him walking through the estate, my mates were going, "Oh no, Rio, there's your dad. Oh my God, your dad."

'I saw my dad and, when he saw me, he just turned back towards home. He knew I would follow. You can imagine what happened when I got home. But if it wasn't for Mum and Dad, maybe things would have gone a bit different.'

Rio has never denied that he got a few clouts at home. He looked on it as part of growing up in that tough environment and believes to this day that a few clips round the ear did him more good than harm in the long run.

As Janice herself explained: 'I didn't want Rio leaving the estate and if he wanted to go anywhere he would have to ask. I didn't want him hanging around on corners getting into trouble. Some nights his friends would try and hide him from me but he always did as he was told when he heard my footsteps. It is about respect and he probably appreciates that now.'

Rio puts it this way: 'I have a very strong family and when I was younger they kept me under wraps. Looking back, that's been great for me. I've grown up with some good mates and there's no way any of them would let me get too cocky.'

Rio's dad, Julian, also encouraged his son's interest in the arts, particularly drama. 'Mum and Dad kept telling me about how many doors were going to open to me,' Rio recalled. 'They were afraid of me getting in with the wrong crowd and going down the wrong road.' Rio loved being the centre of attention, so acting was a natural development.

It was certainly true that Rio was hanging around with a much older, tougher crowd of youths, many of whom had already broken the law on numerous occasions. But Rio remains convinced to this day that 'my mates were good, they kind of protected me; they smoked but they wouldn't let me smoke, and if they were going off the estate to do, like, bad kind of stuff, they tried to leave me behind'. It's likely that 'bad kind of stuff' meant burglaries and muggings.

The arguments between disciplinarian Janice and Rio sometimes reduced the youngster to tears. But he admitted: 'Those rules were for my own good. My parents never said to me, "Don't smoke. Don't take drugs." They just left that to me. Still, if I had tried it, I'd have had to answer to my dad. But there was never anything in it for me. I was always so into sport I couldn't understand why you'd do something that wasn't good for your body.'

One night not long after his twelfth birthday Rio and his six-year-old brother Anton were tucked up in their bunk beds when their parents started one of their regular shouting matches. Rio lay there trembling as the yelling got louder and louder. Anton was fast asleep on the bottom bed. Rio's dad sounded completely out of control. He heard his mum dashing out of the lounge. The old man was on her tail, towering over her.

He seemed like a giant to Rio back then. Rio heard them start ranting and raving at each other again. Then Julian turned around and walked towards the bedroom. The flat went deathly quiet. A few moments later he emerged from the bedroom with a sports bag in his hand. 'I gotta go, I've had enough,' he told Rio's mum, who was standing hands on hips watching him from the kitchen doorway. Rio stood back and observed the scene. He cried himself to sleep that night but made sure no one saw his tears. That was Rio's way of dealing with things – however painful they might be.

The truth is, Rio's mum and dad hadn't really got on for years. These days they're friends. 'You gotta remember he was a young dad with lots of kids,' Rio pointed out. 'The pressure must have been unbearable in many ways.' A few days later Julian came round to tell his two sons exactly what had happened and why he'd left, but it didn't make it any easier to handle.

Janice was determined to keep her kids on the rails. Young Rio was about to hit his teens and it was essential he avoided trouble if he was going to work his way out of the ghetto. Rio has never explained the precise reasons behind his dad's departure but he did say: 'My dad said it would only be for a while. But I knew he was lying and that he wouldn't be coming back. I heard my parents arguing, but I pretended I didn't hear. I cried by myself. I didn't show how sad I was. I wanted them to stay together for ever.'

Growing up on one of the toughest council estates in Europe was never going to be easy for Rio. At school he still got picked on a lot because of his mixed-race background and appearance. A few black kids hated him as much as the white ones because he simply didn't fit in. But Rio ignored the tension and made an effort to get along with everyone, whatever their colour, race, creed or opinions, which helped him thrive in that tough environment.

Janice was, and still is, a strong woman and she went out of her way to educate Rio, especially since she was now a lone parent. She'd say things like, 'You may look different from some of the other kids but you're just the same inside and don't you forget it.'

As one of Rio's classmates said: 'It wasn't easy for kids like Rio. Some kids called him a "bounty", which meant he was black on the outside and white on the inside and all that really hurt.' In fact this was untrue because Rio was immensely proud of his black heritage and in his usual way he shrugged off the name-calling. It made him and his mum even more determined he'd find a route out of the ghetto.

When Rio sang as a chorister at Bluecoat it prompted even more insults, especially after he performed a solo in a carol service one Christmas at St John's Church in Blackheath. But Rio had a potent secret weapon. 'Rio's good with words,' says one of his oldest friends, Leon Simms. 'The guy knows how to survive because of what happened when he was a kid. He could always talk his way out of any trouble.' As Rio grew up he learned to parry the taunts and criticism from other kids. He could handle anything the bullies threw at him and it seemed to make him a stronger person as a result.

But there were times when he felt genuinely scared once he was outside the perimeter of the Friary Estate. He was frightened by what might lie around the next corner. That's when he encountered the police, local white and Asian gangs and lots of temptations, like drugs and crime.

He was disturbed, too, by the sheer weight of hatred against people of his colour and poverty, and promised himself he would never pass on those prejudices to his own kids. But as a result of that inner fear, Rio tended to stick to his own little patch near the estate and rarely wandered beyond it. That caused a few problems as he grew older because many of his best friends refused to venture out into the big, wide world and mingle with people of all colours, races and creeds. He noticed that some of those same friends carried the scars of racism into adulthood.

Rio's ability to get on with his life undoubtedly stemmed from the collision of his parents' genes and the fact he was carefully nurtured through a difficult environment. 'My parents used to build us up. I was called Rio because they wanted me to be an individual. They made us think we were the best; not the best in an ignorant way but that we had talent and we should use it. They told us not to be scared to try things and we're not. But the bottom line for them was that nobody was ever better than us and we weren't to accept anything else.'

One night Janice was fearful for Rio's safety after her customary shouts of 'Ree-ooh! Ree-ooh!' got no response around the estate. There had been a spate of vicious muggings by gangs of older youths in recent weeks and the parents of all younger kids were being extra vigilant. So Janice began roaming the shadowy, badly lit estate trying to find her beloved Rio. Eventually she bumped into one of his friends who told her that he was 'at Ahmed's house'.

Janice takes up the story: 'And sure enough there he was, watching a really important game of Italian football. I couldn't believe it – he hadn't asked me if he could go out. Well, he couldn't get off the chair; you could see he was scared because he knew I'd smack him. He was rooted to the chair, lost in the game of football.' Not even Rio the charmer, who'd been so outgoing since a young age, could talk his way out of this little spot of bother.

The threat of violence often reared its ugly head in Rio's

childhood, but that was the way it was back then. As one of Rio's oldest mates said: 'Mums on the estate were always clippin' their sons. It was the only way to keep some of them under control – and most of them deserved it anyhow.'

When he was at Bluecoat, Rio's favourite book was *The Twits* by Roald Dahl. Years later he explained his love of reading by saying: 'You can learn more about people by reading about them than just by looking at them.' He knew from an early age that reading was vital to his education, especially for boys, who tended not to bother with such pursuits. 'I'd always ask other kids what were their goals in life – you need to be able to read for all walks of life – if you want to be a policeman – or a singer … you need to look at the lyrics! When I was little, I only liked a handful of books. I'd find an author I liked and then read all their books. I also liked biographies. Today I read when I'm travelling, on the coach or the plane. I also read in the toilet! Reading is fun because you get to find out about people.'

And back then Rio already had a very clear idea which celebrities interested him. He even told one friend: 'If I could read their diary I'd go for Madonna's or [the US basketball player] Dennis Rodman's because he's a lunatic.'

Matt Delaney, Rio's PE teacher at Bluecoat, said he was so naturally gifted that he could have excelled at any sport. 'Rio was one of those kids who was talented at everything. Even as a chorister he was a great singer. He also had a great talent for basketball. He was the best football player we had. He wasn't head and shoulders above the rest, but he was very determined and really applied himself.'

Denise Winston was Rio's tutor at the school for five years. 'He was a bit of a Jack the Lad and at one stage he did seem to be falling in with the wrong crowd. But his mother was always there at the end of the phone and if he thought I was going to ring her he'd soon buck his ideas up.'

Later, while he was at West Ham, Rio returned to Bluecoat to hand out an award. He signed autographs for dozens of pupils and still called Matt Delaney 'sir'. Delaney recalled: 'He was still talking about how we won the Met Police five-a-side competition when he was at the school. He's still proud of that. He is such a down-to-earth lad who had great support from his parents.'

According to Leon Simms, who was Rio's close friend at Bluecoat and played alongside him in the school team: 'Rio's always had a funny word to say. Guess it was his way of keeping on top of things. But when he started on a run with the ball there was no stopping him!' Leon never forgot how he and Rio and the rest of the class went on a school field trip to Cornwall. 'Rio and some of us got up to some right tricks. Nothing really bad, but Rio was in the thick of things.'

Also on that school trip – when Rio was coming up to 14 – was a beautiful, ebony-skinned classmate called Latifah. 'She really looked after herself,' recalled Leon.

Rio fell head over heels in love with Latifah and because he was the tallest boy in his class, at almost six feet, he managed to be the first to date her. 'Rio and Latifah were kinda serious for quite a while,' Leon added. 'He was so proud of her because she was so beautiful.'

Rio dated Latifah for almost two years and he has since admitted that she broke his heart. Leon explained: 'Rio was real serious about Latifah. Rio loves women and Latifah was a goddess, man, if you know what I mean.

Latifah was the one ...' Rio's friends say he tried to keep
the romance as low-key as possible because he knew his
mother would not appreciate the diversion from his
school work and football ambitions.

Sport was particularly important to Janice because she
believed it would help keep her son off the streets. And Rio
knew all about the temptations that lay ahead. 'This is a
tough place and, like a lot of areas, there are kids going off
the rails and others trying to stick to their guns and do well
for themselves, academically or playing sports. Fortunately,
the majority of my friends were sports-orientated. There
were others, though, who did a bit of sport but got
involved in negative things as well ... smoking, stealing,
dabbling in drugs. But that wasn't the way I wanted to be.

'I guess I was lucky I had strong friends around me,
many of whom were older. They knew the road I wanted
to go down. They knew I was serious about football and
they wouldn't smoke stuff in front of me. And if they ever
saw me doing anything like that – not that I would – they
would have stopped me. They didn't want to push me
into that.'

One of Rio's most daring late-night pastimes was to visit
a friend in a nearby flat who had cable TV. Rio would stay
up late to watch foreign league matches. 'We'd watch
anything we could. A lot of European football especially.
We were also bunging football videos on all the time. The
player I really wanted to be like was Dutchman Frank
Rijkaard. Not when he played at the back. He was a
midfielder then.' One of Rio's favourite soccer videos was
about the genius of George Best. He would make notes
while watching it and then try to repeat some of Best's
trickery out on the playground the following day.

Watching all that TV football simply reinforced Rio's

determination to make it as a professional player. 'I wanted to play football, and fortunately I had the talent as well as the determination.' But there were other kids on the estate who wanted to earn big money and didn't care if that sucked them into a life of drugs and vice. 'I had a couple of friends in prison. It's unfortunate but it's part and parcel of life for some people brought up in certain environments.'

Rio's closes friend from his childhood, Gavin Rose, said: 'There was a close-knit group of about seven of us and we realised Rio's potential. We always said one of us had to make it as a footballer and it became obvious that he was going to be the one, so he was specially looked after by the rest of us.'

But ultimately it was Janice who deserved the most special praise. 'My mum was really strong,' says Rio. 'She never let me off the estate unless she knew where I was. I had to tell her the time I would be back. We lived on the fourth floor of the flats and because the lift was always broken I always had to run up the stairs to tell her where I was off to.'

Often, by the time Rio got back down, his mates were halfway along the road. 'But I knew that if I went off the estate without telling my mum I'd get a good seeing-to when I got back. It got on my nerves at the time, but I'm grateful now for the way she treated me.'

As Kate Goodwin, wife of local league organiser and coach Dave Goodwin, pointed out: 'There are a lot of dangers living on a city estate and Rio would be the first one to admit that he could easily have gone the wrong way.'

At Bluecoat, still greatly influenced by his father, Rio continued his interest in drama as well as football. 'I always wanted to be the centre of attention. I loved singing, dancing, acting.' When Rio was 13 his school put on a performance of the musical *Bugsy Malone* and he was given the role of Fizzy, the man who swept up the floor of a speakeasy. It was Rio's first opportunity to sing on stage and he belted out a number called 'Tomorrow'. He explained: 'To me Fizzy was the top man and I had to sing that song. I couldn't wait.'

So Rio, complete with a flat cap, braces and boots, immersed himself in the role of Fizzy the sweeper-up. (Ten years later he would face a lot of ribbing from teammates about that first-ever role as a sweeper!)

This is what Rio – in the role of Fizzy – sang to his beautiful leading lady, Velma:

A resting place for bums
A trap set in the slums
But I know the score
I won't take no for an answer
I was born to be a dancer.

Rio never forgot the standing ovation he got from the audience at the end of that night. 'It was wicked, wicked. That ovation just went on and on.' It sent a shiver of excitement up his spine. I want some more of that, he thought to himself.

His classmate and pal Mark Atkinson also never forgot Rio's stage debut: 'I remember one scene where Rio had to wipe my shoes. That's not likely to happen again, is it?'

But Rio's love of acting sparked a more down-to-earth response from his great friend Gavin Rose: 'Let's just say Rio picked the right career in football.'

At Bluecoat, Rio was teased mercilessly about his haircut,

as classmate Tanya Saunders recalled: 'We used to call him Bart Simpson because of his high hair.' Others said it was very similar to the hairstyle of world-famous boxing promoter Don King.

Rio and Gavin Rose often travelled to the school in Blackheath together from their homes on the Friary Estate. Gavin explained: 'We never had the right bus pass, so we'd quickly flash our passes in front of the driver. Once a bus inspector came on the bus and, when he saw our passes weren't valid, he held up the entire bus for about an hour. The same thing happened on the train one December. The inspector said he would lock us up over Christmas. I remember Rio's face! Then he threatened to call Rio's mum and Rio kept saying, "She won't be in! She won't be in!"'

Dave Goodwin's daughter, Daniella, never forgot the day she went to a local fair with Rio. 'We were about 13 and I had this handbag which was my pride and joy. Anyway, when we came off a ride, Rio said he was going to be sick immediately, so I had to empty my prized possession for Rio to be sick in. Later Rio bought me a beautiful Prada handbag to make up for that.'

She also discovered Rio had a passion for window-shopping. 'He came to Lewisham Centre with me because I had £15 to spend. He didn't have any money, but he came around all the shops helping me choose what to wear. He got his own back years later when me and my mum sat in a shop for three hours while four people fussed around helping him choose suits.'

Rio was undoubtedly very popular with the girls and could talk to them with ease, unlike most boys of his age. Many put that down to the influence of his mum. His school friends also recall that he was still seeing Latifah throughout this period. Tanya Saunders explained: 'Rio dated Latifah for two years and she was very beautiful, a trophy. He was very sweet with her. He always showed girls a lot of respect, even though he liked to give you a cheeky grin. The girls were keen on him and he didn't mind. But he was very loyal.'

Mark Atkinson also remembers Rio being very popular with the girls. 'They were always hanging around him.' And another classmate, Yung Chu, recalled: 'Rio loved pretty girls and he had more success than most of us.'

Meanwhile, at the local league matches on Saturday and Sunday mornings, Rio was showing off a different kind of talent. Schools league organiser and coach Dave Goodwin was astounded by the number of club scouts who were turning up to watch the youngster. It could only be a matter of time before one of them snapped him up.

Chapter 3

OUT OF ORDER

When Rio was 14 something happened to one of his Bluecoat friends which is still reverberating around Britain to this day. For 23 April 1993 was the day when a bunch of racist thugs murdered schoolboy Stephen Lawrence at a bus stop near his home in Eltham, south-east London. Rio recalled: 'The whole school came to a standstill when we were told. Stephen was three years older than me but we used to mess around together and have a laugh playing daft games on each other. It was a terrible shock when he died.'

Dave Goodwin noticed the effects of the murder on his young star player. 'Rio couldn't stop talking about it because he took it so badly. I told him he had to let go but he said, "But I knew him and he was a nice person. Why do these things happen?"' Rio needed a father figure to give advice and his coach was that person.

As Rio vividly remembered: 'It was mad. The whole day got frozen. People were coming in saying, "Stephen Lawrence got stabbed." He was a quiet, nice boy, into art and music. He had a purpose and wanted to do something in life. For him to be taken away that way seemed so unreal. People didn't know what was going on, or why.'

There was a lot of anger among black students at Bluecoat. Some talked of taking revenge on the white youths suspected of involvement. But Rio knew that revenge would serve no real purpose. He diplomatically tried to encourage his seething school mates to calm down. He knew from first-hand experience that violence served little purpose. He'd survived on the Friary Estate by treading a thin line between the good guys and the bad guys. There was no point in starting a race war.

Years later Rio had some very strong advice for young people who found themselves victims of racism at school or in the streets: 'At school you've got to tell your teachers. If they don't sort it out, tell your parents, get them down to the school and tell the head teacher. It's got to be sorted out straight away. If you ignore it, it can escalate and become worse and worse. If you don't deal with it, the bullies will think you are accepting it.'

The murder of Stephen Lawrence provoked talk about a wide range of racial issues. Rio knew that for years young black men with flashy cars had been stopped by police more than any other group of people. Later, when Rio took delivery of his first car, he was stopped by police within minutes of driving on to his manor. It happened repeatedly, and they'd always ask, 'Why have you got this car?' and 'Where did you get the money?' As Rio says: 'There is a view that a black man driving a car is a drug dealer or something.' After the tragic murder of

Stephen Lawrence, Rio avidly read up about the lives of his two latest idols – Nelson Mandela and Martin Luther King. More than ever he wanted to understand where all this hatred came from.

By this time Dave Goodwin, as well as being Blackheath and District Schools League organiser and coach, was also an analyst for manager Lennie Lawrence at Middlesbrough. In order to keep on eye on Boro's future opponents he often went straight from Saturday-morning school games to watch senior matches, mostly in League Division One. Before long he began taking Rio along with him, which proved an education for the youngster. 'Dave would tell me, "Watch him, he's a good player, and him too, look at the formation, see what they're doing at corners." So I got a bit of knowledge about the game, and that was really good for me.'

The first club to make a proper approach for Rio and persuade him to consider joining them was Queens Park Rangers. Rio trained for a few months at QPR but hated making the journey across the Thames to west London, so it always seemed unlikely he'd stay with the club. Then word reached the ears of West Ham scout and former star player Frank Lampard that there was a talented young midfielder called Rio Ferdinand available to sign schoolboy contracts.

But before Lampard contacted Rio, Middlesbrough whisked Rio up north to try and persuade the 14-year-old to sign for them. 'They wanted him as soon as they saw him,' Goodwin explained. 'But I sensed that Rio wouldn't be happy so far away from his family. So, even though I worked for Boro, I told him not to make his decision just for my sake.' Rio told Middlesbrough he wanted time to think over their offer.

Then Charlton made an approach to sign him. He went for a trial at the Valley but was so upset by a racist remark made by an opponent during the trial that he told friends he didn't want to join them. Goodwin recalled: 'A couple of weeks later we were playing another team, which included the individual who made that remark. Rio pointed him out to our skipper, who then proceeded to make the best-timed, fairest but hardest challenge I've ever seen in my life and then told him, "Now who's a so-and-so."'

So Rio had a tough side to him after all – and it would have put Roy Keane to shame! One of Rio's old pals commented: 'Beneath the friendly surface, Rio can be a hard character. You have to be to survive that sort of childhood.'

Next followed a chance to go to the FA's National School of Football Excellence at Lilleshall, in Shropshire, but Dave Goodwin believed that once again Rio wouldn't be able to handle being away from his family and London. There were even rumours that Millwall were about to make a grab for Rio, whose Peckham friend Tony McFarland had just been signed by the south-east London club.

Then West Ham traced Rio and asked him to attend a trial. But he failed to turn up despite repeated requests. So one night Frank Lampard arrived unannounced at Rio's home on the Friary Estate and persuaded him that the Hammers really did mean business and that a Youth Training Scheme contract was on the cards if Rio proved a real talent. A few days later Rio travelled to east London for the first time in his life. It would become his home for the next eight years. Though he was grateful to QPR, he knew that a move to West Ham could only be good for his career.

'I was much happier when he decided to start training at West Ham,' says Goodwin. 'He was streetwise and just like any other teenager. But it was just that the situation there suited him better.'

As the Hammers' manager, Harry Redknapp, recalled: 'He never came to us as a kid with a big reputation. He had no England schoolboy honours or anything like that. Dave Goodwin was the scout who first told me about him. But Frank Lampard put in a lot of work to bring him to West Ham and it paid off.'

And all the attention seemed to spur Rio on to produce even more impressive performances for the Blackheath and District Schools League. He was then given a try-out for the England U-15 squad. Afterwards he was handed an assessment that read: 'One pace. Lacks concentration. Good attitude. Mark: B.' His failure to get an 'A' and make the squad left Rio devastated.

West Ham youth team coach Tony Carr was not in the least bit surprised that Rio didn't get into the England U-15 side. 'He was always tall and skinny as a lad but what really stood out was his mobility. He wasn't the type of player to shine in that environment.'

Soon Rio's schooling at Bluecoat was being seriously affected by his training at West Ham. His teacher Angela Rezki explained: 'There were a few times when we clashed with West Ham because Rio would be fit enough to train with them and then tell me he was injured so he had to miss lessons. But he was never big-headed about having to use our facilities, which weren't great, especially when you're training with a top football club. I even had to paint our changing rooms because the school had no money.'

In the last game of his school season at Bluecoat, Rio switched from midfield to attack and then to defence. 'We didn't have enough defenders, so they put me in there.' Everyone watching the game that afternoon was impressed by the way Rio surged through the middle of the defence to inspire attacking moves with great style. Back at West Ham he continued playing just behind the front line.

The strong relationship between Rio and Dave Goodwin helped Rio create a good early impression at West Ham. Goodwin gave many words of encouragement to the youngster, but he insists it was Rio's family who played the most important role in encouraging his love of football. 'They are the rock upon which Rio's later success was based. Rio's family have been tremendous in looking after him. They're a good and close family, but his are closer than most and his mum Janice was really great. My family have also been very supportive and my wife Kate has often had him round here for a meal and he's been on holiday with us.'

And Rio's appetite for food was just as phenomenal as his skills on the pitch, as Kate Goodwin knows well. 'Rio would eat anything, although his favourite was chicken. If eating were a sport he would have won a platinum. He would come into my house and immediately say, "Have you got any chocolate? My belly's aching." The meals his mum cooked for him could have fed a family of four. We treat him and love him like a son, and my daughter, Daniella, around the same age, dotes on him. The other main thing, and I think the most telling, is that he's got this incredible attitude which speaks volumes for him. The most important thing in his life is football. It was then and it is now – nothing has changed.'

Dave Goodwin had always noticed that, from a young age, Rio maintained a strong, streetwise image and was very popular with everyone, though he could also be quite ruthless about his football. It came first, second and last even then.

And Rio's hunger for football was growing by the day. He couldn't bear to be without a ball at his feet for more than a few minutes. He'd stand on his own on the edge of the playground on the estate practising tricks and improving his control.

Rio was soon reading countless books about football. One of his favourites was an autobiography by the legendary Jimmy Greaves. Rio gleaned lots of useful tips by reading it. It helped Rio redefine his ambitions. Greaves was full of dire warnings about drinking and getting consumed by the adulation of fans. Up until then Rio had not realised Greaves had suffered such personal hell as a self-confessed alcoholic. 'At school I couldn't stand reading *Romeo and Juliet*, or thrillers, so I absorbed myself in autobiographies. I borrowed that book about Jimmy Greaves from the school library and learned all about what he suffered and what he put others through. It shocked me to see what could happen to someone who was such a major figure in the game. But it did make him a stronger person.'

Out on the streets of south-east London, Rio and his mates from the Friary Estate still got up to mischief. Nearly every Saturday, after playing football, they would hop on a Northern Line tube train up to the West End and wander past all the incredibly expensive clothes shops in Bond Street. Rio takes up the story: 'But they wouldn't even let us through the doors of those shops. I used to look in the window and think, I want these clothes so bad. But they used to stop me and say I couldn't come in.' He presumed that his colour was the main reason why he wasn't welcome. 'I couldn't ever have afforded to buy anything, but they didn't know that. I could have been a millionaire for all they knew. I used to think, when I make it famous and become a footballer, you're going to want me to come in.'

And when he wasn't hanging out with his mates or training at West Ham, Rio was dating the beautiful Latifah. He made a point of not taking her out with his friends. He liked to keep her to himself even though, as one old friend said: 'Rio loved bumping into people when he was out with Latifah because she was such a looker. But he drew the line at actually letting her hang out with him and his mates.'

One rain-lashed night Harry Redknapp got aboard the West Ham team coach, contemplating a grim five-hour journey back from Newcastle. After seeing the Hammers slump to defeat, their manager wasn't exactly in the best of moods. As the bus headed down the A1, Redknapp took a mobile call from his dad. Harry Redknapp senior had just got back from seeing West Ham's rookies pull off an amazing comeback against Chelsea to lift the Southern Junior Floodlit Cup. And he was full of praise for one particular youngster.

'I've just seen the best kid I've ever seen play for your youth team.'

'Who?' replied Redknapp.

'Guess,' came the old man's response.

Redknapp recalled: 'I went through the names and when I couldn't guess who, he told me, "That young lad Rio Ferdinand."'

The young Hammers had lost the first leg 4–2 at Upton Park and few believed they stood any chance of winning the away leg by a big enough margin to win overall, but they did it.

Redknapp again: 'Rio was still at school back then. In fact, I think the reason he had not played in the first leg was because we couldn't get him time off. I didn't even know he had played in the second leg. But I think Tony Carr, the youth manager, had put him in because we had nothing to lose and to see some of the younger players perform.'

Rio was just 15 at the time and giving three years away to most of his opponents. But Redknapp's dad said he was running 60 or 70 yards with the ball at his feet, showing pace, skill, everything. And for Redknapp: 'He was the sort of player English football had been crying out for – someone who could bring the ball out of defence with style and flair. He was a midfielder when he came to us and we converted him into a central defender. You look at all the greats and they have moved back there. Franz Beckenbauer, Lothar Matthaus ... they began in midfield and looked so cultured when they went to the back.'

The muddy boots in the corner and the grimy tracksuit emphasised the fact that West Ham's training ground at Chadwell Heath, in Essex, was in many ways like a throwback to the old days in footballing terms. But then, for Harry Redknapp, the grind of day-to-day football management had been in his blood for years. He wasn't interested in posh titles like 'Director of Football'. He wanted to always be where the action was and he wasn't shy about telling others. 'Yeah, Director of Football. That's the one to get into at the moment – that's the one they're all aiming for. Players don't want to retire and be managers any more. They want to be Directors of Football – it's definitely the one to have.

'Pick your games, keep an eye on the rest, no real pressure. How many of us would say no? Come in on Saturday, sit in the boardroom, nice cup of tea, nice gin and tonic, say, "Well, this is the way I'll do it. Anyway, I'm off."'

But all this just didn't fit in with the Harry Redknapp philosophy. 'I can't see West Ham going for a Director of Football, though. Director of Traffic, maybe.'

The Redknapp spin on football provides a fascinating insight into the character who has probably played the biggest role in Rio's career to date. 'Until you sit in the manager's chair you do not realise the pressure. A lot of people are happy being Number Two, the assistant or the coach. They look at the manager's job and think, I can do that. Then suddenly they get there, with absolute control and the buck stopping with them. Then they understand the pressure.'

And back in 1995 Redknapp told the world: 'We have a good team spirit here, a good squad and young players coming through who I feel can really be something. Our problem was that we seemed to stop producing home-grown talent. Now we have a group of five or six with chances and two who are outstanding. We've got a kid here called Rio Ferdinand and he can do a lot at the back. He can bring the call out, pass, play, read the game. He's a great kid as well with real possibilities. Then there's Frank Lampard junior, who we've loaned out to Swansea. He's still meant to be a youth player, but he's doing well in their first team.'

Rio even went in goal for a Capital League game against Dagenham and kept a clean sheet. He also had a starring role in the Hammers' Youth Cup Final team in 1995. They might have lost the final, but the word on Rio was spreading fast and some were even tipping him as a squad member for the 1998 World Cup. The same youth side also won the South-East Counties' Championship. Rio hadn't made one first-team appearance and yet the pressure was already mounting. He insisted his top priority was to make his mark on the West Ham team and he continued playing just behind the attack in the youth side.

In the summer of 1995 Rio's former mentor Dave Goodwin took him on holiday with him and his family to the sunshine island of Crete. Goodwin recalled: 'It was close to pre-season training time, so Rio got up at six o'clock every morning and went running while everyone was still in bed. Don't get me wrong: he's not Mr Perfect or Goody Two-Shoes. But he was single-minded about putting football before everything else.'

Back in London, while most teenagers sat at home playing video games, Rio watched even more football tapes to improve his knowledge. And because he wanted to learn more about every aspect of the game, he also continued to go to matches with Goodwin.

Then in a pre-season reserve game for West Ham against St Albans the team was hit by an injury crisis and Rio played a central defensive role. He never looked back. 'It was put on me and I didn't enjoy it at first, but it grew on me.'

The coaching staff quickly realised they had not only an extremely talented ball player but one who was able to defend as well. Rio's career was about to switch direction in a very dramatic fashion.

On 1 August 1995 Rio signed his first playing contract with West Ham on the Upton Park pitch in front of a crowd of 25,000 waiting for the kick-off of the first Premiership game of the season. Janice was there to see the proud moment, and says: 'It was really emotional. I thought back to all those times we had been shopping for football boots.'

Rio signed with West Ham under their Youth Training

Scheme. As part of the £35-a-week deal, he had to attend Kingsway College, in central London, on a part-time basis to do a course in Sports Science. Once he'd successfully completed the YTS, he would sign a professional contract with the Hammers when he turned 17 in November that year.

Harry Redknapp wasn't shy about singing young Rio's praises. 'I think he's got real possibilities to become a good player and I'm delighted he's signed.' He was convinced that Rio would soon make it into the first team, and what particularly impressed him was the youngster's pace and balance on the ball.

Dave Goodwin sat in on Rio's full contract negotiations later that year when he signed a five-year professional deal with West Ham for £450 a week. He proudly explained: 'Rio's friends and his teammates have always looked after him. When the side broke up that was when some of them got into trouble. But Rio was always well protected.' Now the young player was reaping the rewards.

The 1995–6 season turned into a learning experience for Rio as he played regularly for the West Ham reserves and began to adjust to the faster pace and strength required for the adult game. At six feet two inches he was commanding in the air and strong on the ground.

Some of the backroom staff were soon urging Redknapp to try Rio out, but he resisted the temptation for most of that season – until yet another injury crisis forced his hand.

Chapter 4

WATCH YER BACK

Rio's first Premiership chance came as a substitute in the final game of the 1995–6 season, a 1–1 draw with Sheffield Wednesday. It was an occasion he would never forget. 'My first touch – the ball came over to me and bounced near the touchline. I just smashed it up to row Z of the stands and the crowd started cheering and laughing.'

Nobody, including Rio, remembers much more about his first-ever senior appearance for the Hammers. But within days of that first outing with the big boys, Rio noticed reports in the national press suggesting that other Premiership sides were already interested in signing him. It was very distracting at first because his only aim had been to get into the first team and then consolidate his place.

Then he was called up for the England U-21 squad along with teammate Frank Lampard junior. The buzz on the football grapevine was that Rio was definitely one to watch. But it was clear he was going to have a tough time trying to break into the West Ham first team, which at that time featured 11 different nationalities. Redknapp's preferred back two central defenders were Croatian Slaven Bilic and Dane Marc Rieper.

Rio thought the letter that arrived at his home in May 1996 had been addressed to him by mistake. It was an itinerary for the full England squad's Euro '96 campaign. 'I'd only played one game for West Ham. I looked at the letter again and it was me they wanted. I ran round the house screaming my head off. I was making so much noise my mum came charging after me saying, "What's wrong? What's wrong?"'

England boss Terry Venables had been determined to invite Rio to join the Euro '96 squad that summer. For three weeks Rio lived with the squad, trained with the team and stayed in their hotel, absorbing tips from England's finest. 'Nervous? You bet,' he later recalled. 'Have I got the ability? Or will I look out of place? And do you know what? As soon as I got out there and had my first touch it seemed perfectly normal.'

Rumour even had it that Rio marked Alan Shearer out of the practice games, although he was sensible enough to play it all down when questioned. 'He didn't really do much but it wasn't a full-blooded match. He probably could have pulled something out if it was a proper game.'

England got to the semi-finals of Euro '96 and only lost on penalties to Germany. Rio thoroughly enjoyed his taste of the good life and promised himself he'd be back in the squad proper in the not too distant future. Few disagreed with him.

By August 1996 Rio and Frank Lampard junior were both pressing hard for Premiership places in the West Ham team. Harry Redknapp was facing constant injury problems and must have been tempted to blood his two young starlets sooner rather than later. The absence of centre-half Richard Hall – West Ham's close-season signing from Southampton – looked set to open the door for Rio. Lampard was being lined up for his first-ever first-team start because of injuries to John Moncur and Ian Bishop. In the end neither made the starting line-ups for Premiership matches, but Redknapp was confident enough to use them both as regular substitutes over the following few months.

Frank Lampard junior came from the sort of footballing pedigree that meant he was never likely to lack skill. He was eventually to captain an England U-21 side which included Rio, Joe Cole and Michael Carrick, all from the Hammers. Lampard's and Rio's careers followed many similar paths. They both debuted in 1996 for the first team in that same game against Sheffield Wednesday on the last day of the season. Lampard also captained the West Ham youth team that reached the FA Youth Cup Final.

But Rio was soon getting very frustrated about not starting any matches for the West Ham senior team. 'Harry maybe thought I was a bit too young and a bit too eager at that stage. I was desperate to get in the first team. I let it get on top of me, thinking about it too much.'

Rio adored the feeling of a big crowd and in the reserves there were never more than a handful of anoraks on duty. He still says: 'That's what I thrive on – hearing the crowd cheering your moves, pushing you on. The fact that people have paid to watch you makes you rise to the occasion.'

Eventually Harry Redknapp – aware of Rio's unhappiness – shipped him down to Bournemouth, the south coast

Third Division club where he'd once been manager. It turned out to be an inspired move which provided Rio with some essential first-team practice. He also got on extremely well with Bournemouth's veteran manager, Mel Machin.

Rio put in some wonderful performances on the pitch but spending his nights in a £31-a-night hotel on half board was a miserable, lonely existence for a lively young Londoner. He was restless and homesick and even had to take his kit home after training every day and wash it. 'I would sometimes go back to my room at Bournemouth and just sit and watch television in the afternoon. It made me appreciate West Ham and everything about the club. Did me good in other ways too because I learned to face up to all kinds of players.'

And, as this table shows, Bournemouth remained unbeaten when Rio played for them and Mel Machin was soon raving about Rio down the phone to his old pal Redknapp:

9-11-96	(A)	BLACKPOOL	1–1
19-11-96	(H)	BRENTFORD	2–1
23-1-96	(A)	BURNLEY	1–0
30-11-96	(H)	LUTON	3–2
3-12-96	(A)	SHREWSBURY	1–1
14-12-96	(H)	MILLWALL	1–1
21-12-96	(A)	CHESTERFIELD	1–1
26-12-96	(H)	BRISTOL	1–0
28-12-96	(A)	CREWE	2–0
11-01-97	(H)	ROTHERHAM	1–1

Machin christened Rio 'class' – literally. 'I was walking behind him as we went out for training one day and I said, "Hey, Class!" And Rio immediately turned round. He knew who I meant.' The Bournemouth manager added: 'Rio has got so much natural ability and is so quick that he could play anywhere. He went up front at times for us, but his best position is at the back.'

Rio was just going into his third month with Bournemouth when he was recalled by Harry Redknapp because West Ham had injuries. Machin told his old pal Redknapp: 'Don't be frightened to stick him straight into the Premier League. You'll be pleasantly surprised how well he'll cope.' He also told him that Man United boss Alex Ferguson had been on the telephone asking if he could buy Rio. 'I told Alex he wasn't mine to sell,' he informed the Hammers' manager.

'I'll expect a call from him, then,' replied the wily old fox Redknapp, who knew that West Ham were always open to offers for their players if the price was right.

So Redknapp hauled Rio back from Dorset at the end of January and plunged him straight into the sort of first-team action he'd been dreaming about for years. First up was the Hammers' tricky third-round FA Cup replay against Wrexham, earmarked as an opportunity to try out youngsters Rio and his close pal Lampard. There was even talk that Rio might be playing up front because of injuries to three Upton Park strikers.

In the end Rio made his first full start for West Ham as a defender in that game against Wrexham on 25 January 1997. It was certainly a baptism of fire and although Rio bedded well into the West Ham team, the result was a sickening 1–0 defeat. However, he had done well enough to be picked for the Hammers' next game. Redknapp had decided to give Rio a proper try-out in the team to find out if Machin was right.

Rio scored his first goal for West Ham at Blackburn the week after the FA Cup tie at Wrexham. He was – as the old cliché goes – literally over the moon. That night he travelled back down south in the Hammers' coach and went straight round to Dave Goodwin's home. Kate Goodwin takes up the story: 'There was a knock on the door at 11.30 pm and it was Rio, grinning like a Cheshire cat. He said, "Please tell me you videoed the goal." Then he ran upstairs, put the video on and kept rewinding it, doing a running commentary, saying, "And he goes up and he shimmies around the ball, and it's a goal!" for about an hour.'

Just a few days after Rio's sterling performance against Blackburn, Alex Ferguson called Harry Redknapp and asked if Rio was for sale. The response was sharp and to the point: 'Sure, if we can have David Beckham.' But that call by Ferguson was very flattering to West Ham, making them feel they were sitting on a goldmine.

After one home game for West Ham, Dave Goodwin met up with Rio. 'I said to him, Do you fancy a drink, Rio?' He said, "Yeah, in the Boleyn" – the pub next to Upton Park. I think he wanted to buy one for all the fans. They're would have been chaos if he'd gone in. So I had to take him to a McDonald's instead.'

Behind this story lies the key to what drove Rio onwards and upwards. He loved the attention and the adoration of the fans. It was as important to him as any other aspect of the game. Without a crowd he found it very difficult to motivate himself. Rio the people-pleaser, who'd avoided injury as a kid in the ghetto by cracking a joke and playing up to the crowd, now had the ultimate audience.

Harry Redknapp tried to cool the hype surrounding his brilliant young defender by saying: 'We'll start talking about him playing for England after he's had 50 or 60 good games. I'm hoping he'll stay level-headed.'

And Rio knew it was early days. It was essential to keep

learning his craft and he knew he was lucky to have an experienced bunch of other defenders around him at West Ham. Slaven Bilic proved Rio's greatest teacher during that early period at West Ham. 'Slaven played for Croatia in World Cup qualifiers and in the European Championships and played all over Europe. He was the bee's knees in my book.'

It came as a 'mighty blow' to Rio when Bilic signed for Everton at the end of the 1996–7 season for £4.5 million. 'He had given me so much encouragement and confidence both on and off the pitch.'

Another Hammers player who bonded with Rio was Australian youth international Chris Coyne. The youngster had moved halfway round the world to Upton Park when he was still only 16, and he needed all the friends he could get. Coyne had his brother Jamie and fellow Aussie Richard Garcia for company at West Ham when he signed a four-and-a-half-year trainee contract. He linked up with Rio in the Hammers' youth teams alongside Frank Lampard. 'Rio was phenomenal – a great athlete, great on the ball and he was head and shoulders above everyone else. He was a great player,' was Coyne's verdict.

But there was one downside to playing for big crowds – the ugly spectre of racist fans. Rio heard one man in the West Ham crowd shouting 'black this and black that' at the players. He glanced across at a policeman to see if he would do anything, but he was appalled when the PC completely ignored the bigoted 'fan'. Later Rio left the pitch in disgust, although he knew the abuse had been much worse a few years earlier. 'As a player you get a certain amount of racism from crowds here and there, but it is not as apparent now as it was before. When players like John Barnes, Ian

Wright and Viv Anderson were playing it was a lot worse.'

Back in Peckham, Rio suffered from another form of racism when he found himself being stopped after splashing out £20,000 on a brand-new BMW convertible. 'I wasn't really known as a footballer at the time and they'd ask me, "Where'd you get the money for this? Are you dealing? Are you nicking stuff?" I'd then answer, "I earned this car. I wouldn't drive it if I didn't earn it." ' It wasn't until he was properly established in the Hammers' first team that the stopping and searching by police slowed down.

On the pitch, Rio taught himself to be stronger and to go in harder on any opposition players who ever tried to make an issue of his colour. 'Not verbally – I let the football do the talking and embarrass them. I'm not the type of person to confront people but I will try to win the game so I can look them in the eye.'

By this time Rio had settled in so well at West Ham that even the kit man and dinner ladies at the club became his friends. Rio had time for all of them. 'I appreciated everything that West Ham were doing for me. And it wasn't just the coaches who were blinding.'

Harry Redknapp believed he'd finally cracked the difficult transfer market which had nearly finished him off the previous year. Up until then he'd been more famous for buying a succession of dodgy foreigners than developing new, raw young talent like Rio, Lampard and Cole. He wanted desperately to bring the glory days back to Upton Park. 'I've made some good buys in my time and some crap ones,' he said with typical honesty. 'But my aim now is to get good, young lads who will work hard, look after tz

Pearce had just been signed for £2.3 million from

Blackburn and went straight into the Hammers' side alongside Rio, then aged 18, and 23-year old David Unsworth in the heart of defence. He replaced Marc Rieper, who left Upton Park for Celtic for £1.4 million. Pearce, from Surrey, was a West Ham fan as a boy and had joined Blackburn from Chelsea three years earlier for £300,000. Redknapp described Pearce as 'big, strong and quick'. With a rock-solid defence, he was now on the lookout for a back-up striker to join John Hartson and Paul Kitson.

Soon, even Rio's distant cousin Les joined the chorus of praise for the young Hammers defender. He admitted struggling against Rio during Newcastle's home clash against West Ham towards the end of the 1996–7 season. 'I struggled against Rio, but it's not surprising because he's one of the best defenders around at the moment. He's cool, he doesn't get upset by the physical stuff and I can see why everybody says Glenn Hoddle is already an admirer. I think he's ready for England.'

Towards the tail end of the season Rio even showed his loyalty to West Ham by signing a new greatly improved five-year contract worth approximately £4,000 a week. The future was looking bright. But there might be a few hiccups along the way.

Rio's old Bluecoat pal Mark Atkinson never forgot the day Rio returned to his old school to hand out an award. 'Rio arrived in his BMW and I kept my Ford Fiesta parked around the back. I'm envious of all the money he's earning but I'm not jealous of him. I've bumped into Rio out and about. We have a chat and he's still got his feet on the ground.'

It was typical of Rio to show up on his old manor and lend some support to his friends. There was no doubt he

still enjoyed the company of some heavy characters from the Friary Estate, but as they still was to be protecting and nurturing him it was unlikely he'd blot his copybook.

Chapter 5

SWIMMING WITH SHARKS

In April 1997 Rio damaged his ankle ligaments during his debut for the England U-21 side in their 0–0 draw with Switzerland. Harry Redknapp refused to make a fuss, commenting: 'It's unfortunate but I'm not going to make an issue out of it. I would always release players for internationals. If clubs are going to stop letting players go for internationals, then we won't have an England team. If West Ham had prevented Bobby Moore from playing for England in his early years, he wouldn't have gone on to win 108 caps.'

The U-21 line-up that night makes fascinating reading in the light of what has happened over the past five years:

C. Day (Crystal Palace), M. Broomes (Blackburn), R. Ferdinand (West Ham), M. Hall (Coventry), J. Carragher (Liverpool), L. Bowyer (capt, Leeds), C. Holland (Birmingham),

M Carbon (Derby), S. Hughes (Arsenal), D. Huckerby (Coventry), R. Humphreys (Sheffield Wednesday). Subs: L. Briscoe (Sheffield Wednesday), B. Roberts (Middlesbrough), J. Morris (Chelsea), M. Bridges (Sunderland), I. Moore (Nottingham Forest).

England U-21 coach Peter Taylor was very excited by certain players, including Rio. But behind his praise lay a serious issue. The English game was finally starting to reap the benefits of youth. Off-the-field professionalism, superior technique and training methods, plus dietary discipline, were positive aspects inherited from the vast influx of players from abroad.

At last the quick fix of importing established stars on massive wages was starting to lose pace. As Taylor explained: 'I quite like the foreign players being over here as long as they show a good example to the kids. I'm a great Klinsmann fan. I have spoken to people who worked with him at Spurs and they said he was fantastic in everything he did and young players can only learn from that. But I'm not one for having too many in a team. I preferred the old rule with three at the most. We wouldn't want to lose those aspects of the English game, like team spirit, which are recognised as good attributes.' Ironically, Rio's squad at West Ham still featured at least 11 different nationalities.

TV pundit and former Hammers hero Trevor Brooking was particularly impressed by Rio. 'He seems to have every attribute. He is one of those defensive players who can come into forward positions and that's something we must produce more of in this country.' Brooking also felt strongly about the huge influx of foreign players into the Premiership. 'You can argue it both ways. It's not easy to get the right balance because you have got to get results in the Premiership as well as introduce youngsters. Players like Rio must benefit from their presence but it's a long-term impact.'

The irony of the entire debate about foreign players was that the current crop of young talent coming through the ranks had been produced in an environment inspired by the way countries such as Germany and Holland developed their young players. In the 1980s the emphasis at clubs and the FA's National School at Lilleshall was on physical presence and athleticism, rather than on technique and developing personality on and off the pitch, as it was eventually to become.

At that time it was all about results and winning. And while German and Dutch youth and U-21 teams would get steamrollered by their English counterparts, their players would develop into international players used to playing the same system as the national team, whereas British players seemed to stagnate. As Trevor Brooking explained: 'We went through a spell in the eighties when you had to be tall and big. A number of clubs would turn players away for being too small, which was rubbish.'

Now there was a real expectation in the footballing community that players of the calibre of young Rio would develop to full national level by playing a similar 3-5-2 formation with the emphasis on developing ball skills and technique. U-21 coach Peter Taylor even confirmed that the future was more important in some ways than the results for his U-21 squad. 'Of course we want to win but Glenn [Hoddle] has assured me that he wants the young players in and results don't matter. If it was just a case of producing a team just to get a result I would be doing my job wrong. This is a different attitude to what there has been in the past.'

Then Rio's U-21 squad colleague, Leicester City starlet

Emile Heskey, hit the headlines after allegedly getting so drunk he missed the banquet following his club's Coca-Cola Cup victory. 'I had one too many and I didn't get to the party,' Heskey explained. 'I have never drunk very much, nothing major. I don't really like it. It doesn't do anything for me.' Many of Heskey's U-21 teammates, including Rio, were surprised by the vast publicity surrounding what seemed like a harmless incident. But older, wiser heads warned the youngsters to heed the warning signs and be careful to avoid such problems.

Meanwhile Harry Redknapp continued holding together the Hammers despite some precarious moments in the Premiership. His experience, as an adept football manager, racehorse owner and enthusiastic punter, had long since taught him the difficult art of pragmatism. 'I suppose the bookies wouldn't fancy us to go down this time. But something tells me it's going to be even harder this coming season.'

With that in mind, Redknapp wasted no time during the close season of 1997 in strengthening his squad with two more foreign imports plus a number of other domestic players. He explained his spending spree in typical Redknapp style. 'Everyone is having a go – we're all spending our money from the TV deal. We finished above Chelsea last season and look at them. They splashed out a fortune. We're all having to spend up and it's going to be really tough.'

Once again Redknapp made a point of also mentioning his up-and-coming youngsters like Rio and in the process had a swipe at the footballing authorities. 'PFA chief Gordon Taylor has criticised us for signing all the foreign players and is worried about the young players coming through, but I'll have a bet with him now that players like Rio Ferdinand and Frank Lampard will make it. The young players will still come through if they're good enough.'

But for the moment the real focus of attention remained on the Hammers' European hopes for the following season's UEFA Cup competition. Redknapp insisted that team spirit was at an all-time high. 'For the first time since I've been here, there's not a player at the club I would rather see the back of. When I started with Billy Bonds there were half a dozen who were a disgrace. Bill wanted them out, I wanted them out, but it takes time. Now everyone here wants to play for the club. The Premier League is the place to be. It's a very exciting time.'

Rio knew only too well that if he was to become a serious contender for a place in England's World Cup squad the following year, he needed to come to terms with the fact that only two people in his life really mattered – Harry Redknapp and Glenn Hoddle.

Rio's former West Ham teammate Alvin Martin crossed paths with the youngster just before Martin quit Upton Park in 1997. He said then: 'Rio's good enough to go to France '98 and he's the sort who would respond to the challenge of playing against the best. I think he has learned in the past few months that even the smallest indiscretion will be magnified because of the position he is in. He has learned that very quickly. I know him well enough to say that he is a cracking lad. You get a feel for people, don't you? There's something about him that is basically nice.'

During the summer break of 1997 England coach Glenn Hoddle made enquiries about Rio's availability, only to discover he was suffering from an injured foot. And Rio himself went out of his way to dismiss suggestions he might be in the running for a place at the 1998 World Cup Finals in France. 'It all sounds a bit far-fetched,' he said at the time. 'It's nice to hear people say that kind of thing about yourself. But if you sit and drool over that, you could become obsessed. I don't let it get to me.'

But, behind the scenes, Rio's international stardom was already being plotted. His grandparents' nationalities meant he could have played for either Ireland or France, but he'd already made the crucial decision by turning out for the English U-21s. He later explained: 'I was born here, I'm from south London and my mum's English. Simple as that.'

Everyone was full of praise for Rio and West Ham during that summer break in 1997. The previous season they'd produced mobile, well co-ordinated and tactically aggressive performances. They were tight at the back and were being tipped to go even further in the following Premiership season. Ian Pearce's arrival from Blackburn had had a particularly steadying influence on young Rio. His calmness under pressure and astute distribution of the ball helped teach Rio a few important lessons.

It was no surprise that Glenn Hoddle dispatched his Number Two, John Gorman, to White Hart Lane to watch Rio's progress on the second Saturday of the 1997–8 season. Rio's performance as sweeper during West Ham's 2–1 win over Tottenham was so superb it prompted some Spurs officials to describe him as the best young defender in the world. Even Gorman admitted: 'Rio's obviously a great prospect but I wouldn't like to put too much pressure on the lad. After all, he's only had two games this season, but we will be keeping close tabs on him over the coming months.' The Hammers' managing director, Peter Storrie, let it be known he was going to place a bet on Rio winning an international cap before Christmas.

And just to make sure all the praise didn't go to his young head, Rio's feet were kept firmly on the ground by West Ham's assistant manager, Frank Burrows, who always picked the two nine-a-side teams during training. Harry Redknapp later explained: 'The other day it was the "Good-looking" team against the "Uglies" and he picked Rio for the Ugly line-up. Rio couldn't believe it. All through the match, he kept muttering, "It's impossible", but it was a good laugh and he joined in with the spirit of the thing.'

In some ways this incident summed up Rio's Jack-the-Lad opinion of himself. He'd spent so long ducking and diving on the Friary Estate and charming even the most evil of characters that he believed he was now somebody – a force to be reckoned with in football. The only problem was that some others still saw him as a south London kid with a good pair of feet. There was still a long way to go, although you wouldn't believe it from some of the glowing reports about Rio.

Simon Barnes in *The Times* perfectly summed up the grace and artistry that made Rio such a great talent. 'At the age of 18 he is a trifle long in the tooth to be considered an infant, but he is a fine and precious talent. The point is not that he can play football, but the fact that he understands it. He understands the rhythms and the patterns, the well-laid strategies and the sudden inspirations that make up the game of football.

'He is a defender with ball skills, but that fact does him an injustice. A footballing centre-half is usually a big bloke who likes to fanny about on the ball and then gets caught out in some mad foray upfield. The point with Ferdinand is that there are no frills in his game. He eschews the easy back pass and turns forward neatly to lay the ball into midfield, but there is nothing self-indulgent about it.

'Watching him play is an astonishing, rather disquieting

experience. There is something almost freakish about his calm, his understanding. Naturally, people have been coming forward to say good things about him. "Immense skill," said the West Ham manager Harry Redknapp. "Incredible maturity," Roger Cross, the assistant manager of Tottenham Hotspur, added after a game earlier this season.'

Other sports writers soon picked up on the Rio phenomenon. Typical was Henry Winter in the *Daily Telegraph*: 'A new wave promises to race in across the familiar shore. Come the season's climax, when West Ham visit Manchester United, two of the tyros on view could be firmly established in the national consciousness. West Ham offer Rio Ferdinand, a mobile central defender who impressed while on work experience with England at Bisham Abbey. In opposition at Old Trafford should be David Beckham, already a double-winner and now heading inexorably towards England recognition.'

Then, out of the blue at the end of August, the scene was set for Rio to become the second-youngest player, after the legendary Duncan Edwards, ever to put on an England shirt. With Arsenal's Tony Adams and Martin Keown out and Stuart Pearce and Sol Campbell nursing injuries, Rio was called up for the England squad for the World Cup qualifying clash with Moldova in early September despite having just two U-21 caps and 16 Premiership starts to his name.

Everyone at West Ham tried to play down the situation because they wanted to ensure that Rio's transition from ghetto kid to international football star went smoothly. 'The kid's definitely got a lucky streak but you know what they say, "You make your own luck in this life …" ' said one who should know.

The problem was that Rio's luck was about to run out.

Chapter 6

A KICK IN THE TEETH

On 31 August 1997 Princess Diana and Dodi Fayed died when their chauffeur, Henri Paul, smashed a Mercedes into a concrete pillar in a Paris tunnel. Paul's decision to ignore basic rules about not drinking and driving helped deprive the world of one of its most glamorous figures. Flags were immediately flown at half mast throughout the UK and local authority buildings opened books of condolence for members of the public to sign.

A few hours after the Princess's death, in the early hours of the morning of Monday, 1 September, Rio was pulling out of a garage in his BMW in Colliers Wood, south London. His lights were off. Not surprisingly, he was stopped by the police and breathalysed and found to have 55 micrograms of alcohol per 100 millilitres of breath. He was just over the legal limit of 53 micrograms.

Rio told the police officers he had no idea alcohol was

still in his system but that didn't stop them arresting him for drink-driving. Rio had gone out with a bunch of mates following the Hammers' thrilling 3–1 victory over Wimbledon two days earlier and also to celebrate his England call-up. They went out in his car, but returned in a taxi to his home in Peckham because he was worried he might be over the limit. But Rio then made the mistake of having three more drinks at dinner with friends on the Sunday evening before driving home in the early hours. This effectively 'topped up' the alcohol remaining in his blood. Rio's arrest tragically mirrored the circumstances behind the death of the 'People's Princess'. The timing could not have been worse.

As Rio later recalled, when he was stopped and the breathalyser showed positive, it sent a shiver down his spine. 'The thought of being over the limit didn't even come into my mind. I thought it was a routine check because I'd got a flash car. When it came up positive I was sure it was wrong. The second one also came up positive and I just collapsed inside.

'I saw my whole life crumbling. I thought, What am I going to tell my mum, dad and West Ham boss Harry Redknapp? At that point Glenn Hoddle didn't even come into my mind. It was only later, during the three hours I was at the police station, it hit me that I had to tell Glenn as well. I begged the policeman to let me off this one time. I said, "I just want to go home now, please let me go." He knew I'd been picked for England but he said, "You can't expect to be let off just because of that."'

Rio's mum eventually turned up at the police station. As soon as Rio told her what had happened, she said, 'Right, we've got to sort this out.' As usual, it was Janice to the rescue of the son she'd fought so hard to bring up safely and securely. Within three hours of Rio's arrest, West Ham had provided a legal team and he was released on bail.

Janice's take on those events tells us a lot about her relationship with her oldest son. She told one friend: 'He's totally devastated. On Sunday he went out for a meal and later drove some of his friends home only to find he was still over the limit. He usually drinks Coke or lemonade. I don't like alcohol and never have it in the house. We are not drinkers in this house and none of us realised that was possible. We are all so sad. Rio has such a solid head on his shoulders. He has been very strong and positive about keeping away from temptation. He's really walked the straight line.'

Not surprisingly, news of Rio's arrest soon leaked out to the media. But the nation was in such a numbed state after the death of Princess Diana that it didn't make the expected huge splash in the tabloids. That was Rio's only piece of good fortune that week. But the modest projection of the story didn't stop Fleet Street from asking the inevitable question: 'Will Rio still play for England against Moldova?'

With the death of the Princess on everyone's mind, it was always going to be a tough task for England boss Glenn Hoddle to raise the spirits of his team for the World Cup clash with lowly Moldova. In the circumstances he had little choice but to drop Rio from the team. But he insisted Rio stay with the squad. Some suggested that Hoddle never intended to play Rio in the first place and was using the drink-driving arrest to 'teach Rio a lesson'. Whatever the truth, Rio must have felt that his charmed world had just collapsed all around him.

One of the reasons why Hoddle insisted Rio remain with the squad at Bisham Abbey was that 'I wanted him to see what he was missing out on.' He added: 'This being his first call-up it had all the more impact. We have had a long chat. He's very disappointed with what he's done. He feels he let himself, his club and his family down. He's not out for good but if he goes and does something else in a month's time, then there's a problem. I don't want to crucify him.'

Hoddle's sole aim was to provide England with a secure win at Wembley so that they would face Italy in Rome in a far better state of mind than following their earlier dismal 1–0 World Cup qualifiers defeat by Italy at home. Hoddle's career as boss of the national team had begun a year earlier with a 3–0 win in Moldova. A win at home to Moldova would almost certainly mean a draw in Rome would be enough to secure automatic qualification as the second-placed qualifying team with the best record.

Three days later – on 4 September – Rio appeared at Wimbledon Magistrates Court, where he pleaded guilty to drink-driving and was fined £500 and banned from driving for a year. During the five-minute hearing, prosecutor Anne Davies told the court: 'Police stopped the car in Priory Road, Colliers Wood, at 1.30am on Monday, September 1 and found Mr Ferdinand driving. He denied he had had anything to drink that night but gave a breath test which was positive.' Besides the ban and £500 fine, Rio was also ordered to pay £40 costs.

Outside the court he told the waiting press that he thought his drinks might have been spiked with alcopops. He continued to insist that on the day before he was stopped by police he went out for dinner with friends and consumed just two halves of lager before changing to what he thought were soft drinks.

At West Ham, managing director Peter Storrie also

reiterated that Rio was not aware that he was over the limit when he was stopped. 'Rio thinks the drinks could have been changed without his knowledge. He is full of remorse. But he will be back. He will learn from this.'

The day after his conviction, Rio issued a statement to the media in which he promised to pick up the pieces of his shattered career and even admitted: 'I've been so naive. I'm just so sorry. I am being forced to pay a heavy price. It's a harsh lesson for me to learn, being so close to gaining my first full England cap. I made a mistake for which I am dreadfully sorry. I cannot apologise enough. This will show a test of my character. I have to prove to people who have stood by me that I can bounce back.'

Janice was constantly by Rio's side until he joined the England squad at Bisham Abbey. She explained to the press: 'Rio has been punished but I hope he is not hounded. Just let him get on with playing his football. I would hate to think this might destroy him.'

Throughout the most momentous week in Rio's career so far there was never any suggestion that he was a heavy drinker. The incident was seen as a lapse of judgement more than an illustration of a self-destructive lifestyle. This was the other reason why Glenn Hoddle allowed him to remain in the squad get-together at Bisham Abbey.

Yet some were highly critical of Hoddle's decision not to play Rio and accused him of letting his heart rule his head. A number of newspaper commentators were angry with him for treating Rio so differently from the earlier so-called offender Paul Gascoigne, who was accused by his wife of beating her. Many believed that while the whole country wept for Princess Di, public figures like Hoddle should address a strong message to our youngsters. Drink-driving was undoubtedly a terrible offence and, as the nation had witnessed those past few days, it was something that could be so cruel to the innocent.

But it was felt by some that Hoddle had got it all terribly wrong as he searched for one code of conduct for his players whether they were 18 or 38. There seemed to be certain rules for some while others were treated differently. Rio Ferdinand would become the new Bobby Moore – there was no doubt about it – but it would not be because of the handling of this latest horror decision by the England boss.

Some argued that because Hoddle had been quite a lad off the field in his early days, the old adage of 'boys will be boys' still stood. But players needed keeping firmly in their place by a manager who played the game fairly with one and all. Paul Gascoigne's case made Rio's situation seem unacceptable for the simple reason that Gazza should have been old enough to know better than to beat up his wife. To rub salt into Rio's wounds, Hoddle even insisted that his players 'will do it for the country' by turning on the style against Moldova, yet he'd left out his most stylish player.

No one was condoning Rio's behaviour, but it needed to be put in the right perspective. Glenn Hoddle was not only the head coach but a born-again Christian, and that church was there to help, so why did he not sit Rio down and hand out the same treatment he did to Gascoigne? Rio's track record of just 21 first-team matches before leaping from youth football to international stardom was noted as perhaps meaning he knew no better.

One commentator wrote: 'I know what Ferdinand is going through. Hoddle should have given him the biggest rollicking he will ever get in his short career and then told him to go out and put it all behind him. Show me a person, let alone a professional footballer, who has gone through his career without a blemish on his copybook. I always say it is better to get in and out of trouble at an early age so that you can learn from your mistakes, but Ferdinand's is a ridiculous price to pay. It could well mean us losing the best centre-half we have had for some time if we reach the World Cup Finals in France – all because of something that will be forgotten by then. Not only that, but we have two self-confessed alcoholics, Tony Adams and Paul Merson, representing us!'

Within days of Rio's arrest and conviction, others were trying to show encouragement to the teenager to ensure he didn't become too disheartened. In a touching display of loyalty, ex-England manager Terry Venables, now manager of the Aussie Socceroos, told newspapers that Rio and Sol Campbell were two brilliant prospects for the national team over the following 10 years.

Venables had given Sol Campbell his international debut as a sub against Hungary in 1996 as well as including Rio in the Euro '96 squad. 'I believe they will be an outstanding double act. Before too long, the opposition will be calling them the Gruesome Twosome!' he said.

And Venables even pronounced on Rio's drink driving: '... these things happen. Glenn has taken the bull and Rio will have learned a lot from all this. Rio's ability is beyond doubt. I look at him and Sol and see a new type of English defender. They are good examples of the way our attitude towards bringing on young defenders is changing for the better. For too long we failed to train players at the back from a young age to bring the ball out of defence and contribute in a more all-round fashion – as they have been doing in Brazil and Holland for years.

'I have believed for some years that we have to take a

short cut and play players at the back who have come from forward positions. Both Rio and Sol were centre-forwards at one time and that is a real help. At Spurs we always tried to get the kids to play an all-round game and it's the same with Rio at West Ham. These boys have had real education – playing football and not specialising as a stereotype English centre-half or full-back. You specialise eventually. And, as we have seen with Rio and Sol, you are all the better for it. Obviously, it's up to Glenn and any future England coach to decide the best way to use them.

'But I can't see the slightest problem – whether it's three at the back or as the central two in the back four. Both are very mobile, very good on the ball, excellent defenders and strong in the air. You could probably play them both in midfield as well. With boys like these around, the future looks absolutely A1 for England. Glenn's a lucky man.'

Sol Campbell knew only too well how costly the smallest defensive slip could be – and that was on the field of play. His tardy intervention had gifted Gianfranco Zola with a simple goal that enabled Italy to humble England 1–0 at Wembley, leaving the team's chances of qualifying for the 1998 World Cup on a knife edge.

But Campbell later insisted he had used that appalling error as a stimulus to learn and improve. England coach Hoddle even compared Campbell to France's Marcel Desailly. Back at West Ham, Rio had always admired Sol's ability to win the ball and then use it effectively instead of just hoofing it up the park. The entire concept of a defender who did not just automatically locate the roof of the stand on winning the ball was one that Rio fully appreciated.

At the England training camp at Bisham Abbey, Hoddle encouraged old England stalwart Tony Adams to have a chat with Rio. As he later pointed out: 'It took Tony until he got to 30 to find the lesson that Rio has had now. It has to be good for the boy to speak to someone like Tony, who's been through it and can explain what it means.' Adams approached Rio when both players turned up for squad training. A rib injury had ruled the Arsenal skipper out of the Moldova World Cup tie. Three matches short of a half century of caps, Adams was England's longest-serving player and the only international to have played in the same team as Hoddle. Adams knew all about the pressure on the youngsters and how it could affect their future.

Later Adams said: 'I think the most significant change in my time has been towards youth. Although in some ways I think the younger players in the squad are a bit luckier than I was when I was first called up. Today the senior players in the squad are far more helpful to the youngsters. They're more generous and giving. I understand that it can be difficult because there's always someone younger than you pushing for your place. You have to be realistic, though. You have to swallow your pride.'

Adams helped counsel Rio and showed a real concern that the teenager might fall victim to the sort of temptations that landed him in jail for drink-driving. 'Rio is very much a reflection of me. I fear for him,' he said at the time. 'I fear for what this whole business can do to him. If he is in touch with what is good and what is bad then he has a chance to correct it and walk away. Rio does seem to have his feet on the ground but you don't know what's going on internally, do you? You can only see outside but you don't know what is really going on. I can only tell him how it was for me – he's got to help himself. If he wants to use what I am telling him then he does have to go the way I did. He is a great player and a confident player. He just needs to watch and learn how other players cope.'

Rio did penance at Bisham Abbey while the rest of the squad prepared for the World Cup qualifying game against Moldova at Wembley. With the death of Princess Diana still heavily on the nation's mind, Hoddle continued to struggle to motivate his players. 'It will be a difficult, emotional evening but it is an opportunity to lift the nation,' he said at the time. 'The three points are, in many ways, secondary; such a tragedy reminds us it is only a game of football. But she was a very professional lady and we have to be professional.'

Hoddle insisted that Rio's exclusion from the team would have occurred regardless of Diana's death at the hands of an apparently drunk chauffeur. He said: 'With an 18-year-old going to court on the day he was joining up with the squad, I had no option. If I hadn't, I wouldn't have slept well at night. At that age we feel that they need to learn a lesson. It is a signal to any young player.'

So, Rio's chance to be his country's second-youngest player ever had been dashed. It was a cruel reminder to all up-and-coming young players about their future conduct. Rio knew that he now had to fight his way back into Glenn Hoddle's good books, even though that anguish was alleviated to a certain extent by the boss's decision to allow Rio to stay with the England squad.

FA Chairman Keith Wiseman reckoned that Rio's punishment following his drink-driving offence was a credit to Hoddle's style of management: 'This will give Rio food for thought. It will be a lesson learned and he should realise the decision was made for his own good.' Furthermore, the FA denied that Princess Diana's death was a factor in the decision not to let Rio play against

Moldova. 'Rio's case has nothing to do with this,' said Wiseman. 'Glenn Hoddle has certain standards and he expects them to be adhered to. Rio overstepped the mark, he made a silly mistake.'

And Hoddle left the door wide open for Rio when he said: 'I am not saying that he won't play for England in the future. He hasn't robbed a bank and he hasn't killed anyone but between Harry Redknapp and myself we will see how he reacts to what's happened.'

Rio's well-meaning West Ham teammate John Hartson then unintentionally added fuel to the fire by telling one reporter: 'We have all done it. There but for the grace of God ... Rio's bad luck was to be caught. I feel sorry he has discovered so early in his career how easy it is to slip from the heights. Rio's punishment is such a painful one – to be left out by England on the eve of his debut – that the lesson will rub off on us all. I can declare hand on heart that what happened to Rio means I'll never take even one drink and drive.'

But Hartson's remark to the newspaper reporter – 'We have all done it' – raised a few emotional issues with Harry Redknapp. Only seven years earlier the West Ham boss had lost his best friend in a drink-driving accident. Thirty miles south of Rome during the 1990 World Cup, a bus in which the two men were travelling was hit by a drunk driver.

Now Redknapp found himself facing one of his brightest young protégés knowing that he had flouted the law. Redknapp was honest enough to acknowledge his own culpability and that knocking back a few lagers in the players' bar was seen as the professional norm. As he explained: 'We must educate young players. Why should they want to get loads of drink down them when it leads to doing silly things and getting into trouble?'

Redknapp also had no hesitation in saying: 'Rio has been a silly boy, made a big mistake, and now must take his punishment. Glenn Hoddle has my 100 per cent support. We talk to our young professionals at West Ham about the dangers of drink. The days of pouring a crate of lager down their necks after every game are gone. But Rio is basically a sensible boy and I am confident this will just be an unfortunate incident on his path to the top.'

And Redknapp's assistant, Frank Lampard senior, caught the mood perfectly when he reflected thus: 'Rio's a class footballer and he's had lots of good publicity so far this season. But life isn't always smooth. Sometimes it's how you handle the bumps that count. It's up to Rio to come back even stronger. I'm sure he's got the character to handle the situation and recover from it.'

The club's managing director, Peter Storrie, stated: 'The player deeply regrets his actions. He is very young, he has made a mistake and has paid a high price.'

And Redknapp added: 'Rio is a level-headed lad. I cannot see this hiccup taking him out of his stride. I will be very surprised if he does not emerge stronger. As with a serious injury, the way a player can face up to adversity has a lot to do with overcoming the problem. I have no worries on that score about Rio.'

Rio's arrest certainly proved that times were changing. West Ham immediately banned alcohol from the players' bar. And Redknapp made a point of letting everyone know: 'I enjoy a drink myself, but I always get a taxi. You can't tell me that footballers these days don't earn enough money to catch a cab home. If they can't, there's something wrong with them. It's got to be done the professional way from now on. It's our responsibility to educate the kids from as young as 11 and 12 to know how wrong it is. Just think of the advantages, the rewards they can throw away.

'Young lads these days have got to look after themselves because the best players in this country are earning the same money as the best Italians are earning and their attitude is they would never drink before or after a game – a glass of wine at most. If they were caught drinking more, it would shame them, their families and their clubs, so they just don't do it. I'm not becoming a Holy Joe. I like a drink and enjoy a bet. But players now are getting such tremendous rewards that they must be seen to look after themselves so that they can play to the very best of their ability.

'I remember when Kenny Dalglish signed my son Jamie from Bournemouth six years ago, we were talking and he felt there was a problem at Liverpool he would have to deal with. It was just not acceptable to him that players could go out and have a few beers and think it was all right.'

Meanwhile the Professional Footballers Association, no less, was insisting that drinking and driving was not rife among footballers. PFA chairman Gordon Taylor said: 'I couldn't agree that it's widespread. I just find that these days there is more awareness than ever.'

Being kicked in the teeth shook Rio up, but now he saw it positively because he realised that when you are in the public eye you can't do things and get away with it like an everyday person. In some ways the incident was a blessing in disguise because it made him stand up and realise that as a professional footballer he had to keep himself in order. It wasn't as if he was doing seriously bad things off the pitch, but after what happened he understood he had to be careful what he did where he went and who he was seen with.

As Rio later explained: 'It jerked my mind to say to my

friends, I can't afford to take chances because if I get caught it's me not them who is going to look the mug. I still go to clubs occasionally but people shouldn't get the wrong impression. Sure, I got caught out, but the truth is I'm not really a drinker. I prefer to dance.'

However, behind the loyal accolades there were many serious issues at stake. It was rumoured that Rio might miss out on a mind-blowing payday because his five-year deal at Upton Park included some very special incentive bonuses. One of them related to full international caps – and was worth up to £500,000 if he became an England regular.

Now he waited with bated breath to see if he would be included in the next England squad for the crucial World Cup decider against Italy in Rome the following month. There was little doubt that if England did qualify for France '98 it would leave him with a mountainous task to force his way back into the squad.

Rio's arrest also sparked a big debate about the pressures being faced by the nation's young sporting stars. Glenn Hoddle believed that drugs were as big if not a bigger threat than alcohol – and Rio came from a culture where drugs and drug dealers were predominant. As one of his oldest friends told this author: 'It's a miracle that Rio didn't get mixed up with drugs when he was a kid on the Friary Estate. Drugs are everywhere, being offered on street corners. Drug addicts live in rundown flats on the estate. It's impossible not to be exposed to them.'

Hoddle poured out his fears in one newspaper interview: 'For thirty years players finished a match and then went down the pub for fourteen pints of lager. But that was in the sixties and seventies. Today we have to change the philosophy with better habits and eating differently. But it's much harder these days, with players having so high a profile. They've got to change their attitudes.' He said he genuinely feared that drugs such as cocaine, cannabis and LSD might prove too tempting for some young stars. 'There is no reason to say don't drink. But don't overdo it. Don't drink excessively. What concerns me is drugs. That's a much bigger and more dangerous issue than a tipple after the game.'

But the harsh reality was that the harder people tried to deal with the issue of drugs in sport – especially football – the worse the problem became. Many believed that a comprehensive testing programme was the only answer. Evidence accumulated by the Centre for Research into Sport and Society at the University of Leicester seemed to confirm that football had the biggest drug problem of all. The 1997–8 season saw three high-profile positive drug tests – Shane Nicholson of West Bromwich Albion, Dean Jones of Barnsley and Jamie Stuart of Charlton – plus a host of rumours about the use of cocaine before, during and after Premiership games.

Using drugs to enhance performances is almost as old as football itself. Back in the 1920s, the Arsenal side used pep pills to provide what they thought would be extra punch and stamina in their match against West Ham. But the pills left the players so thirsty and out of breath that they stopped using them after that.

Actual drug testing was first introduced during the 1966 World Cup Finals in England. And ever since then the FA has been taking considerable steps towards achieving a foolproof way of detecting drugs. Many believe that footballers get involved with drugs because, the argument goes, the rewards are so high that they are tempted to try anything to get to the top. Drugs appeal because they are a

short cut to success, but this is not something that truly
relates to football. It seems more likely that recreational
drugs are used as a form of relaxation away from the
playing fields and stadiums. Not one of 28 positive drug
tests in recent years was for anabolic steroids.

Down in Bournemouth, Rio's one-time, albeit temporary,
boss Mel Machin insisted to the world that the teenager
would bounce back following his arrest. He even predicted
that, despite the setback, Rio would be an England regular
within a year. His assessment was: 'Rio's a very decent,
level-headed lad with an old head on his young shoulders.
He was still 17 when I took him on loan, but he was 17
going on 37! When it comes to young players, he's the best
I've ever seen – and that's saying something. When I was at
Manchester City I had Andy Hinchcliffe and David White,
who went on to play for England, plus Paul Lake, who
would have done so, too, if he hadn't been so unlucky with
injuries. I said when I had him that he was a certainty to
play for England. After his experience this season, I expect
him to do that within the next 12 months. After all, there's
no substitute for class ...'

Rio was determined to take his punishment like a man
and still make it to the top. He'd learned his lesson.
Nothing would stop him being the greatest. Rio had been
the brightest star to ever emerge from Peckham – a place
where few make it out of the ghetto. Many saw him as a
genuine 'diamond geezer' in the shadowy backstreets of
south London. Rio had the world at his feet – and his call-
up for England should have proved that.

Just a few days before his arrest, he'd even told one
reporter: 'Some of the kids I used to hang around with at
my old school in Peckham ended up inside for doing some

A KICK IN THE TEETH

really silly things. Thankfully I've always had my football
to concentrate on, otherwise I could have ended up like
that. Fortunately I've had my family and friends around me
to ensure I keep my feet firmly on the ground.'

Then he got arrested. Suddenly the road for Rio was no
longer paved with gold. He'd hit a serious pothole, just as
he stood on the edge of making football history. How could
he succumb after seeing what had happened to so many of
his contemporaries? Some had even been kicked out of
football clubs because of their encounters with the long
arm of the law.

Even Dave Goodwin, who ran the Blackheath and
District Schools League side in which Rio was in a class
apart, was tracked down by one intrepid reporter after Rio's
arrest. The coach said: 'I'm deeply saddened and shocked
by all this. Those who know Rio will tell you, without
exception, that this incident is so out of character it is quite
beyond belief. You can be sure his friends and family will
rally round and support him and ensure that he learns from
this experience.'

Goodwin said that Rio's arrest was 'a real shame', but he
confirmed it was nothing in comparison with what had
happened to some of Rio's other teammates when he was a
youngster. 'At least a couple of them had their
apprenticeships cut short at pro clubs because of
misbehaviour. It's all very sad, but sometimes an inevitable
consequence of living in an area like south-east London.'

Rio's arrest also highlighted an attitude that had prevailed
in football for years, much to the detriment of stars such as
Jimmy Greaves and Tony Adams. Add to that Paul Merson
who confessed his addiction to drink and drugs to a
packed press conference in November 1994. Hoddle's

87

decision to drop Rio met with approval from Merson, who said: 'There's no point in saying it was only a minor incident. That minor mistake could have killed someone. But you've got to feel for the lad, particularly as he would probably have played in that match. It's up to the manager what to do, but you can be sure Rio won't go out and do something like this again. He's learned his lesson now.'

Of course, Rio had read Jimmy Greaves's experiences when he borrowed his autobiography from the school library. He knew he hadn't been through half what Jimmy had. 'But it just serves to illustrate what can happen. Perhaps I took my foot off the pedal temporarily,' Rio later reflected.

Even former England captain Bryan Robson lost his licence in 1988 for his second drink-driving offence. Then there was Northern Ireland midfielder Norman Whiteside, one of Manchester United's best-known heroes, banned from driving for two years in 1990 after being caught while four times over the legal limit. Former England defender Terry Fenwick served eight weeks in Ford Open Prison in Sussex for a drink-driving offence as well as being banned for three years. The ex-Nottingham Forest and England right-back Gary Charles was fined £1,600 for drink-driving in 1993. Police at the scene claimed that the player could barely crawl out of his car when he was stopped.

Over at West Ham's London rivals Chelsea, Rio's problems were used as a warning to the crop of youngsters coming through the club's ranks at that time. Young manager Ruud Gullit was keen to reinforce a 'keep your feet on the ground' message to kids such as Michael Duberry, Paul Hughes, Danny Granville, Jody Morris and Neil Clement. To help do that, the management had pinned a photo of Rio under the headline 'Stupid Boy' on the notice board at Chelsea's training ground. Underneath it was written: 'Do you want to become famous this way or do you want to become famous working hard our way?' One Chelsea starlet commented: 'I don't think it could ever happen here. If you started becoming big-headed or flash you would get brought down to earth very quickly. The senior players just wouldn't let you get away with it.'

Meanwhile Rio knew that the only way to answer his critics was to go out there on the field and produce some even greater performances.

Chapter 7

A RARE COMMODITY

On 24 September 1997 Rio got a severe lesson on the differences between the Hammers and the Premiership top three – Manchester United, Liverpool and Arsenal – when the Gunners thrashed West Ham 4–0 in a goal spree mainly inspired by that deadly Dutch duo Marc Overmars and Dennis Bergkamp. Unfortunately for young Rio, his marking of Bergkamp left a lot to be desired. The man with Arsenal's Number 10 shirt and his teammates quickly dampened the spirits of Hammers fans who'd been chanting, 'Boring, boring Arsenal' before the match kicked off.

Rio was left gasping by the magnificence of master marksman Bergkamp. Most punters agreed that no defender in the world could live with the Dutchman in this form and West Ham should count themselves unlucky to be in the wrong place at the wrong time.

Three days later they were set to take on mighty

Liverpool and everyone was talking about the expected clash between two of the country's most exciting young stars – Rio Ferdinand and Michael Owen. The pair had become friends at England U-21 level and Owen had made it clear he was determined to follow Rio into the full squad.

Despite Rio being denied his first full cap because of his drink-driving conviction, the ever-ambitious Owen saw Rio's inclusion in the squad as an incentive to all youngsters. 'It just shows that they are looking to pick young fellas,' he told a pack of word-hungry reporters the day before the Liverpool–West Ham clash.

Ironically, Rio's exclusion from the England team handed some of the impetus to Michael Owen, already a scoring sensation at Anfield. In fact, England boss Glenn Hoddle had already decided to use Owen in a series of friendly games following the crucial World Cup clash with Italy in early October. Now all eyes were on Owen as being likely to get his full debut at a younger age than even Rio or Man United legend Duncan Edwards.

The Hammers came out 2–1 winners over Liverpool and proved that Rio was far from demoralised by his recent troubles. He helped boost the Hammers' confidence with an awesome display of defensive brilliance. As skipper Steve Lomas put it after the game: 'West Ham have always been accused of having a soft underbelly. Now each of us will get hurt for the team. We'll all go in, whereas maybe before others would have pulled out. We have pace in attack through Andy Impey and Stan Lazaridis, a big strong defence with Rio Ferdinand, David Unsworth and now Ian Pearce.'

Everyone at the game – including Glenn Hoddle – noticed how Rio effectively snuffed out master goal poacher Robbie Fowler, although he did have a tougher time against Michael Owen. Harry Redknapp had the good grace to admit after the game: 'Liverpool certainly have some impressive young players in the pipeline – Michael Owen, for instance, who gave our defence a real hard time.'

Hoddle was at Upton Park to run the rule over England prospects Paul Ince, Robbie Fowler and Steve McManaman. He'd already decided that Rio's full debut would have to wait until after the Italy game. But the Liverpool trio's performance that afternoon was overshadowed by the Hammers' Israeli star Eyal Berkovic, who made West Ham's first goal and scored their second.

But when Liverpool pinned West Ham against the ropes during an exciting last 20 minutes, it was Rio who helped see them through for the three points. The *Daily Mirror* gushed after the game: 'Rio performed with such towering authority in front of Hoddle that if he is not given a reprieve it will prove only one thing – the England manager holds grudges ...' For the Hammers it was a breakthrough game after being beaten in their three previous Premiership matches.

Two days later Hoddle was due to name his England squad for the make-or-break qualifier against Italy in Rome on 11 October. As Chelsea's Gianfranco Zola pointed out: 'Italy don't make mistakes on big occasions.' Referring to his country's earlier 1–0 win at Wembley, he added: 'We managed a miracle at Wembley and we can repeat the feat in Rome.' Hoddle had seriously contemplated playing the as yet uncapped Rio, but concluded that he wasn't quite yet ready to face the mighty Italians.

After weeks of off-the-park controversies, Hoddle was delighted to be dealing with purely footballing issues. 'It's the first time there hasn't been some other issue. I hope it stays that way. It would be nice to have a bit of good fortune going into this one. I said we had eight cup finals and if you could pick one where it was all plain sailing this would be it.'

As predicted, he settled for the safe options against Italy. The only mild controversy was the continued presence on the subs' bench of the blatantly out-of-form Stan Collymore at the expense of Blackburn's Chris Sutton, the Premiership's leading scorer. In the end England got a creditable 0–0 draw and were guaranteed qualification to the World Cup Finals.

With England's spine of Seaman, Adams, Ince, Gascoigne, Sheringham and Wright, it looked as if Rio might have to wait quite a while longer before he'd properly break into the team. At this stage the best Rio could hope for was to be an understudy. But if he was diligent enough and kept his nose clean in the future, then who could say what might happen.

The Hammers' next Premiership game against Newcastle looked as if it might prove a testing time for Rio. But Harry Redknapp believed that his young star defender was up to the test. 'I haven't lost any sleep over Tino Asprilla,' he said, refering to the Magpies' Columbian striker. 'He's a terrific player, has a lot of talent and I've a lot of time for him. But young Ferdinand is a tremendous player. And with David Unsworth and Ian Pearce there as well, I'm sure we'll cope. Let them worry about us. Let them worry about John Hartson – he's just as much of a handful. Newcastle's defenders will know they've been in a game after 90 minutes against Hartson and Dowie.'

As it turned out, Rio put in a Gladiator-style display in the clash with Newcastle. By the time the second half came around, he was so full of confidence that he started forcing play into the opposition's half to give all the paying customers his own rendition of 'My Way'. When England hardman David Batty and a couple of fellow Geordie defenders came swinging their boots in his direction, he managed to leave them all kicking at thin air. Even the most loyal of Newcastle fans admitted Rio was a rare commodity. The Geordies squeezed out a miraculous 1–0 victory, but Rio's talent was undeniable as he produced a display that made the cocky Colombian Asprilla look like a Sunday-morning park player.

Many West Ham fans came away that afternoon saying that Rio would one day captain England, just like Bobby Moore. He was also going to show the continentals how to play their own game. Many saw Rio as the answer to all England's problems. It was heavy stuff to put on the shoulders of someone so young.

Bobby Moore had been the only Englishman to skipper a World Cup-winning side and was still the name on everyone's lips at Upton Park. He died from cancer in 1993 at the age of 51. At 22, Moore became the youngest-ever captain of England when he led them out against Czechoslovakia in May 1963. He was later awarded the Order of the British Empire and given the freedom of London. Moore was also the first player to lift three trophies at Wembley in three consecutive years, winning the FA Cup and Cup-Winners Cup at Wembley before that infamous World Cup victory. Moore's 108 caps for his country was a record until Peter Shilton surpassed it in 1989.

As Hammers fan Steve Rapport explained: 'Bobby Moore was on a different plane altogether. It wasn't just that he was the best defender in the entire history of football, the best reader of the game and, probably, the most accurate passer ever to pull on an England shirt. He was also a

general, a true captain and a symbol of an era.'

It was clear that the Bobby Moore tag could turn into a millstone around Rio's neck if he wasn't careful. Rio had been studying videos featuring some of Moore's greatest performances. 'Recently I saw clips of him in action. He just glided forward, didn't he? And that tackle he made on Jairzinho in the 1970 World Cup, well, from what everyone tells me, that epitomised him.'

On 3 November 1997 Rio turned out for the Hammers against Crystal Palace in what must have been one of the most bizarre matches he ever played in. The floodlights went out near the end of the game when the score was 2–2. Both teams were taken off while electricians worked furiously to restore power to the floodlights, but although the North Stand pylons briefly flickered into life and then went off again, the referee David Elleray decided after consultation with police and safety officers to call the whole thing off after 30 minutes of delays.

In the end Rio's international career was always going to thrive because Glenn Hoddle was obsessed with playing a sweeper and he believed Rio had the capability to perform that special role. Indeed, in many ways he saw a mirror image of himself at the peak of his career. Hoddle knew only too well that defending had been the one weakness in Rio's game until that season, but he was convinced that he could adjust to the top flight after around a dozen international games.

Rio was being hailed as the first English League player to stride out of defence with complete composure and assurance since Liverpool's Alan Hansen. As Rio himself later explained: 'When you create an extra body in midfield the opposition look around as if to say, "Where's he come

from?" and if other players are being marked there's not usually a spare person to mark you, so it creates problems for other teams. But you've got to choose the right time to go, someone has got to sit in for you.'

Still quiet and unassuming, Rio was determined to succeed but knew he could still improve every aspect of his game. 'Talking and organisation are things I need to improve,' he said. 'If you're playing in the centre, you've got to be a good talker or lead by example. I'd like to be able to do both. Tony Adams is a fine example and Alvin Martin when I first went to West Ham was brilliant at it.'

And Rio acknowledged that Glenn Hoddle was an important person to learn from. 'He understands the game, every part of it, from the strikers to the goalkeepers. And having played sweeper he can give me pointers on that. I'm not at that stage where I can pick and choose where I play, but if selected, I know I've got a chance to stake a claim to be in the first XI on a regular basis.'

Rio was still a teenager but he wasn't going to let that get in the way of his many ambitions.

Chapter 8
THE VIBE

I n November 1997, less than a year after suffering all alone in that miserable boarding house in Bournemouth, Rio found himself once again a member of Glenn Hoddle's World Cup plans, relaxing in the luxury of the England headquarters – a £110-a-night hotel in Hertfordshire with breakfast an extra tenner. This time he'd been promised a definite slot on the subs' bench against fellow World Cup qualifiers Cameroon at Wembley on the 15th.

Rio cast his mind back to those days and said to himself: 'I grew up – I had to. Bournemouth was one of the best things that ever happened to me.'

Now it was time for the next stage in his learning curve ...

The game against Cameroon was even more significant for Rio after his drink-driving arrest. It meant he'd been forgiven and he fully intended to repay those who'd shown such loyalty to him. Even as he was warming up in front of the Wembley crowd he got emotional about the atmosphere. And that was before he heard yells of 'Rio, Rio' from the fans. 'I'd thought nobody really knew me at that stage but "Rio, Rio" was ringing around Wembley. I was thinking, Whoa, what's goin' on here?'

Rio came on in the fortieth minute for the injured Gareth Southgate and looked at home almost immediately. He drew loud cheers from the crowd for one penetrating move that almost led to a goal. As he later recalled: 'I thought to myself, Go out there and enjoy the game. Didn't I just! It has given me a taste of international football, and now I want more.'

There were aspects of the experience that Rio would never forget for the rest of his life. 'First of all, the national anthem. That's a massive experience. Standing there and listening to it gave me the shivers. Next, running on to the pitch as sub and Paul Ince slapping me on the back. And getting the ball from Andy Hinchcliffe was a big thing – my first touch in international football. Best of all, perhaps, was a run I made through the middle. I brought the ball out of defence and played a couple of passes, and if Robbie Fowler had played it back to me I might have scored. Instead, when I put him through he had a shot. That run did a lot for my confidence. The crowd were shouting my name, and that makes you realise how good it is to be on the international stage.'

England won 2–0, and after the game Hoddle was full of praise for his young debutant, saying: 'He did nothing wrong, everything right.'

Rio himself later admitted a perfectly understandable attack of nerves. 'I've kept a video collection since I was very young and studied all the great players. Suddenly I looked around the dressing room and there was Paul Gascoigne, Paul Ince and Sol Campbell, the players I've watched for the last few years and I was among them. I asked myself if I was good enough to be there and then realised if I wasn't, I wouldn't have been picked in the first place. I've always had confidence in my ability but when I was younger I certainly didn't think this sort of thing would happen so quickly.'

When Rio got home that night he watched a video of the game and criticised every mistake he made by making a note of it on a piece of paper. 'You have to do that to improve,' he later explained.

Rio's next ambition was to actually start a match for the national side. He reckoned he still had a realistic chance of going to the 1998 World Cup Finals in France. By now he had learned that he couldn't constantly be looking over his shoulder worrying about others being picked ahead of him. This was his chance to impress and he was going to have to be selfish if he was to achieve his goals.

Then he remembered Jimmy Greaves's autobiography again. 'Reading Jimmy's book and learning to come to terms with a spell when I did not play well has made me meaner, more single-minded. I knew what I wanted and that was to go to the World Cup Finals.'

In December 1997 Manchester United boss Alex Ferguson once again tried to sign Rio. This time he proposed an unusual pay-now-pay-later deal after alleged secret talks between Hammers and Old Trafford bosses. Under the agreement, Rio would be allowed to stay at West Ham for another two years before moving to Man United. Alex Ferguson had already had a £6-million bid for Rio knocked back. West Ham told the Premiership holders they'd have to pay at least £10 million to land the youngster. 'Ferguson had been keeping an eye on Rio ever since he turned out for Bournemouth. He was like a man obsessed and determined to get his man in the end,' one Man United source later explained.

According to insiders at both clubs, Ferguson was keen to bring in Rio as a long-term replacement for Gary Pallister. The plan was to either pay a suitable 'deposit' or let West Ham have one of Man United's fringe players as an advance.

West Ham later denied there had ever been any pay-now-play-later proposal with Man United. Harry Redknapp hit back furiously, saying: 'It's a load of rubbish. If we were even thinking of selling Rio then we don't deserve to be in the Premiership.' But behind the scenes, there was no doubt that Man United were putting West Ham under immense pressure to sell Rio and they were prepared to try and pull off any type of deal to get their man.

As usual, West Ham's dilemma was that they were desperately in need of the cash to keep the club afloat. But was Redknapp really prepared to sell their best prospect since Bobby Moore? In the end West Ham decided that they would hold on to their 'investment' for the time being. It was too soon to sell him and, in any case, they knew his value would rocket over the coming couple of years. It didn't make business sense to sell him – yet.

It is surely no coincidence that Rio signed a long-term contract with West Ham just days after the Man United stories surfaced in the press. The Hammers knew they didn't stand a chance in hell of hanging on to the talented youngster for that long, but at least they'd get a king's ransom when the time finally came to cash in their chips.

As one West Ham insider explained: 'Under Harry, transfers were a vital part of the club's survival.'

Rio's new deal with the Hammers was worth around £2.5 million over seven years, according to newspaper reports. Not bad for a teenager who'd been on a £35-a-week YST three years earlier and was only on £400 a week when he made his debut for the Hammers the previous year. But news of the new contract simply fuelled gossip about Rio joining one of the bigger Premiership clubs sooner rather than later. Rio insisted all his loyalties lay with West Ham. 'I'm happy to stay here as long as West Ham keep doing well. They gave me my chance in football. I'm not big-headed enough to say, "I've made it" and walk away from them. I want to repay them.'

Meanwhile Janice was deeply hurt by suggestions that her son's background had led to his conviction for drink-driving. She insisted that Rio was 'not your typical teenager who has a bit of money in his pocket and cannot handle it, he has not been brought up that way'. Janice was particularly irked by the suggestion that Rio came from a family of boozers. 'We only have drink in the house on special occasions and he's never been drunk before, he's got too much respect for himself and the job that he does. He's still the same boy he's always been with the same friends and the same outlook. We would never let him get any other way.'

Now, Rio's most painful reminder of his slip from grace was not being allowed to drive a car until the following September. In some ways his 'house arrest' suited the powers that be because it meant he couldn't get out much. But living on one of the worst council estates in Europe didn't exactly fit the image of being a well-paid football star and a lot of those 'bad influences' remained on his doorstep.

At least being 'off the road' meant that Rio read numerous books on trains and buses during his ban from driving, including *The Guv'nor* by Lenny McLean. He loved this true-crime life story of one man's battle for respect in London's East End. Rio could relate to McLean's journey because he often felt as if he was following a similar path himself.

Many in the West Ham and England camps were hoping that when Rio did get his licence back he'd settle down with a nice girl, buy himself a flat and become a responsible adult. Others had already started calling him a 'Spice Boy' with delusions of grandeur. But Rio was determined to prove his critics wrong.

However, his recent conviction emphasised to Rio that he needed to hold on to the most solid base in his life – his family, especially his mum Janice. So he took Janice, her painter-and-decorator husband Peter St. Fort, his brothers Anton, 13, Jeremiah, two, and his eight-year-old sister Sian to see a plush new house miles away from the Friary Estate. Janice recalled: 'Rio was pushing me into all the rooms, saying, "Go on, Mum, have it, have it." I didn't even know where we were. Peter and I had been looking for a house in Peckham but Rio ended up taking me to this house in Mottingham.'

A suburb on the borders of south-east London and Kent, Mottingham was totally different in character from the inner city. The property had five bedrooms and a garden and Rio picked up his mobile and called the estate agents to tell them that he wanted to buy the house within minutes of them all looking at it. 'She's having it,' he proudly told the estate agent.

As for Janice: 'I felt very uncomfortable about the whole thing but he said his dream was to buy me a house.

I was speechless – the entire contents of our flat fitted into one room.'

Rio felt it was the least he could do for the mum who'd been his guiding light throughout his young life. He intended to eventually buy his own penthouse apartment overlooking Tower Bridge but without wheels he was much better off at the house in Mottingham.

And Rio also kept in close contact with his dad, whom he described to one pal as his 'best friend'. Somehow, despite the painful parting between Rio's mother and father all those years earlier, Julian had continued to be a big influence on his life. 'Julian was (and still is) a good father. He's always been there when Rio needed him, offering good sensible advice and never expecting anything in return,' says one close family friend.

Rio was reminded of his drink-driving offence nearly every day as he made the tortuous journey from south-east London to West Ham's training ground in east London by train and bus. 'I had a lot of time to reflect on it, and obviously it was a major mistake. A naive mistake, not an intentional one.'

It was also gutting for Rio to have to keep looking out at the drive of his mum's new house, where his gleaming BMW stood parked. Later he was honest enough to admit that he still liked the occasional drink, although he insisted: 'I don't drink alcopops and I'm not a beer fan. Of course I still go to nightclubs and bars occasionally but I'm not a huge boozer. I would feel terrible if I played badly on the pitch after drinking alcohol the night before – so I'm quite disciplined about it.'

But there was also absolutely no way that Rio would desert his old manor of Peckham. His best friend Gavin

Rose now taught soccer to the kids on the estate playground where they all used to play football.

Rio's closest pal inside football at the time remained West Ham teammate Frank Lampard junior. Most of the other team members were married with children, although Rio also saw quite a bit of Harry Redknapp's son Jamie, who was then at Liverpool, until the midfielder settled down with pop star Louise.

On the financial front, Rio was determined not to squander the millions of pounds that now seemed certain to come his way. He had an accountant to make sure he made some wise investments rather than spending it all at once. 'I knew that if I had it all sitting there in one account I'd probably spend the lot. My huge weakness is clothes. When I went out Christmas shopping to buy things for my family I came back with things for myself.'

But, for the time being, Rio continued sensibly living at the home he'd bought for his mum. As he put it: 'I get my washing done – and there's always food on the table. I have thought about moving out and buying my own place but it is not an option at the moment.'

Rio claimed to all who would listen that he didn't have time for romance, although his past relationship with Latifah seemed to have been conveniently forgotten. 'I don't want all the hassle that goes with commitment and relationships. I've never really had a full-time girlfriend. I tend to get bored really quickly and can't really be bothered to put in all the time.' He was genuinely worried that every time he took a girl out on a date she might be tempted to sell the story to the tabloids if they split up. 'I think it's harder to trust people once you're famous.'

Even so, Rio still hankered after Latifah. One of his closest friends told this author: 'Rio would kill me for saying it, but Latifah was the one as far as he was concerned. He loved walking round the manor with her on his arm and when they split he was gutted. Throughout his teens he would talk about her. Couldn't get her out of his mind. He used to call her perfection on a stick.'

Meanwhile Rio told one journalist that his idea of the perfect date would either be model Helena Christensen or Essex girl turned Big Breakfast TV presenter Denise Van Outen. 'She's a real babe,' said Rio of Denise. Then, giving away his fondness for BBC TV soap opera *EastEnders*, he added: 'Tiffany [Martine McCutcheon] and Cindy [Michelle Collins] really do it for me too!' He surprised many of his pals by saying that he'd love an evening out with TV comic Jo Brand 'because she's so funny. She'd be a brilliant laugh to go out with.' But he swore blind to his mates that he'd never date a famous pop star. 'No. That gets you too much attention. I'd get embarrassed.' He'd watched the way Jamie Redknapp and his wife-to-be Louise had handled the fame game and decided it was not for him.

Around this time Rio was flooded with offers to do modelling assignments alongside his football career. But he didn't want the 'Spice Boy' label to stick, so he turned down every offer. He'd had acting ambitions since he was a kid but they would have to wait – football took priority.

In February 1998 Rio's big mate Michael Owen was called up for his first full England cap against Chile at Wembley. The night before, Rio was swallowing his disappointment by playing for the England 'B' side at West Bromwich Albion's ground. But, typically, Rio put in a sterling performance to show coach Glenn Hoddle that he still deserved to be selected for the senior side. Hoddle admitted to his colleagues he'd bide his time before blooding the man everyone was telling him was the finest English defender in the Premiership.

A few weeks later Rio was featured in a column in London's *Evening Standard* called Sporting Questions, which provided a further insight into the young star's life. In it he described his own character as 'determined, laidback and positive', and denied he was vain 'unless I get a big old spot'. Margaret Thatcher was 'the last person I'd invite to my birthday party'. And he said he had no fears about growing any older: 'Life can only get more exciting.'

Rio had chipped in some cash to help his mum Janice set up a children's nursery in the Old Kent Road, although he told the paper that the job he would least like to have was 'being a headmaster and meeting all those angry parents. Too much stress!'

At this time Rio's all-time sporting hero was US basketball star Michael Jordan and his favourite soccer game was Brazil versus Italy in the World Cup Final of 1982.

His maturity came out when he answered a couple of other questions:

What was your own best performance?

'I believe others should decide on that.'

Do you have any obvious flaws as a footballer?

'I do have – but I don't want everyone to know them.'

By the early spring of 1998 Rio genuinely believed that he was back to his best form in the lead-up to that summer's World Cup in France. He'd had a few poor games a couple of months earlier, but now he had a realistic chance of going to the biggest football tournament in the world even though he'd only been used as a substitute, coming on late in the World Cup warm-up against Belgium.

But time was certainly on Rio's side. When Brazil arrived

in the United States for the 1994 World Cup Final they brought with them a buck-toothed kid in braces called Ronaldo. He was there merely to soak up the experience and it seemed highly likely that Rio would do the same in France if he was picked for the squad. As Rio himself said: 'A mate pointed out the other day that I could play in four World Cup Finals but, to do that, I know I have to take care of myself and look after me body.'

In May 1998 Glenn Hoddle chose his final squad of 22 players for France '98. Rio was one of them. He walked back to his room at the England hotel in Hertfordshire, sat down on the edge of the bed and found himself engulfed in a full range of emotions. For a while he couldn't utter a word. Then came a breathless excitement at what it all meant to him and his family, and he made an ecstatic call home to break the news. 'When Glenn said simply that I was in, it was the most unbelievable feeling. I had been champing at the bit, nervous, expectant, not knowing what to think.'

After his family, he called up his close friend Frank Lampard junior to tell him that he wouldn't be taking a planned two-week holiday in the sun after all. And Harry Redknapp, Rio's ever-loyal boss, said: 'Everyone is talking about Rio going along for the ride and experience, but if he gets the chance in the World Cup he's going to be a permanent fixture. Getting selected for the squad is a marvellous tonic for the lad and it's wonderful for West Ham too. It's been a long time since those three West Ham greats, Moore, Hurst and Peters, helped England win the World Cup but if Rio keeps maturing as I believe he will he could be right up there with them too. Rio is going to get enormous experience over the next month and it's going to help West Ham in the Premiership next season.'

During France '98 Rio and Michael Owen formed an

even closer friendship. Rio was the elder by almost a year. The two made a point of catching up with the latest gossip, swapping a few friendly insults and engaging in a bit of teenage banter. These two young men clearly had the world at their feet. The money in the Premiership meant that neither of them should have a financial worry for the rest of his life. Rio explained: 'Although Michael and me don't share a room we do have a fair bit in common. We tend to knock round together. We play table tennis, snooker and all the usual things.'

But one thing they didn't have in common was music. 'Michael doesn't know anything about music,' Rio said, adding: 'House, garage, soul and swing. I like them all. Michael? He doesn't mind Lionel Richie.'

Rio continued: 'Golf is Michael's thing. He plays a lot of golf.' Owen offered Rio some great advice about how to cope with the sudden influx of fame, a subject on which Rio commented: 'I can't believe how quickly it's happened for Michael. The hype which surrounds him now is on a par with what happened to Ronaldo. Well done to him – he deserves it but it can be tough. I've sampled a bit of it myself but nothing compared to Michael. I know him well enough though to be sure he won't change. He will need to keep an eye on things but he will be okay. I've seen him, remember. He just signs a few autographs when it's needed and then gets on with his life.'

Rio might well have been talking about himself when he spoke about Owen except there was one big difference – Owen was born in a quiet town to a family led by a pro footballer father while Rio was born on a dangerous inner-city estate where temptation lay around every corner. Maybe that's why Rio preferred to switch most conversations involving Owen to himself and how he was coping with stardom. 'There are times when things have become a little hectic for me when I've gone out shopping to Dagenham or somewhere but that's nothing compared with what Michael is going through.'

Although Rio had squeezed into England's World Cup squad, in the end he didn't make an appearance. Some believed he might have had his chance if it were not for that single mistake of being convicted for a drink-driving offence.

England's eventual defeat against Argentina in France left the nation in a state of depression over the failure to progress any further than the last 16. But many observers believed that with up-and-coming young players like Rio waiting in the wings things could only get better.

Old-time England stalwart Terry Butcher – so heroic against Argentina in that quarter-final clash with Maradona in the 1986 World Cup – put it perfectly when he said: 'Young Rio, with his wonderful confidence on the ball, should take his place and operate as England's sweeper. He's definitely the way forward. It's time for England to turn to youth. While we're all down in the dumps, feeling so sick after the defeat against Argentina, the future really is looking bright.'

Rio's fan club seemed to be growing by the minute.

Chapter 9

RAZOR'S THE MAN

In the weeks following his return to West Ham in the close season, Rio had time to wonder if Glenn Hoddle's decision not to play him in the finals had anything to do with his drink-driving arrest. 'The papers don't think about younger players' feelings and how much they can affect them with some of the things they write, but there are a lot of hard people out there and I have got strong people around me and I have put it to the back of my mind. You just have to make sure it doesn't happen twice. You have got to be an idiot if it happens twice. I am not going to do another thing as stupid as that again.'

Many hoped that Rio – still only 19 – wouldn't live to regret those brave words. There was an overriding feeling that he was basically a good person – an honourable kid who'd fought his way out of the ghetto and away from bad influences through sheer hard work. As he himself later said: 'You have got to be strong and have strong people around you to get away from them. It is not even getting away from them, it is just being able to focus your ambition or something and I had an ambition in life to be a footballer. It was drummed into me to have the right manners off the pitch and treat people in the right kind of way and then people will treat you right, too. My dad always said to me when I was younger that you have got to be a totally different person on the pitch to what you are off it. On the pitch, you have got to be nasty and have a lot of discipline and aggression. When I was younger, a lot of people said I was very kind and that they hoped I didn't take it into football. I don't think I have.'

Meanwhile, at West Ham's Chadwell Heath training ground, Harry Redknapp continued to be blown away by Rio's extraordinary natural talent. The Hammers' boss explained: 'We used to do these one-on-ones, where the attacker would face one defender as he went in on goal. Eyal Berkovic said to me once, "I've been here two years and it's a waste of time if you get Rio. I've never seen him beaten." It was true. Even Paolo Di Canio would try all his tricks, but then make a move and Rio would nick the ball away from him.'

At the beginning of the 1998–9 season West Ham's fans proclaimed on their website that Rio was definitely the Hammers player to watch. They wrote: 'Matured greatly during last season, and one of the best defenders around today. A tall player, who isn't afraid to run with the ball and make himself available in the opposition's penalty area during corners ...'

Then Rio further endeared himself to the West Ham fans through reports in the Spanish press that he'd turned down a £12-million move to Real Madrid and had instead stuck to his long-term contract with the Hammers. Now, with lightning-fast striker Ian Wright signed from Arsenal, there was a feeling at Upton Park that great things lay ahead for the east Londoners.

And joining Rio in the back there were so-called hardman Neil 'Razor' Ruddock, who'd arrived from Liverpool for a bargain-basement £750,000, and Chilean international and World Cup defender Javier Margas, who spent his first day at the Hammers' training ground trying to get to know the only fellow South American. The Chilean defender had heard all about the young Brazilian who'd taken the Premiership by storm and wanted to meet him. How was he supposed to know that Rio was his real name, not a nickname relating to his place of birth?

But it was seasoned campaigner Ruddock who would prove to be Rio's most important guiding light. Ruddock quickly concluded that his talented young teammate could handle all the pressure. Within weeks of joining the Hammers, he told one journalist: 'He's a different class. Seeing him every day in training and playing in matches with him, I can see what a quality act he is.' Ruddock, six feet two, well over 12 stone and 30 years old, was a classic journeyman footballer, having started his career as an apprentice at Millwall before joining Tottenham, Southampton and Liverpool as well as being loaned out to a number of clubs along the way.

Ruddock was a tough, blunt Londoner with a strong heart and a no-nonsense approach to the game. Many put him up with Vinnie Jones as one of the classic 'enforcers' of English soccer in the nineties. Rio, the graceful young apprentice with superb ball control and an uncanny ability to dribble and to dummy opponents, could not have been a more different player.

However, Ruddock soon influenced Rio's play on the field. He later explained: 'I think my experience over 13 years helped Rio. I just told him to keep talking, keep talking. Even if it's rubbish you're saying, just keep talking because it helps concentration and others around you. Rio even helps me now.'

And Harry Redknapp obviously liked the idea of 'Razor' keeping an eye on West Ham's most important investment of all time. Before his move from Liverpool that summer, Ruddock had only really seen Rio on television. 'But as soon as I got on the training ground with him I could tell he was an exceptional player. When I came into the team at Southampton I was really helped by having players like Jimmy Case and Russell Osman alongside me. They really brought me on by playing with me and talking to me all the time. That's a big part of the game, something you don't realise when you're young, and I'm sure I can help him just by being there.'

Later Rio acknowledged that he learned a lot from Ruddock. Some at West Ham say to this day that Razor's toughness rubbed off on the teenager and helped his game develop in a different direction. Says Ruddock now: 'Rio was a bit of an artist with the ball, subtle, capable of all sorts of trickery but he wasn't too sure how to handle anyone coming at him at full pelt.' Ruddock taught Rio how to give as good as he got and that, more than anything, helped the younger player to establish himself in the West Ham team during the 1998–9 season.

Rio showed a diplomatic side to his character when – on the eve of the Hammers' early-season home clash with Man United – he made a public appeal to West Ham fans to lay off David Beckham, who was still under a cloud after being sent off in the World Cup clash with Argentina. Rio said: 'Obviously, I do not want him to play well against us, but it would be great if the fans got off his back a bit. People should remember that David did not lose the match for England. Just as the team win games, the team also lose, and David has more than paid for what he did.'

On 17 September 1998 West Ham lost 1–0 to bottom-of-the-First-Division Huddersfield in the first leg of the second round of the Coca-Cola Cup, and Harry Redknapp was left fuming because his side had torn their opponents apart but still failed to score. At one stage Rio ran unchallenged the full length of the pitch before lashing a rising drive an inch over the crossbar. It seemed like a nasty case of history repeating itself for Redknapp and his assistant Frank Lampard senior. Both had been in the West Ham side that handed Huddersfield one of their biggest-ever giant-killing feats in a Cup match – a 4–2 victory in the FA Cup fifth round 25 years earlier.

After the latest game, Redknapp explained: 'I was sitting there watching us miss chances and I feared that might happen. We just didn't take them. They had one break and put their chance away. I would be the first to complain if our attitude was wrong but there was nothing wrong with it at all tonight. Some of the football we played was excellent. It's the first time this season we haven't scored. I couldn't see them scoring but somehow they did. The tie is still evenly balanced and we've got them at home now.'

Rio knew that the current season was crucial to his development as a player because there had undoubtedly been a few occasions where he'd definitely come off second best. 'Putting that right is something I have to sort out in my head and I've got to do things the right way off the pitch as well. If I have to curb a few of the things I'd like to do, then I will, because I have to be right psychically and mentally. The World Cup was a great experience even if I didn't play. My goal for the season is to start getting into the England team as a regular and I know that'll need hard work and dedication. But first and foremost I've got to get things right for West Ham. If I don't, then nothing else will follow.'

A couple of weeks later all Rio's plans were shattered by a leg injury which meant he had to pull out of the England squad for the European Championship qualifier in Sweden.

But none of this stopped Harry Redknapp making yet more predictions for his young defender. 'He will be the best defender in Europe by the time the European Championship Finals are staged in 2000,' he said. 'Rio is ready for England now. He's outstanding but he's nowhere near his peak.' Redknapp urged Glenn Hoddle to select Rio as soon as he was fit again for the up-and-coming Euro 2000 qualifiers.

But the headlines and accolades were just the tip of the iceberg. Among football's elite, Rio's name was on everyone's lips. Meanwhile he kept his Walkman turned up loud and tried to drown out the praise in case it backfired on him. He put it perfectly when he said: 'I turn on to anything; soul, swing, house, garage, reggae. Anything that helps me switch off.'

The buzz on Rio's footballing ability was growing by the day. His twentieth birthday, on 7 November 1998, was marked by a superb article in *The Times* by Oliver Holt. This is just a small taste of what he wrote:

'Ferdinand is one of the few genuine creative defenders to have emerged in this country in the past 20 years, a player who is much, much more than a stopper. He can defend with the best of them – as he showed in his shackling of Alan Shearer during West Ham's 3–0 victory over Newcastle at St James's Park last Saturday – but he also has a great gift for turning defence into attack. Ferdinand is the forerunner of a new breed, the first genuine English sweeper of his generation, a player who can glide forward with the ball. A player like him can change the balance of a team, give them an extra weapon that opponents do not have. Other defenders save attacking forays for set pieces; Ferdinand is always seeking out the opportunity to burst forward.'

In November 1998 Rio, recovered from injury, got his England call-up for the friendly against Czechoslovakia. England won 2–0, although Rio almost let in a goal in the dying minutes. But he knew there wouldn't be too much backlash from Glenn Hoddle because he had encouraged Rio to break with the ball as often as possible. 'It's something you do at the right time, rather than playing a safe ball,' had always been Hoddle's advice. The problem on this occasion was that Rio gave the ball away and goalie Nigel Martyn was forced to make a good save to stop the Czechs taking the gloss off an otherwise fine England performance.

Off the pitch, however, it seemed that even when Rio was keeping a low profile others were determined to try and link him with trouble. The 20-year-old was fast asleep at the house in Mottingham he'd bought for his mother when he was alleged to have been a witness to a fight at the Epping Forest Country Club which ended in a man being slashed with a broken bottle. Rio assured detectives he wasn't even at the club – a renowned hangout for soccer stars, criminals and soap stars – on the night of the attack.

Rio's new agent, Pinhas – better known as Pini – Zahavi, explained afterwards: 'Rio never goes out on a Friday night before a match, so this is a joke. He is a very serious professional. There is no chance of him being there. I think we should wait for the police to complete their investigation and see what happens then.'

This was one of the first times Zahavi had talked publicly on behalf of Rio. The agent already counted Terry Venables, Graeme Souness and Alex Ferguson as his associates and that link with Old Trafford was to later prove crucial to Rio's career. Zahavi – a former sports reporter – brokered his first deal when in 1979 he brought Avi Cohen from Maccabi Tel Aviv to Liverpool. Shortly afterwards he took former Crystal Palace player Barry Silkman, also now an agent, from Manchester City to Maccabi Haifa.

Even Harry Redknapp rated the Israeli Zahavi as 'a man who can get things done'. But many were now asking how Rio ended up on the books of this mystery man from the Middle East. In fact it all started when Rio was just 15 and he met Zahavi for an informal chat at West Ham's training ground. A couple of years later Rio signed a formal agreement with Zahavi, who was also recommended to Rio by his West Ham teammate Eyal Berkovic, who was already with the agent. In time Zahavi came to consider Rio to be 'almost like a son'. He explained how it all started: 'I saw Rio first and knew immediately he was going to be a great player. He had asked Berkovic and he had a feeling he would be better with an international agent like me than a local agent.'

Back in Israel, Zahavi – who came from the same sort of humble beginnings as Rio – was known as a man of his word. A man who kept promises. His old friend Jacob Shachar explained: 'He has kept his promises to all our friends as we have grown up through the years. He is very loyal.'

And Harry Redknapp had no doubts about Zahavi's intentions towards Rio. 'He is a gentleman. Agents have a terrible reputation but Pini is a decent guy. Rio is in safe hands.'

Former client Barry Silkman added: 'I would say he is one of the top four agents in the world and he is one of the few men in the game I would trust.'

Back at West Ham, Rio's best mate at the club, Frank Lampard junior, must have found it difficult at times to cope with the spotlight so frequently being turned on his friend. Lampard, shy, mild-mannered and the apple of every dinner lady's eye at Upton Park, was known as 'Junior' to virtually everyone at West Ham. He spent a lot of time reminding Rio that if it hadn't been for Harry Redknapp, and to a lesser extent his own father, assistant manager Frank senior, neither of them would have progressed so fast.

So when West Ham agreed a new deal with Lampard it seemed that both young players would remain at Upton Park for the foreseeable future. Lampard admitted to friends he was influenced by Rio's earlier decision to sign a new deal with the Hammers and that had helped him decide to stay at the club. It was clear that West Ham wanted to hold on to their two 'investments' and watch them mature into even more valuable players.

But one of Rio's biggest blows came in February 1999 when England boss Glenn Hoddle was sacked after an interview in *The Times* in which he was alleged to have said disabled people suffered because of 'Karma'. The remarks caused public outrage and even prompted Prime Minister Tony Blair to voice disapproval.

Step forward Kevin Keegan, seen by many as the man to

save the England team and bring some more heart and soul into the job after the technical obsessions of master craftsman Hoddle. The only problem was that Keegan was no great fan of Rio Ferdinand. Having moved forward so fast under Hoddle, Rio now faced a new battle to try and establish himself in the England team under a new boss. It wasn't going to be easy.

Chapter 10

ROCKING THE WATERBED

In July 1999 the rumour mill connecting Ri   host of big football clubs started up all over aga   ot of the speculation had been sparked by protracted gotiations between Rio and West Ham about an additional clause in his contract that gave him an automatic 10 per cent cut of any future transfer fee. Rio's agent Pini Zahavi knew only too well that West Ham would one day sell Rio and the player wanted to be certain he'd get his cut of the wedge. West Ham were playing hardball presumably because they wanted to get maximum return from their investment.

So it was no surprise when Roma voiced an interest in Rio. A party of Italians, headed by the club's chairman, Franco Sensi, were rumoured to be on the way to London to start negotiations. But Rio knew that football history was littered with examples of professionals lured by the promise of big bucks in Italy who'd then flopped under the weight of expectation.

Publicity about Roma's interest had a ripple effect among other big European clubs. Real Madrid were reported to be about to make another £12-million bid, and others were waiting and watching developments. Meanwhile West Ham's chairman, Terence Brown, continued to refuse Rio's demand for 10 per cent of any future transfer deals.

Rio himself fuelled some of the speculation about his possible departure to Italy by joining a radio interview with his Hammers colleague Paolo Di Canio at West Ham's training ground. Taking the microphone from his teammate, he told Italian listeners: 'I know the Olympic Stadium in Rome and I know it is a beautiful city. Roma fans are exceptional. I hope we will see each other soon ...'

The following day the national newspapers swarmed around Rio wanting to know if he was about to depart for Italy. He insisted on playing down the stunt by talking about his admiration for his talented young colleague Joe Cole, who was about to break into the West Ham first team.

Despite Kevin Keegan's reservations about Rio's footballing talents, Rio re-emerged as a shock candidate for a place in the England team to face Scotland in the European Championship 2000 qualifier at Wembley on 17 November 1999. He only made it on to the subs' bench in the end, but at least Keegan considered him, which was encouraging after the little contact there had been between Rio and the new England manager. England lost the game 1–0 but got through to the European Championship after thrashing the Scots at Hampden Park in the first leg.

A couple of weeks later, on 30 November, Rio was celebrating Joe Cole's winner in a dramatic Worthington

Cup tie against Birmingham when he was jostled by a steward on the edge of the pitch. 'The steward kept on shouting and then I asked him what his problem was and he pushed me. I couldn't believe he acted the way he did but that's the sort of thing you have to put up with sometimes.' The scuffle between player and club official seemed to show another side to Rio's so-far exemplary character on the football pitch. Was the pressure of not being an England regular getting to him?

With his driving licence now back in his wallet and a luxurious brand-new penthouse flat in London's upmarket Docklands, it wasn't surprising that Rio's skills off the field started to get tongues wagging. In the autumn of 1999 he went on a series of dates with blonde Spice Girl Emma Bunton. The couple became very close and were soon speaking on the phone virtually every day. Emma insisted the romance was not yet fully developed but admitted: 'I am young, free and single and having fun. I've met him a few times as we share the same friends – he's a nice guy.'

Rio and Emma were spotted out in London on at least half a dozen occasions and their friendship was said to be an open secret at West Ham, where Rio's teammates had been ribbing him about his famous new girlfriend, especially since he'd always said he couldn't handle dating a pop star. The pair had first met during a visit to London's Emporium nightclub in mid-August with mutual pals Mel B, Ryan Giggs, David Beckham and his wife Victoria, aka Posh Spice. They hit if off immediately. But Emma – who'd only just split from her long-time love Jade from the pop group Damage – told Rio they should take the relationship one step at a time. Rio's mum Janice proudly told one journalist at the time: 'They seem made for each other.'

Rio was more reluctant to comment on the friendship. All he would tell friends was: 'I do know Emma and she's a nice girl. We get on well.'

Many of Rio's friends insisted he was smitten by Baby Spice and that the couple had even spent a number of romantic evenings at his new flat. Inevitably, many compared the relationship with Posh and Becks. Emma had already let it be known she wanted to settle down and have children in the near future.

But Rio was soon having problems coping with Emma's fame. 'Rio just couldn't handle all the attention she got,' one of his oldest friends said. 'Rio comes from a family where the mother is the one who runs things. In some ways, he felt that his girlfriend's role was to keep out of spotlight, not attract even more attention than he did!'

It seemed Rio was right about his own character: he just didn't suit dating a fellow celebrity. Another old pal in Peckham commented: 'Rio loves the attention – that's why he loves the fans at all the games – but he's not so happy when the person he's with gets more attention than him.'

Naturally, Janice had very strong opinions about the sort of girl who might persuade her son to settle down. 'I think the person he will end up with will be a beautiful, strong-minded woman who loves clothes, music and food. But it will be a while until he settles down – he's still very focused on his career.'

Rio and Emma eventually drifted apart, but it was becoming clear that all Rio's public declarations about leading a quiet private life were a little hollow. He made frequent appearances in the gossip columns as well as on the sports pages. Rio was providing ammunition for those critics who claimed the 20-year-old had been seduced by his new-found celebrity status to the detriment of his game.

After his whirlwind romance with Baby Spice, he was now under a virtually non-stop spotlight. He needed to learn to watch his step.

The football critics began circling Rio because he'd endured a torrid time on the pitch over a six-week period in the autumn of 1999 thanks to a series of uncharacteristic errors while on duty for West Ham. There was a dreadful mistake at Anfield which allowed Liverpool to snatch victory. That was preceded by numerous blunders against Sunderland, Leicester, Aston Villa and, in Europe, against the French side Metz, all of which raised serious doubts about Rio's reputed £12-million price tag.

Rio was honest enough with himself to know he had been suffering and told one newspaper: 'If I knew what was going wrong I wouldn't be making the mistakes. Everyone has bad games but it's how you respond to those setbacks that counts.'

Was Rio yet the finished article? At both club and country level he still quite frequently gave the ball away, leaving himself marooned and his defence completely wrongfooted. And Kevin Keegan continued to believe he was not yet ready for a regular spot in his England line-up.

In early 2000 Rio linked up with his West Ham mate Frank Lampard to play for the U-21 side for the first time in more than two years. The match was against Yugoslavia in a play-off for the chance to be at that summer's U-21 European Championship. Rio shrugged off his apparent 'demotion' by Keegan to prove he was still a very talented footballer, especially at that level, as England won 3–0.

Rio's new riches had given him a Jaguar XK8, designer clothes and a penchant for London nightclubs. But he still believed his football was heading in the right direction and he refused to let the 'Keegan problem' make him downcast. He even saw his return to the U-21 team as the chance to confound his critics and prove he was still worthy of a place in Keegan's senior squad for Euro 2000.

Behind the scenes, though, Rio was growing restless about something else – the lack of silverware at West Ham. He admitted to one reporter: 'I do get a bit jealous when I see others challenging for trophies and I've made no secret that I want to move abroad one day to develop as a footballer and broaden my horizons as a person.'

But it also seemed that Rio still hadn't learned all his lessons away from the pitch. In March 2000 he was accused of booting a girlfriend called Shera Rosun out of his home and telling her to get an abortion. Perhaps not surprisingly, Shera decided to reveal all to the *News of the World* and accused Rio of 'behaving just like a kid. I should have known he could never cope with a baby.'

Shera, 20, claimed that when she rang Rio to tell him she was pregnant there was just silence from the other end of the phone line. 'I wanted him to say everything would be alright. But he told me he was busy and to ring later. Then he stopped returning my calls.'

When Shera finally got through to Rio for a proper conversation, he told her: 'I don't want no kids, do you know what I mean? My mum would kill my ass.' Rio's reference to Janice says it all: his mother was never far from his mind.

Rio's personal habits during his fling with Shera provided a fascinating insight into the 20-year-old West Ham star. Shera claimed Rio constantly gorged himself with sweets and wine gums before all their sex sessions on his waterbed. She implied he was nothing more than a big kid. And after sex, 'Rio stopped cuddling me because he said he couldn't sleep like that. He told me not to laugh at him, then he curled his knees up to his chest and started to suck his thumb. He was in a foetal position like a baby. He said he always slept like that.'

Shera fell for Rio when she was introduced to him at a London nightclub. 'He said he wanted to take me out for a meal, so I gave him my number because he seemed really nice.' Rio called her the next day. 'He had to do a radio interview, so I didn't meet him until 10.30 pm. It was too late to go to a restaurant, so we went back to his flat.'

Once inside the apartment Rio scoffed handfuls of sweets and then put on a video called *Kiss the Girls*. 'We then sat there eating Minstrels. It wasn't very romantic,' explained Shera. 'I'd had a few drinks, so I couldn't drive home and Rio joked that I could either sleep in the bathroom or with him on the waterbed. I thought that sounded great, but he'd put too much water in it because he didn't like it moving around. It was rock solid and not very comfortable. I wasn't planning to make love with him, but he was really nice and I thought, What the hell! I didn't want it to be just a one-night stand and he gave me the impression it meant more to him than that. There are not many guys who can get me into bed on the first date, but I was putty in his hands.'

And despite his childish habits, romeo Rio turned out to be a gladiator between the sheets. Shera revealed: 'When we made love I have to admit it was great. Rio has a lovely bottom. It went on for hours and we made love four times. Then he cuddled me and told me I had a nice figure. He said he'd had enough of women with fake boobs and he loved mine because they are real.'

That's when Rio turned over and started sucking his thumb. 'It looked cute, but it was then I realised he was just a little boy.'

Shortly after their first romp, Rio invited Shera back to his flat again. This time he encouraged her to use the sauna and whirlpool bath. 'We watched *Four Weddings and a Funeral* and ate Minstrels again. I stayed the night and cuddled, but I wouldn't let him make love to me. I wanted to prove to myself he really liked me and wasn't just after sex. He slept in his foetal position again. The next morning we were both in a rush and he said he would call, but he never did. I phoned his mobile several times but just kept getting his message service.'

Weeks later Shera, from Slough, in Berkshire, found out she was pregnant. 'When he finally did contact me it was to find out if I'd made an appointment at the abortion clinic yet.'

In that call, a distraught Shera asked Rio: 'You want me to have an abortion then, do you?'

Rio replied: 'Yeah. So what are you going to do? Are you going to have one?'

'I don't know. What if I want to keep it?' asked Shera.

'What d'you mean, if you want to keep it?' Then Rio paused. 'To be honest, I wouldn't be happy because I don't want no kids. I suppose you want me to keep it as well? I wouldn't be happy.'

Shera explained at the time: 'My mother is pretty strict. She threatened to kick me out of the house if I keep the baby. I feel sick because I'm pregnant at 20 and I'm going to be on my own. I didn't expect Rio to want to play happy families, but he shouldn't just shrug me off. Now I don't know how I can face the future. I just wish I had never met him.'

Rio's trust in women was badly shaken by his whirlwind affair with airport worker Shera, which not only ended up in the *News of the World* but also provoked a lot of banter from his teammates at West Ham.

Then, completely out of the blue, eccentric Hammers star Paolo Di Canio said in a newspaper interview that Rio wasn't yet good enough to play for England. Rio later explained: 'I was surprised by what Paolo said, but I bear no grudge towards him. The simple truth is Paolo is just being Paolo – everybody at the club has a good laugh about him. He's always ready to say things and I guess he always will.'

But a number of Premiership and European clubs were not in agreement with Di Canio. Newspapers were soon reporting that Leeds United were now leading the chase for Rio's talented services.

On 29 April 2000 Harry Redknapp gave his first public response to a reported approach by Leeds: 'David O'Leary has £20 million to spend in the summer and he wants to give me £7.5 million for Rio Ferdinand. But the day we sell Rio and our other young players is the day when this club starts to die. People talk about Sol Campbell, but Rio is a better player than him. He has made a few mistakes, but he is such a special player. He'll be an international for the next 10 years. I have no doubt. And he should certainly be part of England's European Championship squad.'

Three weeks later West Ham's managing director, Paul Aldridge, responded further to the Leeds situation: 'I don't know how many times I have to deny all this. Rio is not for sale. We have not had any discussions with Leeds and there is no truth to the rumour. It has been like this for two or three years now and we are becoming a bit immune to it and it doesn't really bother us too much. It has literally been tens and tens of times and the rumours are tiresome. Rio is an important part of the team and we have got no plans to sell him.'

A couple of days later Harry Redknapp publicly stated that Rio would only quit Upton Park to play abroad and not for a Premiership rival. 'Rio has made it absolutely clear to me that if and when he does leave West Ham, he'll be going to one of the top Italian or Spanish clubs.' Then a fresh round of rumours circulated that Rio was on the verge of signing for Leeds in a £15-million deal. A typically blunt Harry Redknapp instantly hit back: 'I'm sick to death of hearing that Rio's on his way to Leeds. It just isn't going to happen.'

Meanwhile many were speculating that Rio's superb form for West Ham meant he would make England's 22-man squad for Euro 2000 despite Kevin Keegan's reservations. But Rio didn't make it in the end. Many football commentators were shocked by the England boss's decision, and one wrote: 'It seems appalling that someone with Ferdinand's ability will be left at home this summer.'

So Rio, Frank Lampard junior and Newcastle's Kieron Dyer, plus Leeds players Jonathan Woodgate and Michael Duberry, headed instead for the five-star Grecian Bay resort in the popular resort of Ayia Napa, in Cyprus, for a well-deserved summer break. They had all played together for the England Under 21 team. All Rio's pledges about living a low-key lifestyle soon crumbled in the searing Mediterranean heat.

One holidaymaker who joined the young soccer stars during their holiday insisted: 'They were drinking themselves into oblivion most days. They treated the women who flocked round them like pieces of meat.'

By 4.30 pm on the afternoon they arrived, Rio and his friends had positioned themselves at the railings of a local bar to ogle women. Other tourists were soon complaining about their language. Lifeguards had earlier issued a warning to Rio and the others to show respect to holidaymakers on the beach.

Soon the group were lining up shots of neat vodka and taking it in turns to run up to a glass, drink it and then dash back before running to the next one. Four hours later Rio and his friends were virtually the only ones left drinking at the bar.

None of these highly paid professional footballers had even bothered to watch England's game against Portugal in Euro 2000, which was being televised live on a screen in the corner of the bar.

A number of women later accompanied Rio, Dyer and Lampard to their hotel suite. None of these women realised that when one of the players' non-footballing friends held a camcorder and followed them around the bedroom he was intending to turn the footage into an amateur hardcore-porn video. At one stage the 'cameraman' announced into the camera's microphone: 'We are about to encrypt. If you really want to see the following programme you will have to pay £12.99.'

Rio allegedly had another camera hidden at the base of his divan bed while one of the women – a beautiful English blonde – shared her most intimate thoughts with him, unaware everything was being recorded. She lay naked on the bedcover as Rio – also naked – stood astride the bed. The camera then caught them both writhing on the bed. Rio waited until the woman's back was to the camera before waving at the lens as if it was all one big joke. He also pretended to kick a ball and celebrate scoring a goal.

When the woman turned away, Rio raised his hand over her head and jerked a finger in her direction before cackling with laughter. Other scenes showed Dyer and Lampard in similar intimate scenarios. Rio was then heard on the video slurring his words as he boasted that he could keep going for the following 24 hours. 'The way I'm feeling at the moment I could be in a swimming pool.' At least 15 minutes of the video was devoted to Rio making love to the same stunning blonde.

Another scene in the same video showed Lampard in an orgy with two women who seemed to be completely unaware they were being filmed. Eventually he ordered them to look at the camera and they were clearly horrified. A sordid and meaningless attempt at lesbian sex between the two women then followed.

And Rio's reaction when he was later confronted by a tabloid reporter did him no favours either. 'What do you see me doing?' he challenged the journalist. 'The camera wasn't hidden at the bottom of the bed. The girl consented. If I'd been caught degrading a woman I'll put my hands up. But I've never degraded a woman in my life.'

But the women encountered by Rio and his Merry Men thought otherwise. One, Michelle, said: 'It makes me feel sick to my stomach.'

Michelle reported that all the football stars downed beer, vodka and Red Bull cocktails and even refused to buy drinks for any of the women before persuading them to go to their hotel. Rio was also photographed drink-driving as he weaved his way back to their hotel on a rented scooter. Neither he nor his footballer pals even bothered to wear helmets. Would Rio never learn?

Back in London, there was bitter disappointment about Rio's behaviour in Ayia Napa. While he could be forgiven for the drink-driving offence since he was only 18 at the time, the same could not be said for this latest episode. Others implied that while Rio's talent was not in doubt, his attitude towards training at West Ham left a lot to be desired. By contrast, Rio has always insisted that he was a very dedicated trainer.

Even the normally relaxed Harry Redknapp was infuriated by the behaviour of Rio and Lampard. He told one reporter: 'I spoke to Rio. I've told him that he has to be careful. He knows he was in the wrong.' Redknapp had issued a stark warning to his two young stars players. 'They have to be careful because there's always a bird willing to earn a few bob by selling a story to a newspaper about a famous footballer's bedroom habits and prowess, giving him marks out of 10 and some other nonsense. That's how football's gone. Big business yes, but that means there's always someone out there looking to make a few quid by selling a story about you.'

Some felt that Rio's appalling behaviour in Ayia Napa might have been sparked by his disappointment at not being picked for Keegan's Euro 2000 squad. Even Rio himself admitted: 'I was very, very disappointed. I thought I was good enough to be picked. It was a blow to the old confidence, I will admit.' But surely that was not a sufficient excuse to embark on an orgy of drink and sex?

But, despite his holiday antics, speculation was still rife that Rio was on his way to Leeds United. He reacted very coolly to the stories. 'I've come to expect these type of rumours at this time of year. It's happened every season since I've been playing in West Ham's first team, so it's nothing new.' But then he left the door wide open by adding: 'I have never talked to anyone from Leeds. They are a big club with plenty of tradition but, like West Ham, they haven't won anything for a while now.'

Today Rio admits that being snubbed by Kevin Keegan for Euro 2000 was the crunch point in his career that was probably the making of him. 'I'd begun to think I was invincible. To get complacent with my game and I didn't prepare for matches properly. I fully expected to be picked for the team and, when I wasn't, I think it made me take stock.'

Others things also helped Rio 'take stock', as he put it; such as the fact that most other people were not as well off as him. He'd been particularly touched to get a letter from a 14-year-old boy in Ghana. 'He sent a photo of himself. He was really poor, with holes in his boots and a raggy kit. He wrote that he had posters of me all over his bedroom wall. He had looked around the world for a player to give him pointers on his game – and plumped for me. I thought, Wow, this kid's all the way from Ghana and I'm his idol.'

Rio believed that letter put everything into its right perspective. He was incredibly lucky and he had to be more careful from now on if he was to avoid any more pitfalls. 'I put a lot of pressure on myself to do well. My main fear was that I wouldn't be an England regular. If I didn't play for England again I'd have been gutted.'

Chapter 11

SIGN ON THE DOTTED LINE

Rio knew the fast-approaching 2000–1 Premiership season could prove a watershed for him and he admitted: 'Every season is a big one for me, but I want to get the most out of it. Now it's time for some hard graft. I want to get down to the nitty-gritty. It's time my football did the talking.' Behind the scenes, football giants Barcelona were also considering whether to make an offer for Rio. Deep down he knew that unless he left West Ham his England career might well run out of steam. Not being in the Euro 2000 squad confirmed his worst fears and it was a devastating blow to his pride and confidence. Kevin Keegan's decision was a wake-up call for the young defender. It didn't matter how much talent he had; unless it was properly used and carefully developed, then his career could plunge into free fall. And his behaviour in Cyprus hadn't done his standing much good, either.

Many later interpreted the outrageous antics of Rio and his mates as indicative of young men losing control. Rio had good reason to be worried. Perhaps a move to Leeds would help him get away from all those bad influences in London. Also, he could ask for no better a tutor than the boss at Elland Road, David O'Leary. True, the Irishman wouldn't stand for any of the indiscipline that was tolerated at West Ham and he'd probably give Rio a few harsh lessons, but it was no more than he deserved. Rio was realistic enough to know the time was approaching when he had to escape the unhealthy influences on his life.

Harry Redknapp and Hammers chairman Terry Brown knew the day would eventually come when Rio would leave Upton Park. But for the moment they wanted to hang on to their young investment. Rio's value seemed to be escalating at the rate of around £1 million a month. By the end of that year – 2000 – he would probably be worth something like £20 million. To West Ham, that seemed a decent mark-up on a player who'd started with them on £35 a week.

In the summer of 2000 the chairman of Leeds United, Peter Ridsdale, made a point of telling a number of football journalists: 'We haven't made a bid for Rio Ferdinand and will not be making a bid for him.' Not surprisingly, his comments were taken with a pinch of salt.

Back to Harry Redknapp, who on 12 August told reporters: 'The chairman of Leeds is trying to manipulate a deal. It's unsettling for Rio and for this club, and I'm fed up. I know what's been going on. If Barcelona knock on the door we've got real problems because I couldn't say "no" to the boy. But why should we sell him to Leeds? He's better off here.'

Ridsdale then hit back at West Ham. 'Some weeks ago I asked West Ham's chairman if Rio was for sale. He wasn't, so I asked to be kept informed. We've made no bid, nor would we unless West Ham's position altered. I'm disappointed West Ham's manager appears to imply something different.'

Redknapp, facing numerous injury problems the week before the Hammers' first match of the season, at Chelsea, insisted he could well play Rio despite some worries about his fitness. 'I'll have no problem bringing Rio straight back in. He's like a Rolls-Royce – you just start him up and he goes straight away.'

Away from football, Rio found himself linked with beautiful Sky TV presenter Kirsty Gallacher. Rio refused to talk about the relationship, but he did reveal his attitude to love and sex in one newspaper interview. 'I've been out with a few models and I've slept with girls but I haven't had a proper relationship since I left school. If I get too involved with someone, my mind strays off football. You don't have to go out with a girl to have sex with her. I don't need a companion all the time. What I really like is going out with my mates, mucking about and having a laugh.'

Then Kirsty got quite a shock when she interrogated Harry Redknapp about the latest crop of Rio transfer rumours. 'Come on, Harry – what's really going on with Rio?' she asked.

Redknapp cheekily retorted: 'You should know – you've been dating him for three months.'

Kirsty immediately changed the subject, but a Sky insider said later: 'Harry was out of order. Kirsty was very upset but didn't show it. It wasn't very gentlemanly of him, whether or not it was true.'

In fact, Rio's relationship with Kirsty never even got off the ground. He seemed to be determined to stick to his pledge not to have a serious romance in case it affected his football. Rio's main aim was to keep any sordid details about his love life away from the people who really mattered – his family and old friends back in Peckham.

There remained genuine fears that Rio was still too close to temptation to stay on track for soccer stardom. He had lived in London all his life; his friends were there, the club was there and it wasn't clear if he really did know how to say 'no'. Rio later admitted: 'I used to go out raving and partying all the time. My mates used to ring me up and say, there's a party here, a party there, and I'd be the first one to say, "Let's go." I was easily led. I was getting out and about at the wrong times, drinking and everything, chatting up the girls, staying out too late.'

In his heart of hearts Rio knew that things had to change if he was going to climb to the next level of his career.

In November 2000 Rio took a call from the Hammers' managing director, Paul Aldridge, which would change the course of his life. The club was seriously considering an £18-million offer for him from Leeds United. 'It was a big turning point in my life,' Rio recalled. 'There was a lot of speculation, and West Ham were saying they weren't going to sell me, but then I got that call. I was shocked because I hadn't asked to leave but then I thought, If they want to sell me, then I'm going to go. When I heard the size of the fee I thought, Bloody hell, or something stronger.'

Now it looked as if after all the denials, West Ham were prepared to accept a bid. They're willing to let me go, Rio thought to himself. It's time for a new chapter. I've got to talk to Leeds.

On Thursday, 23 November Peter Ridsdale flew to London and booked into the plush Conrad Hotel at Chelsea Harbour. He and the club secretary of Leeds, Ian

Silvester, then got a taxi to meet Rio's trusted agent Pini Zahavi at the Langham Hotel in central London. Half an hour later Rio turned up and introduced Ridsdale to his mother, who wanted reassurance about how life up north would be for her son.

Janice had been privy to all the protracted negotiations behind the Leeds move. 'People were saying of Rio, "West Ham are definitely going to sell him." We even spoke to our friends the footballers Ian Wright and Paul Ince about it and came to the conclusion that if he was going to leave it had to be to go somewhere that was going to take care of Rio.'

And Rio later recalled of his meeting with Ridsdale: 'Five minutes with their chairman and my mind was made up. The key was that I was talking to people whose ambition matched mine. If my family was okay about the move, it was going to happen. Mum and Dad said to me, "Whatever you're happy with, we'll be 100 per cent behind you," which is the way it's been all my life.'

Just before Rio's meeting with Ridsdale, Chelsea had made a last-minute bid to snatch him away from Leeds. Chelsea – armed with £12 million from the sale of Norwegian Tore Andre Flo to Glasgow Rangers – were prepared to go to £20 million. It can now be revealed for the first time that Rio turned down Chelsea because he'd always hated them even as a kid. Rio later told one old friend back in Peckham: 'I don't like Chelsea. They're too flash for my liking.' And Rio always liked being the centre of attention wherever he went. As his old friend explained: 'Rio would have been well down the pecking order after players like Desailly, Zola and Hasselbank. And that's not good news for someone like Rio.'

Puzzled former Leeds boss George Graham – now at Tottenham – was scratching his head at Rio's proposed move to Leeds because he'd never had the funds to finance such a deal when he was at Elland Road only two years earlier. 'I only ever had £14 million to spend on 11 players yet in my first full season we finished fifth in the Premiership,' he pointed out.

At 9.30 am on Friday, 24 November, Rio turned up at West Ham's training ground. It was just over 12 hours since he and Peter Ridsdale had parted company with a handshake. Most of Rio's West Ham teammates were still making their way through the morning traffic and the players' car park had more autograph hunters than cars in it.

Many present at Chadwell Heath that morning wanted to know why Rio – strongly rumoured to already be a Leeds player – had turned up at his old club. And some of the kids hanging around still felt obliged to make one last desperate plea. 'Don't go, Rio,' a couple of them begged. 'We'll miss you. Stay here. You don't wanna go to Leeds. It's better here than up there.' Why was he heading for Leeds? One youngster even pointed out: 'It's not like you're going to Manchester United. Now they really are a really big club.'

Rio felt a bit embarrassed because he knew there was already no turning back. He then sauntered sheepishly into the changing rooms for the last time, but he couldn't train because of a groin strain. There followed a 40-minute session with West Ham physiotherapist John Green in the treatment room. Then Rio spent five minutes chatting with Harry Redknapp in his office. As Rio's boss later recalled: 'By the time he walked out I was none the wiser about what he'd decided.' He thought there might still be a chance Rio would stay at West Ham. 'My wife asked me the previous night if I thought he would go, and I told her I honestly didn't know.'

Other players – such as West Ham's England vet Stuart Pearce – told Rio they'd love him to stay, but most of them sensed he was on his way out of the door. In fact Rio already had a plane ticket to Leeds booked before he set foot in the training ground.

Eventually Rio emerged from the changing rooms wearing a smart suit and carrying a black plastic bag of West Ham kit – memories, souvenirs – which he then put in the boot of his brand-new silver-blue Aston Martin. None of the fans who were there earlier noticed Rio leave. Their attention was on a field on the other side of the building where the first team were taking part in a training session

An hour later Rio pulled up in the driveway of his mother's house in Mottingham and asked her: 'What happens if that's the last time I go to West Ham?'

Janice recalled: 'Rio was very emotional.'

Behind the scenes, Pini Zahavi was still haggling about the amount of compensation due to Rio because he had not requested a transfer.

Two days later – on Sunday, 26 November 2000 – Rio finally signed on the dotted line for Leeds United before watching his new teammates beat Arsenal 1–0 at Elland Road. At a packed press conference before the match, Rio explained the reasons behind his move: 'I am very pleased to be joining such an ambitious club. It came as a big surprise when West Ham accepted a bid for me. The manager's ideas here at Leeds played a big part in me moving here. I saw the squad here, which also had a big effect. I appreciate what West Ham have done for me, although this is a new chapter in my career. Hopefully my career can now start going again.'

That last remark made it clear that Rio believed he could not achieve any more at West Ham. And he certainly wasn't going to let the massive fee bother him. 'The fee involved doesn't concern me. I'm here to play football.'

But the question on every Leeds fan's lips was: 'If David O'Leary ever gets all the members of his squad fit at the same time, who makes way for Rio Ferdinand?' Rio was undoubtedly earmarked as long-term cover for 31-year-old Leeds and South Africa skipper Lucas Radebe. Many believed that Rio had arrived just in the nick of time to save Leeds. Besides injuries, they also had the fast-approaching trial of Jonathan Woodgate and Lee Bowyer to consider. It's not known to this day whether Rio fully appreciated the huge impact that their case would have on the future of Leeds United.

A few hours after signing with Leeds, Rio spoke to his dad on the phone. 'Eighteen million,' said Julian. He paused. 'Who would have thought it when you was a young boy in Peckham? But we didn't pay it. Just get on with it, don't think about it, the money don't mean nothing to you, you didn't make the price. It's not your concern.'

Julian's advice helped him put the transfer fee to the back of his mind. Rio explained: 'My mates don't speak about it, my family doesn't speak about it, the lads at Leeds don't bring it up and I don't carry on like I'm an £18-million player. I don't think I'm greater than anyone else, just one of the lads, as willing as anyone to roll up his sleeves and get on with it. I try to see it in a positive way. If a club shells out that kind of money, they must feel you're a good player and that instils a bit of confidence in you. But that's it, for me it is not an issue otherwise.'

And Rio was deeply irritated that some people presumed his decision to sign for Leeds was only about money. He insisted: 'I am not a money-mad sort of person. I never had much money when I was young and I always found that what I earned at West Ham was more than enough. To my

The young child that would become one of the footballing sensations of his era.

Top: Rio's mother Janice outside the playground of the Peckham school where Rio learned his passion for football.

Bottom left: Rio's birth certificate.

Bottom right: The family together – Rio with mum Janice, brother Anton and sister Sian.

Top: Rio in the Blackheath Bluecoats Secondary School team photo. Rio is second from the right in the front row. At the right-hand side of the middle row is Leon Simms, still Rio's best mate who hangs out with him whenever he comes to London.

Bottom: Rio in his district football team, back row, third from left.

Top: The Peckham estate where Rio was brought up. It is on this estate that young Damilola Taylor (*bottom left*) lost his life. Rio spent his time secretly trying to track down Damilola's killers, and he was also shocked by the death of his close friend Stephen Lawrence (*bottom right*).

Rebecca Ellison – Rio's glamorous girlfriend.

Top and bottom right: The man in action, and (*bottom left*) celebrating his sensational goal against Denmark in the 2002 World Cup with Goldenballs David Beckham himself...

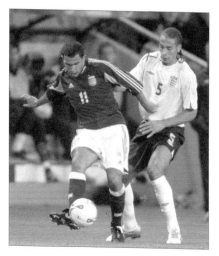

Top: Rio at the West London hotel where in March 2004 his appeal against an 8-month ban for a missed drugs test was dismissed by an independent 3-man panel.

Bottom left: In January 2005, Rio showed his altruistic side when he joined the Stand Up Speak Up anti-racism initiative.

Bottom right: Rio Ferdinand harries Argentina's Carlos Tejez during the England 3-2 win in November 2005, which raised even higher hopes for England success in the 2006 World Cup.

Stylish and contemplative – who knows what the future holds for the world's finest defender?

parents and my mates, the money I earn is absurd. My concern at the time of moving to Leeds was how my family felt about it.'

Besides his mum, Rio's family by this time consisted of his 15-year-old brother Anton, who was about to sign YTS forms with West Ham, Sian, eight, and Chloe, three, and two-year-old Jeremiah. They remained the single most important element in his life. As Rio explained: 'When I ring home Jeremiah hollers into the phone, "Rio, Rio," like they sing in football games. He's mad, just mad. But that was the hard thing about coming up to Leeds, missing family.'

Janice already knew she'd have to make many visits up to see Rio during those first few months at Leeds. Rio couldn't boil an egg without her help. He also struggled with the washing and ironing and just about every other domestic chore.

Within days of arriving in Leeds he was full of praise for the city. 'The people are warm and really friendly. In London, sometimes, the people can be harsher. I have been really made to feel at home up here and the thing that strikes me more than anything else is that everyone's for Leeds. It's a one-club city and everyone here wants you to do well.'

Meanwhile, Janice was telling anyone who would listen that toddler Jeremiah could be the next member of the Ferdinand football dynasty. 'When I go to the nursery to collect Jeremiah, they are always saying to me that his ball skills are amazing for a two-year-old – but they don't know who his brother is.'

One of the most fascinating aspects of the Rio transfer saga was the inclusion of an additional clause in the contract which meant that lump sums would be paid to

145

West Ham after each year he spent with Leeds. This would increase the entire package to a figure approaching £33 million, in addition to his salary eventually doubling to £66,000 a week.

Leeds had bought into a complex transfer deal. Meanwhile many of their fans wondered how long Leeds could afford to hold on to Rio if they didn't start winning some silverware. It was also imperative they qualified for the Champions League each season.

The intrepid Pini Zahavi was still haggling with West Ham about Rio's pay-off. Rio asked the Professional Footballers Association – the players' union – to intervene after the Hammers offered him less than £200,000 as a severance bonus, even though he did not ask for a transfer. Rio was demanding a figure of £1 million.

Other football clubs were genuinely surprised that Leeds had splashed out such a vast amount on such a young defender. Rio took the 29 shirt at Elland Road, opting against keeping the 15 jersey he had had with West Ham. The only thing that really mattered to him was that the move would help him claim a regular place in the England team.

Many in Leeds expected Rio to take up the mantle vacated by the late, great Billy Bremner, who had retired from competitive football just a few months before Rio's birth in November 1978. Bremner played for Leeds a total of 585 times between 1959 and 1976. He was the Roy Keane-style hardman at the core of legendary Leeds manager Don Revie's successful sides of the sixties and seventies. Bremner was a skilful passer, but it was his never-say-die attitude that dominated his play, especially during his long reign as captain.

Rio was hailed at Leeds as the new messiah – the final piece in manager David O'Leary's jigsaw, which would enable Leeds to mount a serious challenge for European and domestic honours. The Leeds players had all been impressed by Rio's awesome display a couple of weeks before his transfer when West Ham beat Leeds 1–0 at Elland Road. O'Leary saw Rio and fellow central defender Jonathan Woodgate as the lynchpins of the team.

Rio immediately made a very good impression on O'Leary, who said: 'Rio wants to improve himself, wants to be the best and, as a lad, I like him. His timekeeping and manners are impeccable and I like that in people.'

But although Rio had moved off his childhood manor, he swore blind he'd never desert it. Even when he'd been talking over his move up north to Leeds, he had made it clear it was a wrench to quit London. O'Leary told him to forget London. 'The manager told me a few home truths and wasn't scared of knocking me back, even though he didn't know the kind of person I was,' explained Rio. 'A different kind of person might have taken offence at what he said, but I appreciated the honesty. What the manager was saying was right. I kind of agreed with it myself. I accept criticism from the people who matter to me. Other people are paid to make their judgements. That's fine, fans have the right to criticise but their views don't bother me. I listen to those who are going to try to enhance my game and that is the manager and coaching staff at Leeds.'

O'Leary made it clear that Rio was already earmarked for an even bigger role at the club. 'A future captain of this club for certain,' he said. 'I mightn't know much about this game but centre backs, I've an idea about them. To me, Ferdinand is quality.'

Rio's new teammates were impressed by the ease with which he settled into Elland Road and they respected his readiness to accept responsibility. Rio was quickly doing his share of the organising and cajoling, reminding his teammates that, along with the easy elegance of his football, there was a definite desire to win.

Chapter 12

MURDER IN PECKHAM

The day after Rio committed his future to Leeds United, 10-year-old Damilola Taylor was murdered while he walked home through the very same estate where Rio grew up. Rio heard the news from a bunch of mates, who hit the phones within hours of the brutal killing of the Nigerian schoolboy on 27 November 2000.

Rio later recalled: 'I thought to myself, Bloody hell, what is going on there? I was brought up a couple of minutes from where Damilola was killed and because you're from there you want to get involved in some way, to get people to sit up and listen.'

Within days of the murder – which made headlines across the world – Rio was asked if he'd help by presenting a TV appeal for information which might help catch the killers. The interview was filmed at his new club's training centre at Thorp Arch, and Rio was given a set of scripted answers beforehand. He glanced down at the answers, carefully folded the piece of paper up and put it to one side. 'You ask the questions,' he told the interviewer. 'I'll be okay.' What followed were a lot of highly emotional, unscripted answers that seemed to get to the core of the problem. They were delivered with an earnestness which made people sit up and take notice back in south-east London.

Damilola's murder highlighted a genuine fear on the Friary Estate about gangs of youths ruling certain corners of the estate after dark. At Damilola's nearby school, his classmates said they were frightened to walk home from school because they might be attacked and they didn't trust the police to help them.

Rio took the Damilola murder to heart. For him the tragedy reflected so badly on the place he loved – Peckham. He explained: 'I love Peckham. It's, like, my place. When I was young and went to school outside Peckham I made sure everyone knew where I was from. I know my life now is a long way from all that, but I can still remember what it's like to want things and to walk down to the shops and wish you had what's in them.'

Rio turned up on his old manor and took a group of journalists on a tour of the estate, where he soon found himself listening to kids airing their views on subjects that were very similar to what he experienced as a youngster. Children complained of being harassed for money, being threatened verbally and physically. Rio even heard that in the weeks before Damilola's murder many of the kids on the Friary Estate witnessed a build-up of problems from certain gangs of youths but residents were too scared to tell the police. Just like Rio many years earlier, most of them had concluded that the police did not care about them because they were black. Many youngsters said that even if they were in trouble they would never ask a white policeman for help.

Rio had two cousins who attended the Oliver Goldsmith School, where Damilola had been a pupil. 'It's a terrible tragedy and the nation has been forced to wake up to what's happening in places like this because of such a horrible, horrible incident,' he told reporters as they toured the estate. But deep down, Rio knew there was nothing new about the Damilola tragedy and he even admitted to the journalists: 'It would be absolutely awful if people believed this was just a one-off incident.' He had seen many examples of this when he was a kid.

After the Damilola tragedy Rio made some very substantial donations to charities in Peckham, hoping that in some small way his contributions might help residents on the breadline. He was furious about what he perceived to be numerous politicians sitting on the wall afraid to get involved in the inner-city problems plaguing Britain. He wanted the outside world to realise that what happened in Peckham was normal life and something had to be done quickly before another similar incident happened.

Rio even tried to get an audience with Tony Blair on behalf of the residents of the Friary Estate 'to sort a few things out'. 'I want to explain to him about the area's problems,' he said at the time. 'The politicians need to start talking to the people who live and work in the area every day.' But the Prime Minister never responded to Rio's offer.

For Rio the situation perfectly summed up what was happening. 'A lot of young kids in these areas are from single-parent families or ones where both parents have to work. By the time the kids finish school at half-past three, they've got three hours to roam the streets while mum and dad are out working trying to put food on the table. When I was younger, I used to go to an adventure playground or I'd go to my mum's friend's house but many people aren't in a position to do that.'

He was appalled by Education Secretary David Blunkett's attempt to link Damilola's killing with today's so-called get-rich-quick society epitomised by the hit TV show *Who Wants To Be A Millionaire*. 'I don't think he knows what he's talking about. He can't ever have been down to Peckham – you have to live there to understand why people don't get involved. Say you saw someone lying there with blood on the ground – you just don't know what the situation is. There could be someone coming down the stairs with a gun ready to finish off the victim. That's the kind of thing you've got to worry about in those situations. It's not as simple as just going to help someone in areas like mine.'

Rio loyally made a point of mentioning his childhood pal Gavin Rose, who was by this time running the Layton Adventure Centre on the Friary Estate. But he pointed out: 'People like Gavin can only do so much because they have very little cash. It sickens me when I consider all that money the Government spent building the Millennium Dome.'

In the middle of the Damilola tragedy, Rio even made a nostalgic visit to his junior school, Camelot, for a Christmas fête. His appearance reinforced the affection in which he was held. 'He has always been true to where he came from,' said one staff member. 'Recently, when some people who owned the shop across the road from the school moved out, he made a point of coming back to say goodbye. We have incredible pride in Rio and his achievements and it's nice a young lad has got the break he deserves.'

When Tony Blair did finally make a much-publicised trip

to the Friary Estate, Rio wasn't able to make it because of Leeds' playing commitments. Some of Rio's oldest friends were deeply offended by what they called the Prime Minister's 'emotional exploitation of schoolchildren'. According to 16-year-old estate resident Leana Davis, Blair was so busy looking at the cameras that he did not pay attention to the kids.

Back in the Premiership, Rio's career at Leeds could not have got off to a worse start when the team were on the receiving end of a 3–1 thrashing by Leicester at Filbert Street. The critics immediately started baying for the golden boy's blood. How could he be worth so much money? Rio himself later admitted: 'You don't want hiccups when you join a new club, you want to be 100 per cent right from day one. The Leicester game was the worst nightmare. I am asking myself, Have I made the right move? I didn't know. I found myself looking at West Ham's results and thinking they were going okay. Then I went training with the lads and the anxieties began to ease. I could see I was among some of the best players in the country and I knew I was in the right place.'

Rio eventually moved into a new house in Wetherby, near Leeds, together with his 2,000-plus collection of CDs, which were to be given a room of their own. His musical tastes were even more eclectic than before and included rhythm and blues, soul, rap, garage, reggae, funk and anything vaguely similar.

Although he still occasionally went out to clubs in Leeds and enjoyed dancing, Rio said: 'I've settled down a lot more. I've got the right people in my life now. My best mates are back home; they aren't on the other end of the phone saying we've got a bop to go to just around the corner. It's a couple of hundred miles now.'

He missed his mum, brothers and sisters but Janice travelled up north to look after Rio at least once a month. And he insisted he was now more interested in playing computer games than chasing girls. He claimed to be virtually unbeatable on a PlayStation.

Rio remained deeply concerned by the lack of arrests in the Damilola Taylor case. He even made a fresh appeal in newspapers: 'It would be nice if whoever did it came forward or if somebody would drop the police a line and let them know who the killers are. It won't bring young Damilola back, but it would help his family to come to terms with what has happened.'

Peckham was, and still is, in Rio's blood. He knew what sort of stuff went down there. Only a few days before Damilola's murder, one person Rio knew ended up dead and another on a life-support machine. Rio didn't claim to have any of the answers to the problems, but he tried his hardest to keep in contact with his mates in the community who knew exactly what was happening on the ground. 'I was talking to my mate Gavin Rose, who works on the adventure playground in Peckham, and he told me some of the things that the kids talk about now. It's like crazy stuff. We definitely weren't talking about those kinds of things when we were that age. It's the community workers and the social workers we should be listening to, not people in suits who've never lived in Peckham, who have never been there and who have never experienced a week in the life of somebody who lives in Peckham, Harlesden, Brixton or somewhere like that.

'They don't know what is going on, then they come up with all these solutions and the people of Peckham sit there and think, What the fuck are they talking about? This is doin' nothin' for Peckham. I love Peckham. I have a Peckham T-shirt here and it's, like, my place. When I was young and went to school outside Peckham, you made sure everybody knew you were from Peckham. Then I got some money and I moved my family out to a quieter place, which was good for my little brothers and sister. But I used to go back, three or four times a week. Obviously, I have left now. From Leeds, it's no longer a bus ride.'

Rio feared that Damilola's murder would make people treat places like the Friary Estate as virtual war zones. 'I don't want Peckham to be abandoned,' he said. The murder spurred Rio on to get even more involved in the problems of inner cities. He was determined to give something back. In the rundown Chapeltown area of Leeds he helped launch a cybercafé for underprivileged children. He also joined RABS – the Revolutionary And Breaking Stereotypes football academy – which encouraged kids in Leeds to grow in confidence. 'I'm somebody who can make a difference simply because I'm a famous face. People take you much more seriously when you come from a poor background. They respect you because of your roots,' he explained. He was realistic enough to know that he couldn't solve all the problems of the world, but he had a lot of very valid points to make and no one could deny his personal knowledge about the problems of living in the inner city.

Meanwhile Harry Redknapp still sung Rio's praises even though he'd joined another club. 'It made me laugh when people said Leeds were paying all that money for potential,' Redknapp told one reporter. 'Absolute rubbish, they paid it for a world-class player. David O'Leary knew it, I'd known it since Rio was at school and now it seems the rest of the world is realising it.'

Just a couple of weeks after finally signing for Leeds United, Rio received racist hate mail from fans purporting to follow West Ham and Leeds. He told one journalist: 'I've had a few letters since the transfer. Some have been nice, but I don't want to go into the others.'

Rio had heard rumours about the racist problems that had plagued Leeds for many years but these vicious letters made him even more curious about the details behind the coming court case involving Leeds players Lee Bowyer and Jonathan Woodgate, accused of attacking an Asian youth outside a nightclub in the city centre. Also, there were reports that Rio's close friend Kieron Dyer had turned down a move to Leeds because he feared he would be targeted by Elland Road racists. Leicester's Emile Heskey, too, was alleged to have refused a move to Leeds for similar reasons. He went to Liverpool instead.

In purely footballing terms, Rio's £18-million transfer to Leeds was still questioned by many fans. Rumours that Ronaldo, of all people, was being lined up to play at Elland Road at least gave the fans something else to talk about. It was claimed that Inter Milan had offered Leeds injury-plagued Ronaldo with a view to getting the player rehabilitated following his long layoff with knee problems. Most considered the rumours to be nonsense since the Premiership seemed the last place for a player to try and mend a damaged knee.

The appointment in autumn 2000 of Sven-Goran Eriksson as England's first foreign football coach was of major importance to Rio because he knew the Swede was a long-time admirer of his skills. The new England coach was very different from the paranoid Hoddle and the heart-on-his-sleeve Keegan, who'd walked out after a disastrous home defeat by Germany in a World Cup qualifying-round game. Eriksson exuded calmness and was even nicknamed by the Italian press 'the rubber wall' because when manager of Lazio he soaked up everything they threw at him so softly and then bounced back a gentle answer.

Not only had Sven heard much praise about Rio, but he had a soft spot for Leeds United after visiting their training camp as a would-be coach more than 20 years previously. And, to cap it all, Leeds were to play Eriksson's club Lazio in the Champions League on 5 December. Eriksson was working out his notice after Lazio had struck a deal with FA bosses that he would not join England until later the following summer. That game would have been the perfect stage for Rio to show Sven what he was made of except that he wasn't eligible for the Champions League until the following February, when the second stage began. As Eriksson explained before the game: 'I think Leeds have an extremely good mentality, always running, always fighting.'

Leeds impressively beat Lazio 1–0 in Italy, which, ironically, forced Eriksson to conclude that 'working out his notice' at the Italian club was not a very practical idea. Within weeks he'd joined the England set-up full time.

Now happily settled at Leeds, Rio was hoping the next stage of his career plan – a regular place in the full England team – would soon follow. He told one reporter at the time: 'As long as I feel I'm doing alright with Leeds, I think things should fall into place. A few of us, Kieron Dyer, Frank Lampard and myself, sat down and picked an England under-23 team. There's massive talent. You look at Liverpool, West Ham, Man United, Leeds, and there's players from other clubs too.

'These players are going to come through and it says a

lot about English football and the coaching that has been going on. It's just a question of nurturing this talent at senior level and in Sven-Goran Eriksson we have a guy who has the credentials. He's done it around the world but particularly in Italy, which is such a hot-bed.'

Rio knew only too well there were no guarantees of a full England place with the likes of Wes Brown, Gareth Southgate, Sol Campbell and Martin Keown around. But he was determined to push hard for selection. 'I made a lot of mistakes when I was younger,' he admitted. 'They were well documented but I now think they were a blessing in disguise. I didn't realise I was so much in the spotlight. I will make other mistakes but I have learned from the ones I have already made. People shell out a lot of money to see you play and you have got to behave in a responsible way. That was hard to grasp at first, but you eventually get there.'

In the middle of January 2001 Rio was struck down by one of the most bizarre injuries to befall any modern-day footballer – something which might cynically be called Couch Potato's Knee. His new boss David O'Leary explained through gritted teeth: 'It was a freak accident and typical of our season. It wasn't even done on the training ground – Rio was watching TV with his foot up on the coffee table in the same position for several hours, and it strained a tendon behind his knee.'

This ludicrous injury sidelined Rio for the weekend's 3–1 home defeat by Newcastle, but he was expected to return for the following Saturday's FA Cup fourth-round tie against Liverpool. For all Rio's undoubted professionalism, there were occasions when he still seemed like a chilled-out kid from the slums of Peckham rather than an international multi-millionaire soccer star.

Rio's first appearance in the Champions League was on 13 February at Elland Road against Anderlecht in the second stage. Leeds won 2–1 and a week later thrashed the Belgians 4–1 away. Rio was then called up for a starting place in England's back four in the 3–0 friendly defeat of Spain. He looked strong and confident alongside Sol Campbell. England's new boss Sven-Goran Eriksson seemed determined to give youth a chance, which was great news for Rio and the other up-and-coming young players.

Behind the scenes, Rio had been working hard at developing his game to that of a flat back four, which was very different from the approach at West Ham. By the time the Champions League quarter-finals began he seemed to have adjusted his game superbly. He was also handed the captain's armband in the absence of regular skipper Lucas Radebe and relished the responsibility.

The emphatic 3–0 victory against Deportivo La Coruña in the first leg of the quarter-finals of the Champions League on 4 April looked certain to secure Leeds a highly unlikely place in the competition's last four. But what made Rio's day more than anything else was that he scored one of the goals. It was a classic. Irishman Ian Harte crowned an impressive evening with a classic assist when goalkeeper Valerón could only flick his sixty-fifth-minute corner into the path of Rio for his first-ever goal for Leeds and his first scored in nearly four years.

Leeds lost the quarter-final second leg 2–0 at Deportivo in front of a hostile 35,000 crowd and just scraped through to the semi-final 3–2 on aggregate. Uncharacteristically, Rio got himself booked for kicking the ball away in frustration in the twenty-third minute. This had followed a tussle with Fran as Leeds seemed to be crumbling under incredible pressure from the Spaniards.

Leeds hung on grimly during the last quarter of an hour as Deportivo battled in vain to score a third goal that would have equalled the aggregate score. No one was more astonished by their success than David O'Leary: 'Frankly, I am amazed that we have reached the next stage of the competition. We knocked out a very good side and rode our luck tonight but it is about time we enjoyed a bit of good fortune after all we have endured this season. Now the adventure continues as we face Valencia. I wouldn't have minded who we faced but I know they are an exceptional side who were only beaten by a world-class side in last year's final.'

Leeds United's latest dream continued, but how long would it last?

Chapter 13

DIAMOND GEEZERS

In *Only Fools and Horses*, Peckham's most famous fictional hero, Del Boy, constantly accentuates the positive. 'He who dares wins, Rodney. He who dares wins.' So it seemed that Del Boy and Rio did have one thing in common besides hailing from Peckham. Del always dreamed of the day he'd make it big, and Rio was determined to be the best defender in Europe while still barely out of his teens.

Just as Del was renowned for an approach to life inspired by the famous SAS motto, Rio was singularly and similarly determined to fulfil his dreams. Such ambition in someone so young was quite startling for many of the older players he came across at Leeds. But there was no doubting his ambition.

Rio's goal against Deportivo La Coruña, followed by one against his former club West Ham and then one against Liverpool, brought his tally to three in five matches – all this for a player who hadn't scored in years.

And Rio credited the Yorkshire countryside as one of his biggest inspirations. 'Believe it or not, I really do love the countryside. I have my farmer's outfit and everything! When we travelled north on the team coach with West Ham we never saw the best bits of places. When I got to Leeds I was pleasantly surprised by the outstanding beauty of the countryside. I am much more content these days sitting in my own house chilling out.

'When we go out at Leeds it's normally together as players for a quiet meal or something. You are much more under the microscope at a club like this and if you try to take liberties the manager gets to know about it very quickly. Mind you, when I first arrived I went into a corner shop in Wetherby, close to our training headquarters, and the woman behind the counter chatted away 19 to the dozen. I couldn't understand a word she was saying. I had to ask her to slow down.

'But it's OK now. The people are blinding. There is only one club in the city. Everybody adores Leeds. The punters sometimes get in your face a bit but you have to expect that sort of thing. To be fair, it's what I've wanted since I was a little kid, so I can't complain, can I?'

Rio's family and friends continued to pop up north to see him. The move to a quieter community seemed to have helped him to keep more level-headed. And his settled state of mind at Leeds was about to help turn him into an England regular. Rio appreciated the gentle art of persuasion practised by Sven-Goran Eriksson. Of the England squad's new Swedish boss he said: 'He's clear and concise with his instructions on how he wants us to play. The coach has created an atmosphere already in which no

player can afford to assume he's too good to be dropped. And I don't see that situation changing. I've played for managers who shout a lot. Not this one. He'll let you sit there and quieten down before he starts talking. Then he'll tell you what he wants in a calm, composed manner.'

Back at Leeds, Rio still got a lot of stick for his vast salary. But he had a very logical answer for the critics: 'I don't think it's really a money thing. It's not our fault that football is the in-thing and people want to pay for it. If working at a bar or in Tesco's was the in-thing, and people started investing in that and paying staff 10 grand a week, those people wouldn't turn down that kind of money. In fact, it's others who act different. Other people call me flash. How many people who got paid that money wouldn't buy things that they liked? Not stupidly, but just a jumper. People just say you are flash because you're a footballer.'

On the clothes front Rio continued to be obsessed with what he wore. Anything from Prada to YMC, but he was particularly fussy about shoes. 'It takes me a long time to find a pair I really want.'

That Spring, England squeezed out a 2–1 victory over fellow World Cup group members Finland. Rio and Sol looked uncomfortable at the back, with Rio even going missing at the corner that resulted in Finland's goal.

But despite this hiccup, Rio's long list of admirers continued to grow. Latest member of the fan club was Big Ron himself – ex-manager turned TV pundit Ron Atkinson. In his column in the *Guardian* he heaped praise on the young defender. 'There was a lot of talk when Rio Ferdinand went to Leeds that he could only play in a back five. Few would doubt now that he has adapted his game to cope as one of two centre-halves. The biggest single difference is that he will be engaging people a lot more. In a three at West Ham, Rio was seldom marking. He had to worry about cleaning up at the back, making interceptions and picking up runners from midfield like Ray Parlour.

'Now he will be more in contact with strikers, getting in more tackles and challenges and having to keep a really close eye on his opposite number. The change will have improved his concentration and his defensive qualities, not least in the air. I remember seeing him play for England against Switzerland and he didn't seem to be able to come to terms with the heading bit. His work in challenging for the first ball has come to a lot.

'Since slotting into a four Ferdinand has reduced the number of runs he makes out of defence. There's nothing wrong with occasionally bursting forward, particularly if you have responsible players like David Batty who can sit in for him. But he knows he can't do it willy-nilly. As the Leeds manager David O'Leary said on Saturday: "The three allows you to take more liberties, to take more chances." In a four your first reaction has to be to make sure you get the ball.'

The build-up to the Champions League semi-final against Valencia was to prove a vital experience for Rio. David O'Leary was still haunted by the way he'd tasted defeat as a player against the same side 21 years earlier in the 1980 Cup Winners Cup Final. But the Irishman believed his young Leeds team could get to their first Champions League Final since 1975, when they lost 2–0 to Bayern Munich.

Valencia knew they would face a tough battle against the Yorkshire club. Goalkeeper Santiago Canizares pointed out:

'Leeds are looking very much like us. They place the emphasis on the unit rather than counting on great individuals In addition they have tremendous desire and a determination. I recognise it because it was what we went through last season.'

But the truth was that Leeds had been the underdogs of the tournament since getting through the pre-qualifying rounds the previous summer. They also had to cope with a torrent of negative publicity generated by the approaching court case involving Lee Bowyer and Jonathan Woodgate.

The first-leg semi-final at Elland Road was played in light rain and Valencia controlled the first half, although Rio stood firm and gave an impressive performance. In the second half Leeds came close to scoring on a number of occasions, but a 0–0 draw on home soil meant all the odds were stacked against them for the return leg the following week.

In the return leg in Spain, Valencia proved too strong for Leeds as Juan Sánchez struck twice and Gaizka Mendieta fired a third to give them an emphatic 3–0 victory in front of a partisan crowd of 53,000. For Leeds, the misery was completed when teenage striker Alan Smith was sent off in the last minute for a tough challenge on the French World Cup winner Didier Deschamps. Defeat was a sad ending to Rio's European adventure, but he and his Leeds teammates had done the team proud.

David O'Leary gracefully conceded that his side were beaten by a superior Valencia team: 'I have no complaints over the result. Valencia were the better side. I now wish them all the best. They're a fantastic side and I hope they go on and win the final. They deserve it.' He was rightly proud of his team's achievements and privately admitted much of it was down to Rio's superb performances as an all-round defender. 'We've come a long way in three and a half years. It's a sign of that when people say they're disappointed we didn't reach the final at our first attempt,' he said after the game.

By mid-April Leeds were sixth in the Premiership table and couldn't be caught by Rio's old teammates at West Ham, 13 points adrift with four games to play. Leeds still had an outside chance of qualifying for the Champions League but needed other sides to slip up badly during the run-in to the end of the season. At least they'd avoided an Intertoto Cup nightmare by guaranteeing they could qualify for the UEFA Cup next season by finishing sixth.

Rio was then named in the Professional Footballers Association's Premiership team of the year. He was Leeds United's sole representative in the final 11. Arsenal and Man United led the rest with three players each.

During the summer of 2001 Rio regularly made it down to London to see some of his old Peckham mates, but he was well aware that footballers, or rather their fat pay packets, were a magnet for the sort of people he needed to avoid. He admitted: 'I've been offered drugs when I'm out in bars, clubs and restaurants. There are always drugs about.' But he never succumbed to temptation and to this day has never touched drugs in his life. However, fame and fortune were bringing other pressures. 'I struggle with the loss of privacy. I can't go out to a restaurant and come out of myself even a little bit. I can have a laugh, but I've got to keep it to a minimum. If I get rowdy – and everyone does sometimes – it's going to be highlighted.'

Rio had grown wary of women and their motives for being nice to him. 'I really don't like talking about it because it makes me sound big-headed, but I do get a lot of women throwing themselves at me – asking me to sign across their chests and lifting up their skirts for an autograph. Of course it's an ego-boost. Even if the girl isn't that good-looking, I take it as a huge compliment. If she's good-looking, that's a bonus. But I've got to watch who I mix with. I usually get a vibe if a girl's interested in me or my money. But it takes a long time to trust someone.'

Then Rio had a night out at that popular watering-hole the Epping Forest Country Club and met an attractive brunette called Rebecca Ellison. She was softly spoken and made no attempt to flash her eyelids at Rio, but he was hooked from the moment he first caught sight of her. This time, thought Rio, I'm going to take it one step at a time.

During the summer of 2001 he courted Rebecca in an old-fashioned manner until he felt confident that she was genuinely interested in him. Then he persuaded her to stay at his house in Wetherby. Rebecca wasn't interested in going out clubbing and Rio liked that. He always responded better when the women he met were happy to stay out of the limelight.

Within two months of meeting, Rebecca was virtually living with Rio at his house in Yorkshire. But, during visits to his old south London haunts, Rebecca was rarely seen out on his arm. One of his oldest pals, Leon Simms, explained: 'We only see Rio down here on his own, man. That's the way he likes to keep it.'

Rio's other big love affair continued to be clothes. 'My mum goes mad when I come home with all my bags. I do the whole works. I love Prada and they know my face well in Gucci.' He had never forgotten the way they treated him when he used to wander into those designer shops on Bond Street when he was a youngster. But Rio still shopped at

those same exclusive stores. 'I can't help it,' he confessed, laughing. 'But when I first went back there, I let them know what had happened. They were hugely apologetic. They said: "Sorry, we didn't know."'

Down in south London, Rio's elderly granny, Angelina Ferdinand, spoke to a newspaper about how disappointed she was that Rio hadn't been to see her in years. 'I was always close to Rio's father Julian and I thought this might bring Rio and I closer. But now I don't see either of them and it breaks my heart. But then Rio is a superstar footballer and it must take up all his time. Rio has never given me any money because I don't want any. All he has ever given me is a football shirt when he got signed to West Ham, which I was really pleased with. I just wish he had a spare moment to spend some time with me. Rio's laughter used to fill this house and now all I have are memories. I feel I don't know him any more – I don't know him any better than the football fans who watch him on TV.'

Rio's career had received the double boost of a highly publicised run in the Champions League plus confirmation from Sven-Goran Eriksson that he saw him as a regular team member. And by the summer of 2001 Rio knew more or less for certain that his seat was booked for the 2002 World Cup Finals in Korea and Japan if England managed to qualify. He even visited the land of the rising sun as part of a goodwill tour, one year ahead of the tournament, accompanied by his mum Janice and Leeds teammate Alan Smith. In his new-found role as ambassador for English football, Rio was given a grand tour of Japan – from karaoke bars to World Cup stadia. His trip was sponsored partly by the Italian clothing firm Verri and he was thrilled when he

was taken to visit a geisha house. Rio loved Japan.

Initially this unlikely threesome didn't know how to handle the country's ancient costumes and traditions. Rio recalled: 'At first we didn't know what was happening but then the old Mama started playing the guitar and singing songs and they started doing some traditional dancing and it was like being in an East End boozer!'

Naturally, Rio and Smith enjoyed a night out singing with the locals at a karaoke bar. 'If Sony had been there they would have signed me up on the spot,' Rio said later. 'I was banging out Bobby Brown like you wouldn't believe!' Rio's trip to Japan also highlighted the problems back home with the recently closed Wembley stadium. 'How can the Japanese knock up five unbelievable stadiums in no time and we can't even manage one?'

And Rio let slip on the tour of Japan that he secretly harboured ambitions to captain England. 'At the moment David Beckham is captain of England and he's doing a great job. But I must admit it's every player's dream to captain his country and I'm no different.'

Typical Rio: always thinking ahead to the next stage of his career.

Chapter 14

MUNICH MASSACRE

The football world was stunned when, in July 2001, Harry Redknapp suddenly quit West Ham because of a dispute over the club's potential summer transfer fund. He had been hoping to strengthen his squad with the remainder of the £18 million he'd raked in from Rio's move to Leeds. Redknapp, a former Upton Park player, had been in charge since August 1994 and was the second-longest-serving manager in the top flight after Sir Alex Ferguson.

Redknapp's loyal deputy, Frank Lampard senior, left shortly afterwards when the club announced that Glenn Roeder was taking over as manager. Lampard's son Frank junior – one of Rio's best friends – immediately left the Hammers and headed for Chelsea in an £11 million deal. Lampard had been unsettled ever since Rio's transfer to Leeds United.

Lampard could have joined Rio at Leeds but chose

Stamford Bridge because he genuinely believed Chelsea were among the biggest clubs in the land. He explained: 'When Rio left and I saw the success he was having I did feel a bit of what I suppose you could call professional jealousy. But just because something suited him didn't mean it would be the same for me. With Chelsea I am surrounded by world-class players in a squad they say is old and isn't but it is vastly experienced.'

It was an important point that Rio took on board. However much he loved Leeds and was grateful for their attitude towards him, there was a nagging feeling in the back of his head that Leeds weren't really up there with the glamour boys. It could be one of the main reasons why they never won anything.

Then Rio got quite upset when Leeds chairman Peter Ridsdale stated publicly that Frank Lampard was not worth the £11 million Chelsea paid for him. In Rio's book that seemed an unnecessary insult. A lot of his mates reckoned Ridsdale was 'out of order'. It was the first time Rio felt things were happening at Leeds of which he did not completely approve.

At the start of the 2001–2 season Rio realised a childhood dream by being appointed Leeds United's captain. Club boss David O'Leary was convinced that the role would make him an even stronger member of the closely knit Leeds set-up. Rio, still only 22, took over from South African Lucas Radebe, an inspirational leader for the club until he suffered extensive injury problems. Rio was given the job of skipper ahead of regular stand-in Gary Kelly and tough guy Danny Mills. Within days the new England boss Sven-Goran Eriksson was hailing Rio as an England captain of the near future.

Rio was understandably well chuffed by the appointment

and the accompanying praise: 'I'm delighted to be honest. As a kid you dream about leading your team out and this is a chance to take with both hands because to be captain of such a huge club is something to be very proud of and my family will be too. This sets me up for the season, knowing the manager and the staff think I am capable of doing the job, which I will do to the best of my capabilities. As I have always said, I came to this club to win things and if that happens as captain then that will be fantastic. But as far as I am concerned it doesn't matter who captains the club, as I think we're all captains out there on the pitch and we win something together.'

O'Leary was confident Rio would be a fine captain. 'Rio has been an absolutely fantastic buy and I'm full of admiration for him. Rio is without doubt a top-class player who can only improve and the price we paid may have brought us some stick but he is already looking like a very reasonable buy. I was lucky when I said I wanted him that I have a chairman who could sign the cheque when everybody doubted our sanity. But after 20 years as a player in the position, I like to think I know a little bit about playing at centre-back, and I believe he is pure quality. I thought he did very well towards the end of the season and grew into being a potential captain and I think he will prove to be a fantastic skipper for many years to come. It's no reflection on Lucas Radebe, who has done a brilliant job. He is a great guy to have around the place, but I just felt Rio's game improved when he did the job while Lucas was out injured last season.'

The next career highlight for Rio would be the mammoth task of facing the Germans in Munich to try to salvage any hope of England qualifying for the World Cup Finals. Rio wasn't worried by the prospect of facing giant German striker Carsten Jancker, all six feet four inches of him. He told one journalist: 'It doesn't matter how they come, tall, short, fat or ugly, as long as they don't score any goals.'

Rio and the rest of his England teammates had been working on the Germans' tactics during training. Sven-Goran Eriksson made them all aware of how the Germans would probably approach the game. Rio had never faced a German team, either at club or international level, so he had no hang-ups about playing against the national side in Munich. Rio would be making his eleventh start and winning his sixteenth cap in Munich. And he knew that his experience with Leeds during their Champions League run the previous season had added greater maturity to his game.

Eriksson had given the entire squad a new confidence in their abilities. Now they had to go out on the pitch and prove it. And they did on 1 September 2001: Germany 1 England 5. Rio's contribution to this outstanding, legendary victory against the old enemy was vital. The opposition were completely destroyed even though they went one up after just six minutes. The opening half-hour was fast and furious as both sides missed numerous chances. Then Michael Owen scored a hat-trick, which, along with goals from Heskey and Gerrard, sealed the Germans' fate and put England back in control of World Cup Group 9.

The historic victory was without doubt the greatest moment in Rio's international career to date. He looked commanding at the back. It was Germany's worst home loss in nearly 70 years and one that made the rest of the footballing world sit up and take notice of Eriksson's gifted pack of young lions.

The events of September 11 in America soon over-shadowed England's great success and Rio was saddened to hear that his great friend Frank Lampard had blotted his copybook by taking part in a drinking binge around hotels at Heathrow Airport on the day after terrorists attacked New York and Washington. Lampard and three other Chelsea teammates found their careers in jeopardy because of one very irresponsible incident. Yet another lesson to Rio to keep his nose clean. Fortunately, he now had girlfriend Rebecca Ellison to go home to each evening. The relationship introduced perfect stability to Rio's life and, hopefully, would help him avoid any more pitfalls and clichéd tabloid revelations. Sadly, that was not to be the case.

On 2 October – just a few days before England's vital World Cup clash with Greece at Old Trafford – Rio and his England teammate Ashley Cole proved they still had more lessons to learn about the art of keeping out of the public eye. They accompanied ex-Arsenal player Paolo Vernazza to two West End lap-dancing bars. Rio's behaviour only came to light two months later when he and Cole were quizzed by police about the night in question because it ended with Watford midfielder Vernazza being stabbed. Detectives spoke to the two young internationals about events leading up to the incident, which had left Vernazza with knife injuries after he surprised an intruder at his home. Although there was no suggestion that either Rio or Cole was involved, Vernazza told police that earlier in the evening he had been to the two lap-dancing clubs with Rio and Cole.

At Old Trafford, England almost threw it all away with a nail-biting 2–2 draw with Greece which nearly ended in disaster until David Beckham curled in a stunning free kick in stoppage time. Meanwhile the Germans' 0–0 draw with Finland left them with the tricky task of playing home and away to Russia in order to qualify for Korea–Japan 2002.

Following England's qualification for the 2002 World Cup Finals, it was back to reality for Rio as Leeds beat

Grasshoppers 2–1 in a UEFA Cup tie. The match came hot on the heels of five successive defeats for Leeds on the road in Europe, plus a first League defeat at the hands of lowly Sunderland the previous weekend.

In the winter of 2001, it can be revealed for the first time, Rio began secretly taking acting lessons. Typically, he was already looking ahead to when he would have to hang up his boots. His heroes in that department were Ian Wright and Vinnie Jones, who'd both managed the switch from soccer to showbiz. 'I really admire what Vinnie and my mate Ian have done. One day I'd love to have a crack at acting, or my other great passion in life, music.'

Rio adored being in the limelight and his new position as skipper at Leeds meant even more TV interviews and public appearances. He believed he came over pretty well on the small screen, so acting was a natural move.

On Friday, 10 November 2001 Rio turned out for England in their 1–1 friendly draw with Sweden at Old Trafford. It was hard for the team to lift themselves after getting through to the World Cup Finals following their draw with Greece. Sweden certainly showed what a difficult team they are to break down. But the World Cup was now beckoning and Rio saw it as the ultimate showcase for his talents.

During the 2001–2 Premiership season, Rio devoted large amounts of time and effort to improving the prospects of youngsters whose future appeared as bleak as his own had once seemed. Already an accomplished and confident public speaker, he became a regular visitor to schools in London and Yorkshire, where he addressed racial issues and tried to encourage youngsters to work their way out of the ghetto.

Rio also became deeply involved in the Prince's Trust and

the National Literacy Trust, whose director, Neil McClelland, was impressed by his enthusiasm. At Christmas 2001 Rio persuaded Leeds to stage a dinner at which players were to paint designs on plates for a Prince's Trust charity auction. The team had just crashed to an appalling defeat at bottom-of-the-table Leicester, but Rio cajoled his dispirited teammates into a spot of artwork and in the process raised £25,000. The community affairs manager at Leeds, Emma Stanford, was full of praise for the club captain: 'Rio's got tremendous attitude. He'll stay and talk football with children who have cancer, for example. He never talks down to the kids. He speaks their language and they're transfixed by him.'

Just after Christmas one of Rio's oldest Peckham mates – 21-year-old Gillingham striker Marlon King – was given a one-year road ban and a fine of £650 for drink-driving. King was one-and-a-half times over the limit when police stopped him in Streatham, south London, the previous September. It seemed a shame that he hadn't taken any notice of what had happened to his friend Rio back in 1997.

Many cynics believed that the trial of Leeds United's Jonathan Woodgate and Lee Bowyer in January 2002 was proof that the saying 'British justice is the best money can buy' was spot on. The two millionaire players walked out of court as free men after an Asian, Sarfraz Najeib, was left battered, bleeding and unconscious in Leeds city centre. One of Woodgate's friends was found guilty of the attack and sentenced to six years.

Woodgate, described by one witness as having jumped on the victim, though clearly the jury didn't believe it, was convicted of affray and the judge sentenced him to 100 hours of community service. Bowyer, though blood had been found on his jacket and the judge accused him of telling a series of lies under police investigation, was cleared of all charges. However, because of those lies, the judge imposed on Bowyer the obligation to pay £1 million in costs. Woodgate would also have to pay the same amount.

Rio has never spoken about the trial, but many of his friends in Peckham wondered how he felt about still playing alongside Bowyer, who already had 'form'. As a 19-year-old who'd just joined Leeds from Charlton six years earlier, he'd been fined £4,500 for attacking Asian staff at a McDonald's restaurant in east London.

In Leeds a small hard core of supporters who'd led racist taunts at Elland Road for so many years tried to claim that Rio, undeniably black, had been bought by the club because he was a whiter shade of black. It was sickening stuff which was rightly condemned by all sides.

After the trial, the family of Sarfraz Najeib were left mystified as to why the words shouted at him, 'Do you want some, Paki?', were not stated in open court. For some reason the prosecution decided that bringing racism into the equation would muddy the legal waters.

Although Rio had arrived at Leeds after Woodgate and Bowyer had been arrested, he still could not avoid the controversy. Chairman Peter Ridsdale later claimed that Rio had only been bought as 'cover' for Woodgate in case he got jailed. That in itself was upsetting to Rio because he rated himself a better player than Woodgate. Others in the club were even suggesting that Leeds bought Rio partly because they wanted to improve their racial mix. There were already other black players in the squad, but the club wanted to appear 'colour friendly'. In fairness it seems unlikely that they would go as far as spending £18 million on a player just to prove that point.

But Rio continued to feel the undercurrent of racism while playing for Leeds. The bigoted remarks yelled during home games deeply offended him and left him totally bewildered that this sort of behaviour was still tolerated in modern society. Rio believed that cutting out racism in British football was as important as any other issue in the game and joined the football-linked project Show Racism the Red Card.

Rio felt so strongly about the race issue that he agreed to take part in a 20-minute video which combined football action with interviews of players on their experiences of racism in football. The video was targeted at youngsters at schools across the country. Rio also hoped that other countries might take note of what was happening in Britain. 'When I was growing up, no one bothered. It's changing and it's changing for the better.'

Rio saw Muhammad Ali as the ultimate role model, regardless of colour or religion, because he was always his own man and stuck to his beliefs. As another black professional player pointed out: 'Ali was a black guy and he won a gold medal and threw it in the river because he wasn't appreciated at all for being a man, you know what I mean? He was considered less than a man really because he was black. You've got the best fighter ever, in the history of the world, and he couldn't go and have a cup of coffee. Yes, racism has got better and you know hopefully in 20 or 40 years' time there won't be any.'

Meanwhile racism continued at football matches. Around this time Rio was deeply angered when he went to watch a match with a white friend. 'After about 20 minutes a white player was injured in a tackle with a black player. This bloke sat in front of me in the stands then started screaming, "You black this and you black that. Go back to where you came from."

'I sat there thinking, Where is this bloke coming from? What is this geezer on? And I remember my friend being really embarrassed. Then I thought, No, I can't have all this, and turned round to a policeman who was standing nearby. I asked him if he was going to do anything about it, but he just shrugged his shoulders to indicate there was nothing he could do.

'Then the racist abuse from this so-called fan started again just before half-time and the bloke turned to me and said, "Not you, mate, you're okay. It's just those on the pitch." I just thought, You stupid idiot. I just wanted to punch him, but I thought, No, I'm not descending to your level, so instead I walked out. Looking back, that was the best thing I could do.'

But Rio did have some words of encouragement for numerous up-and-coming Asian players. 'They are at the same stage of the cycle that black players were at 20 years ago. If Asian boys want to play football they've got to know there is a place for them in the English game. There are a lot of Asian leagues but I don't think there should be separate ethnic leagues. I think there should just be football leagues so scouts can see everybody playing, rather than segregating them.'

As Garrett Mullan, co-ordinator of Show Racism the Red Card, explained: 'Racism is like a cancer. If it is allowed to spread then it becomes more difficult to remove. That is why our campaign is important. Footballers are role models for young people and if they are leading a campaign against racism in football then this will assist education against racism in society. We want all schools, youth and community groups to order our video to spread the message as wide as possible.'

In Peckham there had even been arrests in the hunt for little Damilola Taylor's killers. It seemed as if the perpetrators were at last going to be brought to justice.

Chapter 15

SURVIVAL OF THE FITTEST

The FA Cup third-round tie between Cardiff and Leeds at Ninian Park in January 2002 proved yet another turning point in Rio's career. The game itself was a disaster for the Premiership side, but, more importantly, it ended in scenes of crowd trouble that shocked the footballing establishment. And for Leeds boss David O'Leary it was the moment when his career at Elland Road began to slide backwards.

The trouble began when, towards the end of the second half, Cardiff's owner, Sam Hammam, set off on a walk which took him to a place behind the Leeds goal. He raised the temperature by urging the home crowd, but at the same time was seen to incite the away supporters to throw missiles in his direction. It was bedlam. But then he stoked things up even more by claiming that his club were superior to Leeds and tried to turn the tie into Wales versus England. At the end of the 1–0 victory to the home side, police had to use batons and dogs to force back hundreds of Cardiff fans who'd gathered next to the away section. Leeds chairman Peter Ridsdale was forced to pull O'Leary away from Hammam.

The Leeds players were stunned by the way in which Cardiff fans were permitted to swarm on to the pitch just seconds after the final whistle. Hammam insisted the supporters were entirely justified to celebrate this famous giant-killing act. But O'Leary commented: 'I just thank God my chairman does not do what he does.'

Rio watched all the crowd trouble with bemusement. The result was a disaster for Leeds' season and he was starting to wonder how much longer he could stay at a club that promised so much but delivered so little.

Then, following that controversial FA Cup defeat against Cardiff, Rio joined a long list of Leeds players needing treatment for injuries. He was told he'd definitely miss the top-of-the-table clash with Newcastle plus a home clash with Arsenal the following Sunday. But he was hopeful he might recover in time to face Chelsea and Liverpool.

On 3 February 2002 Leeds intended to teach a few lessons to the mighty Liverpool, who were suffering from a dreadful loss of form which had resulted in nine consecutive winless League games during a stretch lasting from 12 December to 19 January.

But Leeds were smashed 4–0 at Elland Road and looked dejected as they left the pitch. Having lead the Premiership at the turn of the year, they now seemed to be in free fall. Since beating West Ham 3–0 on New Year's Day, they had lost three games and drawn once, not a good record as the season shifted into fourth gear. Rio's old U-21 colleague Emile Heskey of Liverpool ran rings round the Leeds back three as he notched up a brace in the second half of that Elland Road match. And to make matters even worse for Rio, he knocked the ball into his own net after he clipped a bending free kick from Danny Murphy.

When Leeds were knocked out of the UEFA Cup by Feyenoord in the fourth round, the team seemed to be suffering from the biggest loss of form since O'Leary had taken over from George Graham nearly four years earlier.

But there was one statistic Rio had good reason to be proud of: by the end of February 2002 he had not been booked for an astonishing 76 League games. He explained this away by pointing out that he preferred to show his skills than his studs to opponents. 'I don't go out to hurt someone. I only ever get booked for dissent and usually all I get is a warning like, "Any more of that and you're booked." A few refs can take it, some can't. As a captain, I get a bit more leeway.'

Rio had no inclination to show aggression either on or off the field. He'd survived on the Friary Estate by walking away from aggravation. Now he was applying the same principles to the football field. Rio preferred performing all the trickery: the nimble moves, the neat back heels. As he explained: 'Around where I lived, everyone was trying to be Alessandro del Piero or George Weah or do the type of tricks that Dwight Yorke does.'

In some ways Rio still longed to have the number 10 on his shirt: 'Playing just behind two strikers, trying tricks.' He still used to play his video of George Best highlights over and over again, focusing on some of his most outrageous tricks. Rio had never forgotten the day he played up front for West Ham in a testimonial and scored one goal and set up another. Even when he played so-called 'fun' games at Leeds in training he'd go straight up front.

Off the pitch, Rio had finally matured into a genuine role model. 'We're being paid a lot of money to do something we really enjoy and, for 15 years out of my life, I have to make sacrifices to achieve things. It's taken me a while to realise that. Things like not going out on Friday night or having a laugh at my mates' houses until the early hours of the morning, even if it's a Monday. I don't do that now. I stay in and watch any kind of football, or talk shows like *Jerry Springer*. I'm not a saint. I do go out and have meals but I don't come in at all hours.'

Rio was careful not to refer to his live-in girlfriend Rebecca Ellison because he didn't want to expose her to the sort of publicity nightmares he'd faced over the previous three or four years. But the new, more settled Rio had definitely developed more of a social conscience. He felt strongly that there needed to be more facilities for kids on estates like the Friary. He never forgot how his mum encouraged him to go to the council-run adventure playground on the estate knowing there were volunteers working there from 10.30 am to 5 pm every day. 'Kids need that sort of thing to stay off the streets,' he explained.

Rio remained determined never to forget his roots. In the spring of 2002 he spent time with the 9-year-old son of a friend called Charlie Sauvoury, who suffered from acute asthma. He managed, as usual, to make the entire family feel he had a special connection to them. Afterwards he raced back to his mum's house in Mottingham for some of her finest home-made cooking. As Kate Goodwin, wife of Rio's schoolboy coach Dave, commented: 'He is still the hungry little boy he was when he first walked through my door.'

Rio was the principal organiser of Leeds United's £50,000 sponsorship of 10 runners, whose hard-sweated earnings would be shared between the Outward Bound Trust and the Damilola Taylor Trust. 'I have tried to do as much as possible for the Damilola charity,' Rio said, adding, as he'd sought to emphasise often before: 'But this kind of tragedy has been happening for a long time on the streets where I was brought up. Not always incidents of kids dying, admittedly, but certainly kids getting stabbed and people getting shot. It is not a nice thing to say but that has all been part and parcel of living down there. Damilola's death has simply put it under more scrutiny. Now action, money and Government intervention is needed.'

Then, on 25 April, came the shock news that two teenage brothers accused of the murder of Damilola Taylor had been acquitted on all charges, including murder, manslaughter and assault with intent to rob. The court's decision left Damilola's parents and many on the Friary Estate deeply shocked. Rio made another visit to Peckham just after the Old Bailey decision and was angered to find that many of the old problems on the estate had returned with a vengeance, despite a period of calm following the murder of Damilola.

Rio was given ample recognition for his work in the community when the local council granted him the Freedom of the Borough of Southwark. He received a scroll which he fully intended to hang on the wall of his lounge. He would also be invited to all ceremonial occasions in the borough.

Meanwhile the 'other' Rio still managed to find time to enjoy the good things in life. He now lived with Rebecca in one of the smartest villages in Yorkshire and ferried himself to training in the snug-fit cockpit of a brand-new £120,000 dark-blue Ferrari. Rio also owned a top-of-the-range Jaguar and a Range Rover and dined at the best restaurants. He wore even more designer clothes, Gucci T-shirts, Victor Victoria cargo pants, discreetly accessorised with a Patrick Cox Wannabe belt, and of course a hefty gold Rolex on his wrist. It was all such a far cry from those humble beginnings in Peckham.

'I often think how fortunate I am,' he recalled. 'The other day I was walking round Covent Garden with my friends and there was this guy sitting on the pavement begging for money. It just hit me right there and then how lucky I've been – that I didn't have to go down the wrong road, that I had given talents. But I've had to work hard to get where I am and, luckily, I've had the right people around me and the determination to do something positive.'

Even Rio's dad was now thriving, having successfully built up a fashionware business. Julian had remained a big part of Rio's life and attended many of his matches. He also escorted Rio's younger brother, Anton, to and from the youngster's coaching sessions at West Ham.

What should have been a night to remember for Rio when a special Leeds United dinner was held in his honour turned into a disaster as stand-up comedian Stan Boardman told a string of racist jokes. Boardman even cracked a tasteless gag about the assault on the Asian student for which Bowyer and Woodgate had stood trial.

Rio and many of his friends and family who attended the dinner were appalled. Leeds later insisted they had no idea that Boardman was planning to tell a racist type of joke. A spokesman for the campaign against racism in football said: 'It was deeply insensitive. Someone at the club messed up.'

Rio refused to comment about the furore that followed publication of what Boardman said, but must have wondered if his future still lay at Leeds United. One friend explained: 'Rio was very upset by Boardman's remarks and he couldn't understand how Leeds could have booked him.'

Then Leeds lost 1–0 to Fulham on 20 April, which killed off any hopes of the club qualifying for the Champions League. Their season was basically over. Thank goodness Rio still had the World Cup to look forward to.

Just before the end of the 2001–2 season, Rio was reported to have met a beautiful singer called Roberta Whitney in a London club. His live-in love, Rebecca Ellison, remained back at his home in Wetherby. One newspaper reported that Roberta told friends she did not go out with men already involved with other women. She explained: 'I don't really want to talk about Rio at the moment. I didn't know he had a girlfriend when I gave him my number.'

Rio's place in the squad for the 2002 World Cup was already assured as he'd been in all Sven-Goran Eriksson's England teams to date. But there were some other genuine surprises when the 23-man squad was announced in May. Included were midfielders Joe Cole of West Ham and Owen Hargreaves of Bayern Munich. With typical understatement, Eriksson told reporters: 'We have some difficult matches but an extremely exciting time ahead of us.'

Alongside Rio and the many other youngsters named in the squad, there were also some highly experienced players, including Arsenal's central defender Martin Keown, who won a place ahead of Liverpool's Jamie Carragher and 36-year-old Teddy Sheringham. The squad broadly reflected the strength of England's top clubs, with champions Arsenal and Manchester United supplying four players each and Liverpool three, including strikers Michael Owen and

Emile Heskey. Despite Leeds' disappointing season, they still provided Rio plus three others. Only 10 of the squad, Rio among them, survived from England's 1998 World Cup campaign in France.

Every pundit recognised that Rio was part of a first-choice defensive pairing with Sol Campbell. Gareth Southgate and Martin Keown were second-string alternatives. Eriksson's faith in youth meant that the squad had an average age of 26.3, and 25.1 among the outfield players.

Convinced that his former West Ham teammate Joe Cole would be the surprise package of the World Cup, Rio told one journalist: 'Some people might think he's just going along for the ride but he could have a big part to play. Joe's someone who can change a game in an instant and I think he's come on a lot in the last year. He knows when to play the right ball into the box now instead of messing around and beating a man just for the hell of it.'

Rio had never forgotten watching Cole's development when they were at West Ham together. 'I remember the day he joined the first-team squad for training. I knew a lot about him but watching him that day was amazing. We played a two-touch game and he scored a hat-trick.'

A few months later Rio had even watched Cole in a West Ham reserves match against Southend United. 'Joe got the ball and did a trick which I cannot even describe – except to say I've only seen it once before, by Ossie Ardiles in the film *Escape to Victory*. It was astonishing stuff and I screamed out laughing. He's so skilful it's frightening.'

Rio and Cole had kept in close touch since their days together at West Ham and both were obsessed with the beautiful game. As Rio later explained: 'When he's not playing it he's watching it like me, studying skills and wanting to learn and try something new.'

Just before the squad departed for Japan, Rio was told by Sven-Goran Eriksson that he would lead the team in the World Cup Finals if David Beckham didn't return to fitness in time following his much-publicised foot injury. Eriksson believed that Rio had already proved his leadership qualities while skippering Leeds.

Rio was bewildered by the enormous public reaction to Beckham's injury. It seemed to be on every front page for weeks. 'When I saw Becks go down, it made my heart jump. It was a scary moment for any of us hoping to go to the World Cup. You had to feel desperately sorry for him. We know we work in a risk business and sometimes the odds catch up with you but you have to think there is more in the world, surely, than having an injured footballer filling the front pages and TV bulletins. With all due respect to David, he should be in the sports section. It's been madness, hysteria really, and Becks wouldn't want all this attention. You think of the Israeli issue, global disasters and people dying, and you know where football should be placed.'

As the England squad arrived at their base camp in the Far East, stories about Rio leaving Leeds started to surface in the UK. Rio even admitted to the Sun: 'You are always flattered when big clubs are interested in you.' The club in question was undoubtedly Manchester United and they'd already tabled a £20 million offer. Leeds' financial problems and their failure to qualify for the following season's Champions League ensured that the big boys were now circling the club like vultures.

In Japan, Rio was more concerned with publicly defending his one-time West Ham teammate Trevor Sinclair, who'd been criticised for going home after he was released from the squad when a first-choice team member recovered from injury. Rio said: 'There's no question in Trevor's mind that he will come back if required. I spoke to him the night before he left. It's a joke that people have made so much out of it. His wife is six months pregnant and everyone else would have done the same thing.'

Amid all the speculation linking him with Man United, Rio refused to comment any further. Back in London it was rumoured that the club were about to up their offer to £25 million. With five days to go until the start of the World Cup, it was then reported that they had put £30 million on the table. Throughout the world of football there was astonishment. Was any defender really worth that sort of money? And had Leeds decided that if they could virtually double what they'd paid for Rio just 18 months earlier then the deal would be green-lighted despite the damage it might do to their future?

Rio – with four years on his contract still remaining – was understood to have a quick-release clause, although it was not activated for another year. In the middle of all this was a deeply unhappy David O'Leary, well aware that his most talented player could be about to leave the club.

In the Far East, some were saying that Rio had misgivings about the turbulent times he'd experienced at Leeds the previous season. One member of the England party explained: 'Rio isn't too happy about some of the things that have happened at the club over the previous few months, but he's a loyal fellow so there's no way he'd air those feelings in public. And he insists he's staying put at Leeds.'

On 30 May Leeds and Man United took the unusual step of issuing a joint statement to refute stories that Rio was on his way to Old Trafford. Both clubs were angry about claims that the 23-year-old player had been sent a copy of a proposed contract for a seven-year deal worth £60,000 a week and rising to £110,000. Leeds were also upset about a claim that they still owed West Ham millions of pounds from when Rio moved up north.

The joint statement between the two clubs read: 'No deal has been struck between the clubs and contrary to the story ... Manchester United wish to point out that they have not made an illegal approach by forwarding a contract to Rio Ferdinand in Japan or a list of houses in Cheshire for his perusal ... Leeds United are taking legal advice regarding the totally false allegation that £4 million remains outstanding from Rio Ferdinand's transfer from West Ham. Leeds paid West Ham £12 million on signing the player and the balance of the fee was paid in full ... on the first anniversary of Rio's recruitment, last November.'

But would both clubs keep their agreed truce so that Rio could get on with the business of helping England win the World Cup?

Chapter 16

THE WORLD STAGE

In football they say that Manchester United boss Sir Alex Ferguson always gets his man in the end. So the charm offensive that the club put into action after the England squad arrived in the Far East for the 2002 World Cup was no surprise. David Beckham, Paul Scholes, Nicky Butt and Wes Brown all urged Rio to join them in the quest for more trophies the following season. As the squad carried out their final preparations on the Korean island of Jeju, Rio talked to family, close friends and associates back in London, including his powerful agent Pini Zahavi, who'd been on first-name terms with Alex Ferguson for years. Man United would stalk their man until they could pounce at the perfect moment. The denouement might not have been as cold and calculated as they had hoped, but the end result was all that mattered.

The World Cup tournament they'd all been waiting for

had finally arrived. Unlike at club level, there was no way the superpowers of soccer could buy their way to success. This was all about skill, training, technique and spirit. And Rio had bucketloads of all of these. Fan trouble was feared, but in the event it never materialised. In fact, scenes of English fans singing along with the Japanese would become a feature of the tournament that brought tears of joy and misery to the eyes of the watching millions back in England. The World Cup draw hadn't exactly been kind to England as they were in the co-called 'group of death' with arch-enemies Argentina, plus Sweden and Nigeria.

In the middle of all this, Rio heard rumours from London about Juventus planning to make an eleventh-hour bid for him. But that was completely overshadowed when David O'Leary suddenly quit Leeds. Many believed his decision had been caused by the club's refusal to guarantee the manager that they wouldn't sell Rio. However, the day after O'Leary's departure, Leeds chairman Peter Ridsdale still insisted that Rio was not for sale.

O'Leary had been under severe pressure for at least six months because in the 2001–2 season Leeds had yet again failed to win anything. Injuries and repeated indiscipline among some key members of the team had not helped his position, either. So it wasn't considered such a big surprise when the Leeds board, tired of O'Leary's constant round of excuses for under-achievement, finally lost their patience. Many believed that he had been earmarked for the chop much earlier that year when extracts from his book appeared in a tabloid newspaper within 48 hours of the end of Lee Bowyer and Jonathan Woodgate's second lengthy trial at Hull Crown Court. Appearing to profit from such a nasty episode did O'Leary's reputation no good.

One insider at the club told the *Observer*: 'The directors

thought he was bringing embarrassment to the club.' Others cited Leeds' 1–0 defeat by Fulham on 20 April because it killed off any hopes of the club qualifying for the Champions League. 'That's when they made their mind up. They watched the game and said, "God this is rubbish." Leeds had played boring defensive football. It vindicated concerns that some of the players had expressed that the tactics were too defensive,' added the inside source.

But the last straw for the Leeds board came when O'Leary used his weekly column in the *Sunday People* to warn that if Rio's widely expected transfer to Man United went ahead then he could hardly be expected to get Leeds into the Champions League.

With only a few days to go to England's first group match against Sweden, news reached Japan that Scandinavian stars Freddie Ljungberg and Olof Mellberg had been involved in a nasty punch-up during training. That really cheered Rio up because it was a perfect diversion from the transfer talk back home and the fallout from O'Leary's departure. He gleefully told one journalist: 'We think what's happened with these Swedes is blinding. It's unfortunate for them that it got out. But you can look at it another way. It either means it will have a damaging effect on their squad or that they are hyped up for the tournament.'

Rio's first-ever game in the World Cup Finals on 2 June proved a bitter disappointment for England, who were extremely lucky to escape with a 1–1 draw. They started well against Sweden, but in the second half were ripped apart by a well-organised side. Rio's biggest contribution came when he put a header over the bar from a David Beckham corner in the thirty-seventh minute. He also unintentionally unsighted keeper David Seaman when Andersson scored the equaliser for Sweden at fifty-eight minutes. But after the game most pundits agreed that Rio looked solid at the back.

In south-east London, Janice and her husband Peter, along with Sian, nine, Anton, now 17, and Jeremiah, three, screamed at the telly as they watched Rio turn out against Sweden. 'It was amazing,' Janice later recalled. 'I got goosebumps on goosebumps – you know when you feel like you are there and you get bellyache. I just had this overwhelming feeling of being so proud – you just smile until you can't smile any more.'

Everyone in the household was shouting and jumping up and down as the match progressed. 'For me to watch my son walking out for England in the World Cup was more than I could ever have imagined. It was my most exciting time, the feeling that came over me was incredible.'

Immediately after the 1–1 draw, Janice's phone rang and an excited Rio came on the line. 'It was brilliant, Mum. I'm trying to savour every moment.'

Then little brother Jeremiah grabbed the phone and started telling Rio: 'It was you, Rio. It was you on the telly.'

Janice then told Rio just how proud the people of Peckham would be. 'Well done, son.'

'Thanks, Mum.'

The next World Cup game – against Argentina – was hyped to the hilt with all the usual emotional baggage of the 1982 Falklands War plus Diego Maradona's 'Hand of God' goal that helped knock England out of the 1986 World Cup and David Beckham's infamous red card in Argentina's penalty-shootout victory at France '98. The Argentinians had gone into the match as favourites, and were further strengthened by the fall of the holders, France, who lost the tournament's opening game against Senegal.

A draw would be creditable, but a victory would probably secure England's passage into the next round as group winners. That would mean avoiding France and gave a clearer route towards the semi-finals. The pressure was on. The English team wanted to emulate the heroics of the 1966 World Cup Final triumph over West Germany at Wembley. Bobby Robson's Gascoigne-inspired 1990 side came closest, losing an agonising semi-final penalty shootout against Germany at Italia '90. The sense of anticipation surrounding Eriksson's current squad was reminiscent of that which accompanied Robson's 1990 side.

The dream win came true for Rio with a 1–0 victory over Argentina. England were suddenly hailed as potential winners of the World Cup. A Beckham penalty late in the first half was enough to do it. Rio and defensive partner Sol Campbell performed superbly. Argentina had more possession, but England created more chances. Rio's only slip of the game enabled Pochettino to get in a free header but Seaman blocked it brilliantly on the line.

Rio's reading of the game against Argentina was so good that he undoubtedly played a vital role in preventing them from scoring for the first time in 21 internationals. Rio's Leeds and England teammate Danny Mills hailed him as 'one of the true greats of football' after his awesome performance against Argentina. Neither Gabriel Batistuta or his replacement, Hernan Crespo, was able to produce a single worthwhile on-target shot between them.

Mills said after the game: 'We have always known that Rio Ferdinand is a great player. I believe he can go all the way and become one of the true greats. This is a fantastic stage for him to show what he can do. Hopefully, we can progress in this tournament and he will have an even greater opportunity to prove what a great player he is. Rio and Sol at the back were winning everything against Argentina. Every time the ball came into the box, they were heading it away. They were awesome – and long may it continue because we will need them playing like that in every game.'

Rio made a point of dedicating the victory against Argentina to the fans but, typically, he then stressed the importance of keeping a lid on the hype and expectation levels with a point still needed against Nigeria in Osaka on the following Wednesday to guarantee a place in the second phase.

He said: 'That result was a big thank-you to all the England fans who have stood by us. It was for them and the supporters back home who watched the game on television. They deserve it. We are very proud of what we achieved, but we know there is still a lot more to do and I just hope that people do not start building up the expectations too high. There is a long way to go but it was an extra-important victory and I am delighted we are getting better and better with each performance.'

The Argentinians were so upset they hadn't even wanted to swap shirts after the game …

Rio had paid for his mum and his brothers and sister to fly out to Japan for England's 'group of death' clash with Argentina, and there Janice met up with Rio's dad, Julian. She recalled: 'We must have looked quite a sight. All of us were sitting in a line in the stadium wearing England shirts. We were just like any other supporters, except our kit had "Rio" written on it. Sian had her face painted red and white and she was draped in an England flag bibbing a horn. Every time he got the ball, we'd all shout, "Re-Oh! Re-Oh!"'

Janice went on: 'When Beckham lined up to take that penalty everyone was holding their breath. All the people had stopped cheering, all the babies had stopped crying. And as he went forward a million flashlights lit up the stadium. I could have done a somersault.'

Rio was hailed as England's best player during the 0–0 draw with Nigeria. He showed great authority and on at least two occasions intercepted Nigerian attackers with superb skill and tenacity. Both teams were exhausted by the early-afternoon heat. Man of the match Rio told a packed press conference afterwards: 'We came here to get out of the group and now we have done it we want to go as far as possible.'

When she was back in London, Janice got a call from Rio saying that following his fantastic performance against Nigeria more big clubs were rumoured to be interested in him. She told him to put it all out of his mind until he got back to England after the World Cup. Janice was so proud of her son: 'It's every parent's hope in life for their children to have a fantastic life – and Rio's got that because he's worked hard for it. But he could still come home from the World Cup, go back to Peckham and be the same Rio.'

The newspapers in England had a field day about the clubs allegedly lining up to try and buy Rio. They dubbed him 'the world's most wanted defender'. Rio assured Sven-Goran Eriksson he wouldn't allow all the speculation to affect his performances in an England shirt.

Rio fully appreciated how much expectation rested on his shoulders with the 10,000 fans who'd travelled to Japan to follow England. He'd also heard through calls to his friends back in south London that everyone was rooting for the team. 'We have to put a smile on everyone's faces and want to keep it there,' he told a packed press conference just before the second-round clash with Denmark. 'We've been watching the scenes in places like Trafalgar Square on the BBC and I can tell you it brings you out in goose pimples. The atmosphere there must be incredible and we don't want to let anyone down.'

And even more proof of Rio's importance to the team came when it was revealed that he would be one of England's five nominated penalty takers – an immense vote of faith considering he hadn't taken one in a competitive match in his entire career! Rio had been on the bench in 1998 when England's second-round clash with Argentina went to penalties and David Batty – now with Leeds – missed his penalty, which cost them the match. 'I felt for Batts when he missed but he was able to deal with it and it didn't affect his life.' Rio was super-confident he could deal with the same sort of pressures, and no one disagreed with him.

Rio and his England pals cruised into the World Cup quarter-finals with an emphatic 3–0 victory over Denmark and Rio scored the opening goal, thanks to a fumble by keeper Thomas Sorenson. (FIFA later ruled that the goal was Rio's, not Sorenson's.)

Rio's header from David Beckham's corner was off target, but Sorenson knocked the ball off his own chest and over the line. It was the perfect start for England, and a nightmare for Denmark, who even while singing their national anthem had looked nervous. After the match, Rio admitted it was a lucky scramble that led to his goal. 'My first thought was, What a rubbish header. I should have headed it in with the 'keeper touching it. Fortunately, it went in off him and there's no better feeling than scoring your first goal for England.'

Goals by Liverpool's Emile Heskey and Michael Owen sealed the victory, although Rio did make one minor slip which let Danish striker Ebbe Sand through on the right just before half-time. However, Rio recovered and was also helped out by good old dependable Sol Campbell. Now the scene was set for a mouth-watering quarter-final clash with Brazil.

After the game Rio even kept hold of his beloved England shirt despite the fact that everyone else swapped theirs with the Danes. 'No way was I going to lose my shirt from a match where I scored,' he later explained.

Sven-Goran Eriksson's assistant, Tord Grip, rated Rio one of the team's star performers. 'If you want to know why the defence is so strong, you need only look at Rio. He wins the ball just like Bobby Moore. His timing is perfect, so clean. And he is good on the ball.'

Back in Manchester, officials at Old Trafford were rubbing their hands in glee at the prospect of Rio wearing a red shirt for the opening Premiership game of the season if they could thrash out a deal with Leeds.

Rio's favourite team after England was Brazil, so to have the South Americans as quarter-final opponents was a dream come true. 'Everyone knows how much I love Brazil and meeting them will be wicked. Ronaldo looks back to his best and I love to see a player like that doing well. When he is fit there is no one better in the world.'

The hype before the game against Brazil was virtually non-stop. And the world's press were hailing the performances of the English defence starring Rio and Sol

Campbell as the linchpin of the success they anticipated for England.

Many noted that against Denmark, Campbell marked close to his Danish attacker Ebbe Sand while Rio stood back and observed the game. Rio moved the other England defenders around him and whenever an extra Dane popped up in attack, he seldom showed much interest. He would watch while Campbell and Mills dived in. Rio was definitely a supervisor, not a cleaner. Like David Beckham, he had blossomed into a leader during Sven-Goran Eriksson's early days in charge of the England team. Rio had been encouraged to marshal the defence and he relished that role.

In London, Chelsea's Jimmy Floyd Hasselbank – appearing as a TV pundit because Holland hadn't qualified – reckoned the two best centre-halves in England were Rio and Arsenal's Martin Keown. He explained: 'With Keown you end a match covered in bruises but with Ferdinand you almost don't notice.'

Rio was hailed as the thinking man's centre-back, more interested in the direction of the attack than whoever happened to be in his vicinity. Many compared Rio to Italy's Alessandro Nesta – tall, fast, comfortable on the ball. In the air, it was noted that both Rio and Sol Campbell had completely nullified the Argentinian attack. The two defenders had also scored two out of England's five goals so far.

As England's World Cup campaign progressed, England's loyal fans warmed to Rio and regularly chanted his name, a rare honour for a defender. 'Re-Oh! Re-Oh!' reminded him of his mum back on the Friary Estate when she wanted him home. Meanwhile Rio's England teammate and close friend Kieron Dyer proclaimed: 'I honestly believe that on present

form we have the best player in the world in Rio Ferdinand. Not just the best defender, but the best player.'

Many of the England players had seen ex-England international Viv Anderson state on television just before the World Cup Finals began that Rio was 'not world-class'. Halfway through the Nigeria game, Anderson was on the small screen once again and announced: 'I was wrong. He is world-class.'

Journalists labelled Rio as one of the two or three best defenders at the tournament. One German reporter even claimed Rio was acquiring the same mythical status as goalkeeping superstar Oliver Kahn, who discouraged strikers even before he dispossessed them.

But Rio still had his faults. It was pointed out that he was not a great tackler. Said *Observer* journalist Simon Kuper: 'He almost always remains upright. This contributes to his elegance, but sometimes a centre-half needs to get his shorts dirty. Just before half-time against Denmark he allowed one of their attackers to nip dangerously past him to the byline, and when Sand or Jesper Gronkjaer brought the ball into the box, Ferdinand tended not to confront them but to stand off, trying to guide them away from goal. At moments like that you wish he was more of an old-fashioned English centre-half.'

A couple of days before England were due to play Brazil, Rio sauntered in for another routine press conference brimming with confidence at England's World Cup headquarters on Awaji Island, an hour's drive from Osaka, in western Japan. He was as relaxed as ever in front of the cameras and the assembled pack of journalists: 'It's absolutely great being here, but what I really wish is that, for just an hour or so, I could be back in England enjoying all of this as much as the fans are. We're hearing about how fantastic it is but, here, we're a bit cut off. I'd really like to be there, you know.'

Then Rio told the press he was bewildered by all the back-page talk of an injury crisis in the England camp. 'I keep hearing there's all this despair going on but it doesn't feel like that in our hotel.'

In fact, Rio spent much of his time thrashing teammates Joe and Ashley Cole at pool. As he explained: 'They are getting absolutely stuffed and, if my form on the pitch is as good as it is on the pool table, I will be happy. The whole mood generally is very upbeat.'

The next morning's training session in the town of Higashiura was held in swelteringly hot weather and featured an England squad training game called The Greens v The Yellows v The Whites. Two teams were playing, and one goal usually won it within a minute or two. The winners would then stay on to play the next side. Twenty minutes after the first game had started and they were still hard at it. Rio had magnificently repulsed attack after attack and hardly even built up a sweat in the process.

As striker Teddy Sheringham remarked dryly: 'He's having a great World Cup, isn't he, even in bloody training. Look at him, not a bead of sweat on his forehead, as cool as you like – can't even get past him in the seven-a-side.' Not many had managed it in the 11-a-side, either.

Rio had become a popular figure among the vast travelling press pack because he seemed so at ease with the media. He then made a point of telling them that he expected the England side to go all the way and win the tournament.

He told the journalists: 'Let's make it clear, we would not be happy with just a quarter-final place. There is absolutely no way we would settle for a brave defeat on Friday. There have been too many times in our history when things haven't gone that well, have been like failures, and now we have a great opportunity to put that right. We certainly don't want to be sitting in our homes in a few weeks' time thinking about what might have been. We don't want to be looking back with any regrets. We won't settle for just anything because we definitely have the talent within the squad to go all the way to the final. This is not us being arrogant but we are very confident and we have a great belief within us. We are all young lads together and we want to do well. For us, losing on Friday would be a disaster. We really want to continue as long as we can in this tournament.'

Rio insisted that the best was still to come from the England side. 'The team is developing well and the longer we are together, the better we play. If you look at the age of the side, a lot of players are not at their peak level yet. But we have also got people like David Beckham, Sol Campbell, Paul Scholes and Nicky Butt who have been playing at the top level for years. It means we have got a really good mixture, a really good blend, and there is a lot more to come from this team. But rest assured that on Friday we will have one thought – to get into the semi-finals – and we will be really gutted if we don't make it.'

The difference between the characters of Rio and Sol Campbell was perfectly summed up by the way the two players publicly responded to their next challenge – Brazil. Asked how he planned to defend against the ultimate attacking force, Campbell said: 'You just defend, you know, you just do your job.'

Rio's take was a lot more eloquent: 'Well, playing against

Ronaldo is so special because he is one of my heroes. He's in the same category as Batistuta, they are exceptional. You are testing yourself against the absolute best in the world and it needs 100 per cent concentration the entire match. Let that slip for a second, and you are in big trouble. Ronaldo and Rivaldo play as a pair, but they are also brilliant individually, you never know what's coming next. It's going to be a challenge, but we are getting much better match by match ...'

Rio and his England teammates' hopes of going all the way to the final were crushed by a brilliant footballing display by the Brazilians, who came out 2–1 winners. England scored first through Michael Owen, but then Rivaldo got one back just before half-time and England were soon up against the ropes.

In the second half, Ronaldinho's clever free kick completely fooled David Seaman, and England never even looked like getting back into the game. They even failed to cash in when Brazil were down to 10 men after Ronaldinho was sent off in the fifty-sixth minute for a foul on Rio's Leeds teammate Danny Mills.

With just over 10 minutes to go, Eriksson sent on Darius Vassell and Teddy Sheringham in place of Owen and Ashley Cole. Rio was dispatched into attack as another striker in a desperate attempt to claw back a goal. But it was all to no avail ...

The first 44 minutes had gone according to plan and then, as so often happened, England were breached at just the wrong time. However, those watching made a point of saying that none of the English defenders failed in their duties.

At least Rio walked away with two mementoes from that

final England game: the shirts of Rivaldo and Roberto Carlos, which he gave to his brother Anton after the match. As Rio later explained: 'I got Rivaldo's shirt myself and then Roberto Carlos asked for mine, so I swapped another one with him. It's really something when a player of his stature comes looking for my shirt.'

Afterwards Rio was one of the players randomly chosen to have a drug test, and there he encountered free-kick scorer Ronaldinho. Rio asked him if his goal was a shot and he just laughed and said, 'Yes'. Rio responded by saying, 'No way.'

So England were out of the tournament. Down but certainly not disgraced. And Rio emerged with an even bigger, worldwide reputation. Many continued to talk about him being in the same class as Fabio Cannavaro and Alessandro Nesta.

Was there no limit to Rio's talent and ambitions?

Chapter 17

END OF AN ADVENTURE

Rio was carefully packing his clothes in the hotel bedroom that had been his home for a month in Japan. The sea outside was lapping against the shores of Awaji Island and for the first time there was no longer a World Cup Final on the horizon. The adventure was over.

He threw his England T-shirts into a bag and then carefully packed his treasured CD collection. He'd tried his hardest to take each game as it came, but the final had always been lingering there in the back of his mind. He'd dreamed every night of lifting the World Cup and now the reality had dawned and it hurt him immensely.

This had been England's greatest chance to win the trophy since 1966. The memory that would probably stay with him the longest was the victory over Argentina. After all that had happened between the two countries it was the sweetest, defining moment.

But Rio was haunted by England's lacklustre second-half performance against Brazil. As a complete pro, he knew they could have done better and he couldn't understand why they didn't get the ball back from the Brazilians, who were down to 10 men for most of that half.

When Rio and the rest of England's World Cup squad flew back to London, team boss Sven-Goran Eriksson singled out Man United's Nicky Butt as his star man, but most of the talk in Korea and Japan had been about Rio. Michael Owen had been a bit of a disappointment and he claimed he was not fully fit for the match against Brazil. 'I could run but I couldn't go flat out. My biggest regret is that I couldn't go into this game in peak condition,' said Owen, who'd scored against Brazil despite not fully recovering from a groin injury.

Many newspapers, magazines and websites ran their own assessment of how the England players performed in the 2002 World Cup. Rio got nine out of 10 from nearly all of them. The England News Pages website wrote: 'Ferdinand showed that he is one of the best central defenders in the tournament and was England's best player (along with Nicky Butt). He was tremendous in the games against Argentina and Nigeria and was unlucky not to make it into the international World Cup 2002 squad.' But although many rated Rio the best defender of the tournament, FIFA did not choose him as part of their final-16 All Star Team.

Rio had a lot of thinking to do on his return from the World Cup. The previous season at Leeds had definitely not gone according to plan. They'd won nothing, failed to qualify for the Champions League and were still haunted by the Bowyer and Woodgate court case. Then they'd sacked their manager. Rio reckoned the club had made a complete hash of handling the media. The low point came with the publication of David O'Leary's book *Leeds on Trial*, which opened the club up to the media spotlight when it least needed it.

But would it be any better at another Premiership club? Rio asked himself. While many clubs were stockmarket-listed companies, the inescapable fact was that their share prices went up and down depending on the success of the team on the field.

So what tactics would Rio adopt as the speculation about his future reached fever pitch? Should he go on the attack and make his feelings about Leeds known? That would mean taking over the story, which was a risky business if any future transfer collapsed. Rio was in a dilemma, but his heart was telling him it was time to move on.

In order to escape the intense media attention, he set off with England pal Wes Brown, of Manchester United, for a sunshine break in the gambling capital of the world, Las Vegas. Brown's presence ensured that Rio would be kept carefully informed of Man United's quest to sign him from Leeds.

On Monday, 24 June Man United's chief executive, Peter Kenyon, claimed he'd held talks with Leeds about signing Rio. Kenyon told the club's official website he'd spoken to his Leeds counterpart, Peter Ridsdale. Leeds knew Rio's value had rocketed because he'd performed so superbly on the world stage. Kenyon said: 'Over the next few weeks things will start to develop but there is nothing at the minute. At this stage Ferdinand is not for sale.'

Ridsdale then put pressure on Rio for a decision by saying that he would have to request a transfer before the club would consider selling him. Leeds were rumoured to be £30 million in debt and desperate to sell some players in order to balance their books.

There was also that additional clause in Rio's contract between West Ham and Leeds which meant that lump sums would be paid to the Hammers after each year Rio spent with Leeds. This would eventually increase the entire package to a figure approaching £33 million, effectively doubling Rio's salary to £66,000 a week. Clearly Leeds could not afford to stick to this contractual obligation.

Meanwhile newspapers suggested that Rio would stay at Leeds if the club could offload Robbie Keane to Sunderland and Lee Bowyer to Arsenal. Rio – back from Las Vegas – continued to play down the speculation and publicly insisted he was still happy at Elland Road. 'I've heard all the speculation about me possibly leaving and as far as I'm concerned it's up to Leeds,' he said. 'If they want to keep me I will be staying. If they decide to sell me that's different.'

Then Man United executive Martin Edwards told BBC Radio Five Live it was 'no secret that Ferdinand is a great player who would certainly improve our squad. Whether Leeds are prepared to sell him is another matter.'

The pressure was mounting.

Rio felt that Leeds were changing direction as a team. David O'Leary's departure had disappointed Rio because O'Leary had been an important figure in his development as a player. Now Rio would have to start again when a new manager was appointed. He had watched all the antics from a distance and grown increasingly concerned that Leeds had, in the words of the departing O'Leary, 'gone from being the second most favourite club of most neutral supporters to being the most hated club in the country'.

It was clear to Rio that life at Leeds had turned into a virtual soap opera, with almost weekly, dramatic events. There had been the acrimonious defeat at Second Division

Cardiff City, Ridsdale's extraordinary post-match discussion with Leeds fans during another defeat, this time at Goodison Park, and defeat in the UEFA Cup. Leeds had been top of the Premiership at the start of 2002 and yet only just managed to scrape into the following season's UEFA competition.

O'Leary had also alienated some of the Leeds fans. He'd lost the backing of some players in the dressing room, and they'd even told Ridsdale they no longer thought O'Leary was the right man for the job. Those players included Mark Viduka, Harry Kewell, Robbie Keane, Danny Mills and Erik Bakke.

But Rio wholeheartedly approved when he heard that former England manager Terry Venables looked certain to be appointed the new manager at Leeds. Rio felt he owed Venables for letting him join the Euro '96 squad when he was no more than a kid. He respected Venables immensely and he was looking forward to hearing what the cockney coach had planned for Leeds.

So, with the appointment of Venables, Rio found himself in a terrible dilemma, unable to work out whether he should join Man United or stay at Leeds. The reasons to stay included:

1) To Become a Leeds Legend. Rio was a big fish in a small sea at Elland Road but at Man United he would just be one of a vast number of superstars.

2) To Pay Back the Club's Loyalty to Him. Rio knew that Leeds paid over the odds when they bought him from West Ham and without their support his career might not have gone so well. He felt a definite obligation.

3) To Please the Fans. Rio had a fantastic rapport with the Leeds fans and it might not be the same at Old Trafford.

Former Leeds star Eric Cantona had a horrendous time whenever he returned to Elland Road.

4) To Be Part of Something New. With new boss Terry Venables in charge, Leeds looked as if they might go on to greater things.

On the other hand there were four good reasons to go to Man United:

1) To Win Trophies. If Rio went to Old Trafford he would be virtually assured of some medals.

2) To Play in the Champions League. Assuming Man United got through the two-leg qualifier in August, they were definitely expected to be challenging for the title.

3) To Earn More Money. Rio's current Leeds salary of £30,000 a week would be more than doubled by a move to Man United.

4) To Play with Great Players. Rio had already got used to David Beckham, Paul Scholes and Nicky Butt during the World Cup, but Ryan Giggs, Ruud van Nistelrooy and skipper Roy Keane could be added to this illustrious roll-call.

On 13 July Rio took his agent, Pini Zahavi, to meet with Terry Venables at a London hotel just a couple of days after Venables's appointment as the new Leeds boss was confirmed. Venables insisted Leeds was still the right place for Rio to continue his footballing education. But as Rio later explained: 'Mr Venables never asked me to say whether I would be staying or not. But I couldn't have given him an answer there and then because there was a lot to think about and I'm sure he understood that.'

Venables assured Rio he had big plans for the club. Rio added: 'As a person and a coach he's up there among the best of them. He said the sort of things I expected and you can see he wants to do well. This is his chance to stamp his mark on a club and he wants to do everything to make it a big success.'

But Rio also knew that he would double his salary to more than £60,000 a week if he went to Old Trafford. It was particularly tempting since Leeds had already made it clear they could not improve on his current £30,000-a-week deal despite those clauses in his original contract that included an increased weekly wage after a set amount of time at Elland Road.

Rio still insisted that money was the least important issue. 'Of course I think about it but it's not the be-all and end-all and besides I'm already being paid good money by Leeds.' Rio's biggest priority was to win medals and he knew he would never feel properly fulfilled in footballing terms until that happened.

On 14 July Rio rolled up at his mum's house in Mottingham in his brand-new £168,000 Aston Martin. He wanted the family to help him decide whether he should join Man United. Rio listened avidly to Janice as she explained the importance of loyalty. He heard Julian talk about the need to keep his feet firmly on the ground no matter how many millions of pounds were thrown at him. He even talked to his kid brother Anton about how it might all affect him. Anton was a very similar character to Rio. He'd even attended the same school as his elder brother, Bluecoat Comprehensive, and was now following in his footsteps at West Ham.

Rio explained at the time: 'I honestly didn't know what I would do. But my family would play the biggest part in helping me make up my mind.' He also listened to his kid sisters. He realised this decision was important to a lot of people – the clubs, the fans, everyone – but in the end he

believed he had to do what was right for him and his family.

Meanwhile Sir Alex Ferguson openly admitted he was getting nervous waiting to see if Rio would join Man United. 'We're waiting to see how things develop at Leeds. If he's available then we're interested but it is not clear.' Rio was well aware that the whole transaction was now 'down to the wire' and that everything had to be settled sooner rather than later.

In the middle of all the feverish speculation about his transfer, Rio was to be found at an anonymous, weed-strewn football pitch near the Friary Estate, in his beloved southeast London, lending moral support to his close boyhood friend Gavin Rose, now 25, who had just been appointed coach to the Dulwich Hamlet youth squad. Later Rio popped over to the Friary in his Aston Martin but there was no danger of the vehicle being vandalised because a bunch of kids volunteered to guard his car in the hope of being bunged a fiver by their favourite superstar. Dozens of children from the estate gathered round Rio asking hundreds of questions about football.

But it was clear to Gavin, who'd grown up with him on the estate, that Rio wasn't after accolades from the kids. 'At the same time, people took the mickey out of him because they knew him as a person, not a big star, and they knew he'd never completely leave his roots. He spent the whole morning here and we didn't even discuss Manchester United, to be honest,' said Gavin. 'Rio knew a couple of the lads who were training and I think he was more interested in watching their progress.'

Rio had even phoned Gavin every other day while he was in Japan for the World Cup. 'We discussed the matches, of course, but he was just as interested in finding out what was happening in Peckham,' explained Gavin. 'You see it's very important to him to keep in touch with his real mates. He still comes back whenever he can, and I'm sure he always will.' Over the previous year Rio had turned up regularly at the youth adventure project in Peckham also run by Gavin.

Later that afternoon Rio attended a five-a-side tournament on Hackney Marshes because a few of his oldest friends were playing. Then he headed back to his mum's house in Mottingham for some of her tasty home cooking.

On 18 July newspapers claimed that bidding for Rio had opened at £28 million. But Peter Ridsdale still insisted he'd rejected his captain's written transfer request. The Leeds chairman was said to be determined to hold out for £35 million for Rio. 'We are a public company and I have a duty to shareholders to maximise the value of our assets. If we receive any reasonable bid for any of our players, including Rio, they will be considered.'

Yet, behind the scenes, the deal was virtually complete. Pini Zahavi was confident that Rio would be playing for United when the Premiership opened in early August. 'He would be happy to join Manchester United,' he said. 'He wants to play in a bigger and better club and he wants to play in the Champions League.'

However, Rio – who'd been deeply concerned about the reception he'd get upon his return to Upton Park after the move to Leeds – was now worried that the Elland Road crowd would be much more resentful. He admitted: 'The last three days have torn me apart. I love Leeds United. They took a huge gamble in signing me and I will never forget that.'

The spin-offs from Rio's expected transfer to Man United were enormous, even though the deal wasn't yet officially complete. Agents from all over Europe were knocking at Leeds' door offering their clients for cut-price deals, though one agent, Fernando Hidalgo, made it clear: 'But it all depends on whether Ferdinand's transfer to Man United goes ahead.'

Then Lee Bowyer's proposed £7 million move from Leeds to Liverpool collapsed despite newspaper photos of Bowyer smiling with Gérard Houllier. Bowyer's reported attitude was said to be the stumbling block. There were also legal problems following that earlier, controversial trial. It was announced that civil proceedings had been launched against Bowyer for lawyers acting for the family of the Asian youth injured in the attack. Proceedings were issued in the High Court in London seeking damages for assault, battery, conspiracy to injure and conspiracy to pervert the course of justice. The Leeds soap opera rolled on.

By 20 July there was total deadlock between Leeds and Man United over Rio's value. Ridsdale was said to have rejected an improved offer of £30 million. In the middle of all this, David O'Leary – Rio's old manager at Elland Road – was rumoured to be joining Juventus as right-hand man to Marcello Lippi. O'Leary was highly rated in Italy after Leeds' successful run in the final stages of the 2001 Champions League.

On that same day, Rio was scheduled to join his Leeds teammates on a flight to the Far East, although his involvement in the trip was in doubt because of rumours that Man United were about to complete his transfer. Peter Ridsdale still insisted: 'I have had one conversation with Manchester United but it did not move the situation on any further. We have still to receive a bid of a level that we would find acceptable.'

When Rio didn't make the flight to the Far East it was even more clear that his days at Leeds were numbered.

Chapter 18
A BOLD STEP

On Monday, 23 July Rio completed his move to Manchester United for an astounding £33 million. Sir Alex Ferguson had finally got his man and Leeds had got a healthy profit of £16 million over just 18 months. Rio – now on a new wage packet of more than £60,000 a week – announced the transfer at a packed Old Trafford press conference and cited the ambition of Man United's England stars to win more medals as a major factor in his decision to move. 'I've seen the boys with England and they are as hungry as ever,' he explained. 'They said it's like they have not won a championship yet and they want to do so again. When you are with England the United boys stay after training and work on little things. They are the players that are at the top and that is something I want to have. To be able to say I have played alongside the best and the hungriest players around is important to me.'

Rio admitted to the assembled press pack that he knew his move was a bold step – especially because of the fierce rivalry between the two teams. 'I made a decision to come here, as I thought it was a step on the way to improving me as a player. It wasn't an easy decision. I spoke to my family about loyalty. But at the end of the day, it is a short career and opportunities like this don't come around all the time.'

Sir Alex Ferguson even revealed to the press conference how he'd tried to sign Rio when he was a teenager on loan to Bournemouth from West Ham. He conceded that it would have saved the club a fortune if he'd got his man all those years earlier.

Also at the press conference on that day was Rio's girlfriend Rebecca Ellison, his mum and young sister. It was Rebecca's first real taste of the public spotlight as the lover of the world's most expensive defender. She looked calm and serene throughout the media gathering and made a point of watching proceedings from the back of the hall at Old Trafford. Then the couple went off house hunting in Cheshire's stockbroker belt. Back in Yorkshire, where Rebecca had been living with Rio for the previous nine months, a neighbour said: 'Rebecca is a lovely, friendly girl. She is very ordinary – and I mean that as a compliment.'

Rio's mates in south-east London were all asking the same question: 'Rebecca who?' As his pal Leon Simms explained: 'We never heard nothin' 'bout her 'cause Rio never brought her on the manor. But, hey man, that's cool. She's his little lady and that's fine by us.'

At Leeds there were rumours that ex-Man United star Jaap Stam was being lined up to replace Rio. Chairman Peter Ridsdale confirmed some of the money from Rio's transfer would go towards purchasing new players. New manager Terry Venables was also reported to be interested in AC

Milan's Brazilian World Cup winner Roque Junior as well as Valencia's talented Argentinian Roberto Ayala.

The following day the Ferdinand clan got further good news when 17-year-old Anton was offered a three-year professional contract by West Ham manager Glenn Roeder, who said: 'I have always felt that Anton would develop more slowly than his brother, but he has improved significantly since last Christmas. My intention now is to get him into the reserve team as soon as possible because he needs to be playing against more experienced opponents. That's the only way he will learn. But he will also be available to play in our most important youth games.'

Anton's first taste of senior football occurred when he played in the Hammers' pre-season friendly against Leyton Orient at Brisbane Road just a week before signing the new contract. Anton was just as modest as Rio when it came to assessing his future: 'It was a great experience for me and hopefully I showed the manager a little of what I can do. Rio's success gives me something to aim at. He's set the standard for me. I've seen what he's got from football and I'd like some of that, too. I want what he's achieved but I know it will take a lot of hard work.'

In Manchester, more behind-the-scenes stories about the 'deal of the year' were unfolding. One important aspect for Man United – besides Rio's obvious skills – was his nationality. Old Trafford chief executive Peter Kenyon explained: 'Rio's nationality is important because the backbone of our team is built on English players. There are more wet, cold days than there are hot, sunny ones and British players know what to expect. We have always said we want to keep the core of our team English. We know their international commitments and they are not going to suddenly depart on long-haul flights around the world every five weeks. These things are disruptive, irrespective of skill. The team spirit thing has worked for us. The Premier League is a tough league and in some respects is unique. It is not going to take Rio three months to acclimatise.'

So, while most of Europe was facing a slump in soccer finances, Man United continued to add to their enormous turnover. Since the Bosman Ruling in December 1996, wages in football had grown annually by an astounding 30 per cent, a trend that only started to slow down in the summer of 2002. Yet even now only half of United's turnover was spent on wages, an almost uniquely low figure among Champions League teams. 'I think the financial lessons of football are tough,' added Kenyon. 'The top players will always command top wages and transfers. Wage controls and wage restraint are up to each individual club to decide.'

Kenyon also explained: 'Any business has got to use its strengths and ours is that we have little debt. There is a fallacy that just because you are a plc you can't invest in players. We do because that is our core activity. But we are never going to bust this club in search of a player. We knew that Rio was one of the best centre-halves knocking around, certainly there were no others like him at that age and we think this will represent a fantastic investment.'

Typically, Sir Alex Ferguson was more concerned with his failure to win a trophy for the first time in four years than any of the financial aspects of the Rio transfer. 'It is important to remember that, despite what some people think, we have every right to improve ourselves. We have the right to be best of the best. There is nothing wrong with that. It doesn't matter what your view of Manchester United is. There is a thirst among the players and there was disappointment here last season. We hope to make amends for that.'

But he did admit that a 'tricky transfer' deal had been made easier by Leeds' obvious need to reduce their debts. 'Leeds are a big club, big rivals to us and Ferdinand had four years left on his contract. These were massive hurdles but we were always hopeful because of Leeds United's financial position and because Rio wanted to come here.'

And Ferguson's take on Rio was typical of the man. 'Improvement is the key word here,' he said. 'He is 23 years of age and we are confident he will mature and develop into one of the best centre-halves in the world. His ability on the ball has been there to see since he was a kid. To understand the fee, you have to look at his age, his nationality, his position and potential. Then the rest is easy.'

The transfer of Rio to Manchester United turned the spotlight once again on his Tel Aviv-based agent Pini Zahavi. Behind the scenes he was considered one of the most influential figures in the game, part of an international network which connected many of football's biggest movers and shakers. The close association between Rio and Zahavi had already once been richly rewarded when Rio was sold to Leeds for £18 million and Zahavi pocketed at least £1 million in fees. Now the pair had made an even bigger fortune thanks to the immense wealth of Man United.

In the middle of all the delicate negotiations between Leeds and Man United, Zahavi had deliberately turned up the heat by telling journalists: 'Rio needs to move to a bigger and better club.' It was an indisputable statement of fact yet only the obtuse would have not weighed up the effect it might have on Leeds fans. It also seemed the seeds of this transfer saga were sewn long before United's failure to win the Premiership.

But not everyone was impressed by Rio's move. The *Daily Mirror* published a 'fascinating' comparison between what Rio said when he left West Ham on 27 November 2000 and what he said on leaving Leeds on 22 July 2002. Headlined 'NEW CLUB ... SAME OLD CLAPTRAP', it read:

'I never wanted to leave West Ham. I have said that all along, but once they accepted the fee then it was up to me. Now I am at a club where I can realise all my ambitions of winning medals and playing in Europe.'

and:

'I'm leaving a great club in Leeds, but I made a decision to come here as I thought it was a step on the way to improving me as a player. I wouldn't have come if I didn't think I was going to win top honours in the game.'

But among the managers of many of Man United's rivals there was a sneaking admiration for the way the Old Trafford team had finally pulled off the transfer because Rio would have been top of every coach's shopping list – if they had the funds available.

Gérard Houllier was full of praise for Rio in the days following his world-record transfer. The Liverpool boss said: 'I wasn't surprised what United paid for Rio Ferdinand when you consider their turnover. In football what appears expensive today sometimes seems to be cheap tomorrow. When the player is quality the price is always right. At the World Cup, Rio showed he had something special. I think if United had had Rio last year they could have won the Champions League.'

In the weeks following Rio's transfer to Man United it became clear that the huge fee involved was unlikely to be matched in the foreseeable future. Everyone in the Premiership and throughout Europe was looking to trim squads, not buy new players.

European champions Real Madrid made half their first-team squad available for transfer, although they did buy Ronaldo in late August 2002 (for approximately £30 million) after protracted negotiations with Inter Milan which included the agreement of a bizarre instalments deal. Former Liverpool ace Steve McManaman was reportedly available for nothing just so that the club could get rid of his astronomical wages and there were rumours he might go to Inter as part of the Ronaldo deal when the transfer window reopened in December 2002.

In Italy, the financial situation at clubs such as Roma and Lazio was so serious that the start of the Serie A season had to be postponed for two weeks. A drop in TV revenues in Germany, Italy and Spain meant that many top clubs were in serious trouble.

Perhaps not so surprisingly, Peter Ridsdale let it be known that, fine player though he might be, Rio would not be missed at Elland Road. The Leeds chairman insisted that the club only bought Rio in the first place because of the uncertainly and possible prison sentence hanging over Jonathan Woodgate following the assault on Sarfraz Najeib. Ridsdale described Rio as nothing more than a stopgap for Leeds. A man keeping another player's seat warm.

He even suggested that Leeds ended up using Rio rather than the other way round. Ridsdale was careful not to criticise Rio personally but found it difficult to hide his anger at Rio's alleged conduct during the protracted negotiations with Man United. He insisted that, when he first received an approach for Rio from Man United's Peter Kenyon, he was resolved not to sell Leeds' star player. 'All the speculation started after that but I can assure you that speculation was not prompted by Leeds United,' he told one journalist. 'I'll leave it up to you to decide who started it.'

Ridsdale claimed he met Rio when he came back from the World Cup on the Monday before he went off on holiday and he told Ridsdale he wanted to leave the club. Rio has never confirmed or denied this meeting took place. Ridsdale added: 'That, by the way, was the very same day he put his name to an article in a national newspaper saying he wanted to stay.'

In addition, Ridsdale insisted that when Rio got back from his holiday in Las Vegas, he then put in a written transfer request saying not just that he wanted to leave Leeds but that he specifically wanted to join Man United. The chairman explained: 'At that point we had not received an offer from them that we considered even close to being viable so it was all a bit puzzling. But when the offer went up to £33 million, an offer which I don't believe will be repeated in the foreseeable future in the British transfer market, I think as a public company it would have been very questionable for us to turn that offer down.

'When you combine that with a player who says he wants to go in the first place, the two things together make it impossible to say no. There is an argument for saying we have got a certain amount of strength in the central defensive area anyway.'

Ridsdale knew only too well that many Leeds fans were angrily accusing him of selling the club's best player. 'But you have to take a view on whether that is actually the case or not. You could argue what we have done is cover for Woodgate for 18 months in case he was not around. Now we have got him back and we have made a healthy profit on a player we only bought as cover in the first place.'

He even pointed out the earlier case of how Leeds sold Jimmy Floyd Hasselbank, then considered the club's best player. 'That raised a few people's eyebrows but we stormed to third in the League that season without him. I don't really want to criticise Rio because he did a great job for us. We took a big gamble when we signed him but he was great in the community, great on the field and great for England. But the reality is that he has gone and yet there are still a lot of Premiership clubs who would be happy to swap places with us when it comes to strength at the back. I'm so relaxed about that.'

The only comparable move between Leeds and Man United in recent years had involved the fiery midfielder Eric Cantona, who moved in 1992 for a bargain price of £1.2 million and then went on to inspire a decade of unrivalled United success. That was deemed to be a terrible mistake. Many Leeds fans feared the same could be said of Rio's move to Manchester.

After hearing about Ridsdale's attack, Rio hit back in typical fashion, saying: 'A lot of my mates thought his comments were out of order but it's water off a duck's back. I can handle it. It's time to let bygones be bygones and for him to get on with his life and me to get on with mine. He knew my feelings and I knew his. I wish he could have just left it at that. I've always said I respect the people at Leeds and I enjoyed my time there. But after a lot of soul searching I felt it was an opportunity I couldn't turn down.'

Rio remained in touch with some of his former teammates and many of them even rang him in the days following the transfer to wish him luck. Rio explained: 'They haven't asked why I've gone or had a go at me for it. I wouldn't have held it against any of them if they'd left. We all know that transfers happen in football and that people move on. It's just part of the game.'

He had left Leeds because he was made an offer he knew

he couldn't refuse. Man United remained the most glamorous club in the world and he knew he could win the biggest prizes at Old Trafford. Rio hoped that Leeds fans would not blame him even though he feared there might be quite a backlash against him for a while. He also hoped they would understand the reasons for his move. He'd carefully weighed up so many factors and listened hard to Terry Venables – a man he had the utmost respect for. And he fully appreciated what a big gamble Leeds took on him when they paid West Ham £18 million 18 months earlier.

But all Rio's advisers were saying that he had paid Leeds back handsomely and with interest over that period. He hadn't short-changed them once, but times had changed at Elland Road. They were seriously cash-strapped and in the end money spoke louder than words.

However, Rio's fears about a backlash from fans were soon proved true. Leeds supporters cancelled their Player of the Year presentation to prevent Rio collecting the award. Rio had topped the season-long poll, voted for monthly by members of the Leeds supporters club. Fans chief Ray Fell said: 'In the circumstances it would be folly to invite Rio and hand over the award to him. In this case we have decided to cancel the Player of the Year presentation to Rio and instead we will make a presentation of some sort to someone we feel more worthy of it. His name will be put on our list of winners because the fans voted for him at the time. They loved him when he was happy to play for Leeds United, but that is now in the past.'

Over at BBC Leeds dozens of fans vented their anger by flooding the station with text messages. They included:

'I remember Jack Charlton being paid over-the-top praise by a sycophantic journalist. With his inimitable style he said, "My position is the easiest on the pitch," i.e. central defender. Rio is not irreplaceable.' John Brook, Leeds.

'Man U and Ferguson seem to think they are above any regulations. Any other team would have been brought before the FA for what they have done, but the authorities and media love them. Is it any wonder that all genuine supporters dislike them?' Ian Goldman, Leeds.

'Goodbye, Rio and, as they say in show business, "break a leg".' Dave, Leeds.

'Rio will be missed after all he is a world class player, however if he wants to be a Judas and go to Man U so be it. After all, we can all show Judas what we think of him when he visits with the scum.' Des, Wakefield.

'We got in the Champions League with no help from Judas. He stayed a season and guess what? We failed to qualify. He should remember this: At Leeds, every time (and it happened most games) he made a cock-up when trying to be too elaborate there was big Nige or Robbo to save his blushes. At the scum his errors will be exposed by the French clown that is Barthez. Woody is twice as good, younger and we have the best young keeper in the world. Good riddance, Flopiland.' Gez, Leeds.

And so it went on. BBC Radio Leeds received countless indignant messages about Rio's move to 'the scum', as many Leeds fans referred to Man United. If Rio thought his move would be achieved with the minimum of anger, he was seriously mistaken.

Chapter 19

THROWING DOWN THE GAUNTLET

Rio's move to Manchester United was intended to address the weakness at the back of United's defence that had contributed to nine League defeats the previous season. But French stalwart Laurent Blanc was about to turn 36 and there remained many questions about the unit in front of Fabien Barthez. United may have pulled off the transfer coup of the summer by snatching Rio from Leeds, but Arsenal boss Arsène Wenger had also been carefully strengthening his already gifted side and they still looked the stronger team. Wenger warned: 'If I didn't believe this side could have more success, I would be wasting my time staying. This is only the beginning.'

Wenger also cleverly stepped up his traditional war of words with Sir Alex Ferguson by saying that Rio wasn't worth £33 million. It was a backhanded compliment from the Arsenal boss. Ferguson was on the winner's rostrum at

Aintree Racecourse celebrating a victory by his miler Rock of Gibraltar. He grinned, gave interviews willingly and even cracked a joke about Wenger's comments.

A few days later Ferguson got his own back by suggesting that the much sought-after Gunner Patrick Vieira 'would like to play' for United. No doubt the aura of invincibility at Old Trafford had been shattered, but United would still hammer more teams than most. However, had they become vulnerable to Ferguson's constant tinkering with the team? The big question now was, had Rio joined a team that had already peaked?

Rio, David Beckham, Nicky Butt and Paul Scholes were all given an extra two weeks' rest after the World Cup. Over the previous year Rio had become particularly close friends with Man United defender Wes Brown – a friendship that was further cemented when they went on holiday to Las Vegas after the World Cup. But now, having moved to Old Trafford, Rio was threatening to force Brown out of the first-team picture. Yet Brown, 23, sportingly hailed Rio as the best centre-half in the world just days after his £33 million transfer was completed.

'And he's going to get even better,' Brown told a group of football reporters. 'He's a great buy and I'm sure this season he'll prove to everyone why we bought him. People say it's a lot of money, but he's only 23 and has got many years in him. He's strong, fast, good in the air and a good reader of the game – he's a huge signing for us and pretty much the defender you dream about having. He's proved to everyone over the years how much of a great player he is. He topped that off with the World Cup where he put in a magnificent performance throughout.'

Another one of Rio's new teammates, veteran Frenchman Laurent Blanc, insisted he couldn't wait to line up alongside the new boy. Blanc had delayed retirement plans for another year so as to work with Rio at the heart of Man United's defence. 'My desire and the desire to win things at Manchester United is one of the reasons why I decided to come back to play one more year and cancel my decision to retire. I'm looking forward to playing alongside Rio, who is an outstanding player for his age.'

Man United's outgoing defensive stalwart Denis Irwin was also full of praise for Rio. 'They needed a centre-back and Rio is as good as anyone out there,' explained the veteran, released on a free transfer to Wolves at the end of last season after 12 years at Old Trafford.

Rio quickly made it perfectly clear that one of his next ambitions was to succeed Roy Keane as Man United's skipper. He even told one reporter: 'I will only get it if I deserve it.' It wasn't a very tactful statement to make to his new teammates, but Rio's ambition never stood still. No sooner had he achieved one thing than he was moving on to the next. And there was no doubting his determination when he wanted something.

Just a few days after arriving at Old Trafford, Rio persuaded Sir Alex Ferguson – the ultimate tough-guy manager – to let him make his Man United debut against Bournemouth in a friendly testimonial to their manager Mel Machin after just two training sessions with his new teammates. Machin happened to be on the phone to Ferguson when Rio was in his Old Trafford office and the deal was done on the spot.

All eyes were on Rio from the minute he stepped out to warm up with his teammates at Bournemouth a couple of days later. And they included Juan Sebastian Veron, Ryan Giggs and Ole Gunnar Solskjaer. Eight-and-a-half thousand packed into Bournemouth's Dean Court ground to see the return of their prodigal son. This pre-season friendly of little sporting significance was even beamed live on MUTV across the world, with China among the countries transmitting the match. A global audience of some 60 million was believed to have tuned into Rio's Man United debut. That meant 60 million people had paid a fee to watch him, even though he only ended up coming on for the final quarter of the game.

The money spent on Rio's transfer would soon be recouped. The bare facts were that Bournemouth's most expensive signing in the team against United cost the equivalent of 12 days' worth of Rio's wages. Same sport, different worlds. No surprise then that Mel Machin's first words to his one-time trainee were, 'My word, you've grown' when he saw Rio just before the kick-off. The Bournemouth boss did add: 'Rio is now fulfilling the promise he showed.'

Rio was in fine form when he attended a press conference after the game, which United won 3–2. Rio even sportingly refused to allow the press to forget the main purpose of the match. He said: 'This is Mel's day. He deserves all the praise in the world.' Rio saw it as his way of thanking Machin for his help when he'd played at Bournemouth as a 17-year-old. 'It was great to get out there and I really enjoyed myself. I'm relieved I got that one out of the way. I am now looking forward to the challenge ahead. I just want to get the season started and to start playing football with United. I told Mel I was going to play in this game and I was determined to honour that. He did a lot for me when I was at Bournemouth all those years ago, and I really wanted to come out and join everyone in paying tribute to him.

'It was great to get on the pitch at last and I really

enjoyed it, even if I did only get 17 minutes. The United fans gave me a great reception. I am really looking forward to getting the League season started now and getting United back where they belong. I'm nowhere near match fitness – but this is just the beginning. It's a chance for us to get to know each other and play together against good opposition, so we're looking forward to it.'

And one-time Old Trafford manager Big Ron Atkinson had no doubt United were on to a winner with Rio: 'He will solve one of their problem areas – but they still require extra defensive cover and need to resolve how to fit Juan Veron into their midfield. And they need someone to link up with Ruud van Nistelrooy.'

Clearly, Rio and his agent Pini Zahavi had come out the real winners from his transfer to Manchester United. He was on a salary of more than £60,000 a week, putting him up there with the club's top names, including David Beckham. His five-year contract also granted him ownership of his image rights, allowing him to negotiate lucrative commercial deals. Then there was the small matter of the £3.3 million the club had agreed to pay to cover a pension contribution to the Professional Footballers Association, plus a payment of the agents' fees.

Naturally, all this haggling didn't stop Rio splashing out £190,000 on a Bentley GT Coupe to match the tastes of his superstar teammate David Beckham. Some at Old Trafford immediately dubbed the new teammates the Bentley Boys. With a £110,000 Ferrari and that £168,000 Aston Martin already in the driveway, plus a two-seater Mercedes sports car and a 4x4 Escapade, Rio still went for the Bentley, a brand-new model not even in the showrooms yet. Rio put down a £50,000 deposit to make sure he got one of the first off the production line. Rio was told to expect delivery of the car, complete with white leather seats, walnut dashboard, DVD player and mini-TV screens, by mid-winter of 2002. By that time he hoped to have settled in a Cheshire mansion. Local estate agents were already on the lookout for a property with a pool, gym, snooker room and jacuzzi.

But despite the high salary, flashy motors and beautiful brunette Rebecca on his arm, it wasn't all smooth sailing. Rio received at least 10 death threats in the days following his transfer to Man United. Senior officials at the Professional Footballers Association were alerted, as well as the police. Two meaty ex-SAS bodyguards were immediately assigned to protect Rio whenever he was at the club's training ground or Old Trafford. One source at the club explained: 'Rio usually just shrugs this stuff off – but these letters are more sinister. They have gone too far.'

Many believed the threats had been fuelled during Leeds's close-season tour of Australia and the Far East when a handful of Leeds fans started waving banners saying 'Rio is scum' and 'We're going to get you.' Televised in England, these scenes provoked a number of bigoted Leeds fans who seemed hell-bent on proving the club's race issue was far from dead. Rio was disturbed by the threats but a kid from Peckham's Friary Estate was not that easily scared. As he told one old pal in south-east London: 'I've had a lot worse before. These people don't scare me. They're just crazy, from a different world. Not even worth talking about.'

But at Rio's mum's house in Mottingham a security guard was also on duty because of taunts made in the street to members of Rio's family. As he told his friend: 'Now that does bother me. They're havin' a dig at my family and that's completely out of order.'

Sir Alex Ferguson was warned by his financial bosses at Man United that he would not be able to buy any more big names following the vast outlay on Rio. He even admitted: 'We're not well off with money so that we do a Real Madrid and just buy anyone. We do worry about debt. We're a plc. It's a different culture. So if I want to buy two or three players I might have to sell. If I see the right players available I could do that. It's a buyer's market at the moment and there are a few very good players available who you could get for a lot less than this time last year.'

That left chief executive Peter Kenyon to interpret his manager's words: 'The reality is that whether you pay £10 million or £30 million it has to be in line with what you can afford. The reality of the situation to date is that you can't just keep spending and adding players to the squad.'

But Kenyon did reveal that Rio's transfer deal had been carefully structured with a series of delayed payments over the next five years. 'You don't spend £30 million on a player lightly, but it was a real target. We decided at the end of last season that the area that needed strengthening was the defence. We have a payment structure that covers the next 12 months and a performance-related element for the next five years. We will be delighted if over the five-year period we have to pay that.' While Kenyon called it a '£30 million deal', the total spent on Rio was at least £33 million if all the 'extras' are included.

And, typically, Ferguson was soon issuing a warning to Rio and any others who might think they would be automatically selected. 'It's simple. If players perform, they'll go in. If they don't, they won't. Performance is everything. You can't go beyond that. Reputations don't matter, I'm sorry. I'm the manager of the biggest club in the world, with the biggest support base in the world, and my loyalty is to them. I've also got loyalty to the players, obviously, but the bottom line is I've got to produce a winning team. That's where decision making comes into it. I've been given that job and I've never shirked it.'

Not surprisingly, Man United were quickly installed as the bookmakers' favourites to win the 2002–3 Premiership. Ferguson pointed out: 'We should be favourites to win the Premiership because we have the best players. We have been the best over a number of years. Some people say there has been a shift in power to Arsenal but that is only after one season. It is up to us to get back on track and win the League again. I have to produce a winning team. It is a hard business being at the top and only the very best can do it. Some individuals keep driving themselves. They get annoyed with themselves when things are wrong and that's what you like to see.

'But some take it for granted and if you do that you eventually run out of time. You give them every chance because you trust them and because they have always responded in the past when we've had a bad season. Now they must respond again. But if they keep failing there's nothing you can do. You pick them but they drop themselves. If that happens again maybe you change the whole team – more likely you just change one or two.'

And Ferguson would drop Rio Ferdinand if he deserved it. 'I've been given this job and have never shirked it. You might think it's hard, the players might think it's hard. but it's not. I remember that this club went 26 years without winning the League and since then things have changed around here. But there are still some fans, some people at Old Trafford and even some directors who don't remember the Manchester United who once came behind Liverpool.'

Summing up his attitude for the coming season, he

continued: 'Last season we were very unlike Manchester United and that will not happen again. We won't lose nine games again this season and we won't lose six at home. Last season was littered with mistakes – individuals' mistakes. One match it would be one individual making a mistake, the next it was someone else and that's what we have to eradicate.'

Over at Leeds United, new boss Terry Venables had decided after all not to splash out much of the £30-million-plus fee for Rio on new players. Rio's old defensive partner Jonathan Woodgate lined up alongside Dominic Matteo in the middle of the park and produced a good performance during a pre-season friendly 1–0 victory over Barnsley. Woodgate was so quick and commanding that many believed Rio might not be so sorely missed after all. Leeds fans claimed that Woodgate could soon be challenging Rio for his England shirt. They chanted for an international call-up after three pieces of world-class defending by Woodgate during the first 45 minutes of play against Barnsley.

A couple of days after the Barnsley victory, Terry Venables confirmed that Matteo would succeed Rio as the long-term captain of Leeds. The new Elland Road boss made his decision after the 28-year-old ex-Liverpool player skippered the side during their three-match tour of the Far East and Australia.

Venables continued to put a brave face on the loss of Rio. 'When I was at Barcelona, that job was as big as it gets anywhere in the world. And my first decision there was whether I kept or sold Maradona. But as soon as I saw the financial situation he just had to go – he couldn't stay. But we made £4 million on the transfer and we won the League, so the loss of one player is not necessarily devastating.'

He urged his new Leeds superstars to smash the stranglehold that Man United, Arsenal and Liverpool had on the top of the Premiership. Just like O'Leary before him, Venables said he wanted to make sure his side mounted a serious challenge for the title. He also demanded that his team gain a Champions League place at the end of the season, even without superstar Rio.

The Leeds boss did imply that Rio wouldn't be missed when he told journalists: 'As I have said to many of the players here, I don't look at the opposition. I don't care who they have signed. I am only concerned about what we are doing ... no one else.'

When Rio finally moved to Man United, Venables had been deeply hurt. He'd hoped that the loyalty and patience he'd shown Rio by encouraging him to join the Euro '96 squad when he was an untried teenager might be repaid. But he was also pragmatic enough to know that there was no sense in dwelling on the past. Within days he was even voicing an interest in buying Rio's home in Yorkshire, a converted barn.

Still on the house-buying front, Rio was eyeing up a des res close to Old Trafford. Teammate David Beckham had already offered Rio a temporary home at the Beckhams' flat in Cheshire, which he and pregnant Posh had left for a bigger, family property.

Rio and Rebecca were soon looking over some flashy pads in the picturesque village of Hale Barns, already home to new teammates Roy Keane and Nicky Butt. Rio was particularly taken with a £1.4-million house called Summerfield which had five living rooms, five bedrooms, a huge pond, a 40-foot swimming pool and a massive kitchen.

Despite the warnings from United's money men, Sir Alex Ferguson was still pushing for a fourth striker to join Ruud van Nistelrooy, Ole Gunnar Solskjaer and Diego Forlan. He also wanted further cover in defence. 'It would be nice to have a fourth striker and we're also a couple of defenders short. We've lost three defenders – Denis Irwin, Ronny Johnsen and Ronnie Wallwork – and we've only bought Rio.

'[Chief executive] Peter Kenyon knows there's weakness and it's a buyer's market at the moment. I think any player would want to come to our club. It has a romance about it and an attraction to most players in the game. I get calls all the time from agents saying their players would love to come here and they are good players I'm talking about. But we're only looking at the very best so, most of the time, I'm not interested. However, if those one or two were available we'd ask ourselves how we could get them.'

Then it seemed as if Rio might be joined at Man United by his other new, young England World Cup teammate Darius Vassell after wage negotiations with his club, Aston Villa, broke down. But that deal ended up on the back burner because of the £15 million price tag Villa put on Vassell.

It was clear at Old Trafford that David Beckham was still feeling the effects of his broken left foot. With United just a few weeks away from their Champions League pre-qualifier, Ferguson was taking no chances. 'I need them to play in the next couple of games to give me an indication of the right team to pick for our Champions League qualifier. I have a team in mind, subject to how well the England players progress in the next few days. When you have just got back to training and only played a couple of pre-season games, there can be a dip in performances.'

Rio didn't even fly out with Man United for their next

pre-season friendly against Norwegian side Valarengen. Alex Ferguson believed it better for Rio to stay behind in England and then link up with the squad for a four-team tournament in Amsterdam the following weekend. In that pre-season friendly event, Rio's full debut for Man United ended in a 2–1 defeat by Ajax. Ironically, Rio made way for his close pal Wes Brown in the fifty-eighth minute. But Alex Ferguson insisted he was pleased with Rio's performance: 'Rio looked assured at the back. He read the game well and I'm happy with him.'

Dutch ace Ronald Koeman – now Ajax coach – was not so impressed: 'It's a bit too early to call him world-class. You are only that when you have proved yourself over a number of years at the highest level. The whole attention will be on him and everything will be analysed. It's not every player who can handle that extra pressure. Some so-called quality players can't handle the life and expectancy of being at a big club.'

Koeman also made a pointed reference to the amount of cash United had paid Leeds for Rio. 'It's usually the strikers, the goalscorers, who grab the headlines and who cost the most money. But there was a problem with the Man United defence last season and, with Ferdinand in it, it will be better this time.'

For Man United's friendly with Parma at that same Dutch pre-season tournament, Rio partnered John O'Shea in defence, with Roy Keane on the bench and David Beckham taking over as captain even though regular stand-in skipper Ryan Giggs was in the side. Heavy rain was accompanied by loud claps of thunder, and with the stadium roof open, the players found themselves sloshing around in the mud. United took the lead in the twenty-third minute with a stunning move featuring some wonderful interplay between Veron, Rio and Beckham before Nicky Butt spread the ball wide on the right to the advancing Wes Brown. He beat one defender and then whipped in a low cross which was steered home by the left foot of Giggs, who'd slipped ahead of his marker.

Minutes later Rio managed a deft feint on the ball before bursting off on the left wing to create space from which he picked out Solskjaer for a speculative overhead kick that stunned the Italians. United eventually coasted home 3–0.

On 10 August Rio wrenched his left ankle after twenty-three minutes of Man United's 2–0 win over Boca Juniors, leaving Alex Ferguson without his £33 million centre-back for a least two weeks. Rio would definitely miss the first leg of the following week's Champions League qualifier against Zalaegerszegi in Hungary and he was unlikely to play in United's first two Premiership matches.

Meanwhile Rio's interest in acting had turned into a serious hobby. After taking those secret acting lessons while at Leeds, he was delighted to be offered a part in the second series of ITV's *Footballers' Wives*. During the summer of 2002 he filmed on Waterloo Bridge in central London, and one member of the production team told reporters: 'Rio was strolling over the bridge with cameras following him. He was obviously a big hit with the production company. One of them even said if Rio ever thinks of quitting his day job there's a career for him as an actor – he's a natural.'

Back in the real world, Alex Ferguson's pledge to win the Premiership had upset other clubs, such as Newcastle, who insisted the championship was up for grabs – despite the high-profile signing of Rio. Chairman Freddy Shepherd said: 'One man doesn't make a team and, no, I don't think it means the title is definitely set for Old Trafford. Juan

Sebastian Veron came in for £28 million last year and was supposed to guarantee them the title, but they ended up finishing third.'

Rio missed United's first two Premiership games, home to West Brom and away to Chelsea, through injury. But that didn't stop him popping over to Peckham to see some of his pals the day after watching United's 2–2 draw at Stamford Bridge. One of the 'crew' he met up with was old friend Leon Simms, who later explained: 'Rio's as cool as ever. We all hung out after the Chelsea game. He seems very happy to be at United. The same old Rio. He ain't ever goin' to change, man! You gotta remember that this manor is home for Rio and always will be. This is where his real mates are and I can't see him ever leavin' all this behind.'

But perhaps surprisingly, there were still very few of Rio's south-east London friends who knew anything about his live-in love Rebecca Ellison. 'He didn't mention her and she's never been down here with him,' added Leon. 'But that's up to him, he's a good guy and kept in touch with all of us. He's never let it all go to his head.'

When Rio was recently asked if Rebecca was 'the one', he replied: 'Well, I can sit in a room with her for more than half an hour and not get fed up.'

Many people, including Rio's mum, credited Rebecca with being a calming influence on Rio's character. She seemed very quiet and reserved. One friend explained: 'Rebecca's taste seems in great contrast to that of Rio's love of white disco suits. She prefers an understated dress sense with high-necked Victorian blouse and discreet Fendi handbag and not a blonde highlight in sight.'

While in London for the Chelsea match, Rio also heard from his old friends that Latifah, the girl he was so smitten by when he was a teenager, was travelling the world as a dancer. 'He always wants to hear how she's been,' adds another close friend.

But Rio's taste in barbers was slightly less exotic. In the middle of August he took a trip down to Moss Side – in many ways the Manchester equivalent to Peckham – for a haircut that cost £7. He drove to one of the toughest parts of the city in his £180,000 Aston Martin Vanquish, which was never likely to go unnoticed. Barber Joseph Campbell, 43, explained: 'He went for a low cut on the top, faded even more closely at the sides and back. He wanted some colour too, but we don't do that, so I suggested somewhere else.'

Jamaican-born Mr Campbell – who'd previously cut former Man United star Andy Cole's hair – described Rio 'as a very nice chap – very down-to-earth'. Tactfully, he refused to reveal the size of the tip Rio left, except to say it had been more than the cost of the haircut.

Rio finally made his competitive match debut for Man United in their second-leg Champions League qualifier at Old Trafford against Zalaegerszegi on Tuesday 27 August. Trailing by 1–0 after a late goal by the Hungarians in the first away leg, United were undoubtedly facing their most important match of the new season. If they didn't progress into the Champions League proper, then it could cost the club as much as £40 million in lost revenue.

As it turned out, the opposition were thrashed 5–0, but Rio looked far from comfortable at the back of the United defence. Halfway through the second half he made a terrible blunder, giving the ball away in front of his own goal, but was saved by a superb tackle by Laurent Blanc. Shortly afterwards Alex Ferguson took Rio off and he was given ice treatment on a swollen ankle although many in the crowd wondered if he had been substituted before any more disasters occurred.

Rio produced a solid display for England in their 1–1 draw with Portugal in a friendly at Villa Park on Saturday, 8 September. England's goal was scored by Rio's former Leeds teammate Alan Smith. The game was somewhat overshadowed by the inclusion in the England squad of Lee Bowyer and Jonathan Woodgate after their two-and-half-year ban because of the Leeds assault case.

But the most significant event happened a few hours after the game. Rio couldn't resist motoring down the M1 from Villa Park for a night out in London's sleazy Soho. He arrived at the trendy Sugar Reef bar with five friends. Yet again, Rebecca was nowhere to be seen. Now all this might have happened without Rio's bosses at England and Man United ever knowing about it except that a terrifying brawl broke out in the middle of the club and worldly Rio helped break up the scuffle.

Rio was sitting quietly in the VIP area with his friends when one of them got into an argument with another clubber. The row then escalated and Rio's other pals joined in as the player remained seated. It soon developed into a free-for-all with tables and glasses flying in all directions. One clubber was injured and needed first-aid as a team of bouncers rushed over to split up the nasty confrontation. Rio disappeared into the night minutes after the trouble had flared up. A customer, 29-year-old Rosil Bento, said afterwards: 'I couldn't believe what was happening and that an England player was there. The fight was really scary and women were running and screaming trying to get out of the way.'

It seemed that despite all the pledges and the 'calming influence' of Rebecca, Rio still couldn't resist the lure of the bright lights of his home city. As one friend pointed out: 'We all know Rio's still the same dude he always was and that also means he has the same habits. The guy likes to see his old friends from Peckham and he doesn't often take Rebecca out with him in London.'

But Rio's first big test of character on the pitch would come the following Saturday, 14 September, when Man United were travelling to Elland Road for an important Premiership clash. Many in Leeds had compared Rio's departure with that of Eric Cantona 10 years earlier. In fact it was said that Rio's much-hyped return to his old club would prompt a new bitter song from the most ardent Leeds fans: 'The old Judas is dead, long live the new Judas.'

David O'Leary – Rio's old boss at Leeds – predicted that Rio would brush off the crowd's anger and get on what he does best – play football. And O'Leary provided a fascinating insight into Rio's character: 'The great thing that impresses me about him is his mental strength. And I think he's getting stronger and stronger.'

As it happened, Man United lost 1–0 to Leeds, but their defeat couldn't in any way be blamed on Rio, who gave a faultless display, despite non-stop heckling from the crowd. The names didn't seem to hurt Rio, although he did appear slightly edgy on the ball. More hurtful was the fact that many pundits at the ground came away applauding Jonathan Woodgate's performance at the heart of the Leeds defence. As Matt Lawton wrote in the *Daily Mail*: 'Of the two defenders Woodgate was by far the superior on an afternoon that proved a touch traumatic for the former Leeds captain.'

But the question on everyone's lips following United's second defeat of the season, which left them tenth in the

Premiership, was whether the Old Trafford bubble had burst. After five matches the team had managed its worst-ever start to the Premiership. And those who assumed the arrival of Rio would see Alex Ferguson's side return to the top of the League already appeared to be very much mistaken. It really looked as if Ferguson's empire was starting to fall apart. The biggest test of Rio's character was yet to come.

Rio's appearance, on a list of the top ten richest foot-ballers in Europe, seemed to confirm his extraordinary rise to the top. At number four, with an estimated fortune put at £5.8 million, it must sometimes have seemed like a fairy tale to the young star.

Now 24 years of age, the time had really come when his future talents would have to be superseded by his existing skills. No more Rednapps or O'Learys to heap praise upon the up-and-coming star. Now it was sink or swim time and he was playing among the sharks in every sense of the word.

In one magazine interview Rio even admitted, 'I do feel blessed. I've got the money to look after my mum, my dad, my family and those people close to me. If I want to go out and buy them a present, I can. And why not?

'If you want to stay in touch with reality and be true to yourself, you have to remember your roots, what they are all about and what they mean to you. It keeps you grounded. But I'd still be playing football if I wasn't being paid for it.'

Rio's sensitive side came into play following his move to Manchester United when a replica of his United shirt and name was used to advertise an arms company. Using the slogan 'Who do you think spends this much on defence every season?' BAE Systems' advert was a blatant intrusion into Rio's life. He immediately ordered lawyers to pursue a case against the company with his spokesman telling journalists: 'It's fair to say we're not happy. There is no way Rio wants to be associated with an arms company.' But the incident did highlight one surprising issue; Rio apparently had not registered his name and shirt number as a trademark. However, the advert had used a slightly different strip from the actual Manchester United colours so it did not breach any laws.

Back on his childhood stomping ground, Rio came to the rescue after hearing that the junior football club where he once trained was in danger of folding through lack of funds. The Red Lions Boys Club in Surrey Quays needed to raise £5,000 to cover debts and service bills. The young players also needed new kit. Rio's new agent Danny Crerand played down the player's involvement. 'I've sorted out what Rio is going to do,' said Crerand. 'But it's a private matter and I don't want to go into it.'

In November 2002, it seemed that Leeds United were unlikely to ever receive the full reported £30 million from Rio's transfer. The only way this would happen was if United won the Champions League, Premiership and FA Cup plus the League Cup, twice in the next five years – an extremely tough feat.

In fact, the deal between Manchester United and Leeds had involved a downpayment of just £13 million in July when Rio signed with another £13 million to be paid a year later. It was also reported that Leeds had been very keen to give their fans the impression the transfer was for £30 million cash in order to 'water down' their fans' anger at the deal.

United's Premiership title bid had got off to a rocky start with a run of injuries and mixed results. Initially, they excelled in the Champions League but failed on the domestic front. But their league challenge firmly got back on track with a victory over Liverpool at Anfield with Diego Forlan scoring both goals in a 2-1 win. In December 2002, United also managed impressive victories against Arsenal and Newcastle United. In the Champions League, United beat Juventus both home and away and were undefeated in the Premiership.

Rio's old West Ham mentor, Harry Redknapp, revealed that the only Manchester United player he'd select for his own side would be his former young player Rio. The then Portsmouth manager made his comments on the eve of his side's third round FA Cup defeat at Old Trafford in January 2003. 'Man U have got many outstanding players but Rio is extra special. Yet he was never really an outstanding talent as a kid.'

The new year also saw United reach the Worthington Cup Final and they thrashed West Ham 6-0 in the FA Cup. However, United's Champions League campaign came to an end in the quarter finals when they went out to Real Madrid on 8 April 2003.

Rio's move to Manchester United seemed to pay dividends that very first full season when United clinched the Premiership with 83 points. Sadly, Rio's old pals at West Ham ended a disastrous campaign with relegation. As Rio held aloft the Premiership trophy at the end of the season he must have been elated that his move had proved so successful.

Rio's first season with Manchester United was full of ups and downs but it must have seemed a great move by him as his former clubs Leeds and West Ham struggled to survive in the Premiership.

But United's European adventure – which saw them

knocked out of the Champion's League to the supposedly invincible Real Madrid (themselves knocked out in the semis) did undoubtedly expose Rio to some of the fiercest criticism of his career.

Onetime Leeds and Man U favourite Johnny Giles wrote one highly critical article at the end of April, 2003, headlined 'THE TWO Rs EXPOSE HUGE GAPS IN RIO'S KNOWLEDGE OF DEFENDING'. The article claimed that Rio's boss, Alex Ferguson, could not avoid asking some awkward questions of Rio's performances at the back. Few had forgotten how United's survival in the earlier stages of the Champions League had been guaranteed only after French veteran Blanc managed a brilliant edge-of-the-penalty-area tackle after Rio had, yet again, let the opposition off the hook.

As Giles pointed out, 'Rio at 24 is young enough, but the worry is that a big part of a defender's performance will always be not so much technique as attitude of mind. Watching Ferdinand, you sometimes have to wonder if he has the potential to develop that defender's instinct and mindset. Part of his problem is that all footballers have a tendency to become creatures of habit and, in the Premiership, this can be a major problem when someone like Ferdinand, who in an average league game looks quite masterful, has to step up his effort against players of the quality of Raul and Ronaldo.'

During United's two quarter final games against Real Madrid it was certainly true that Rio sometimes looked as if he was lost in a minefield and, undoubtedly, Ferguson had noticed his shortcomings on the European stage. Now people inside football were asking for the first time if Rio could really make it in the big time. Could he acquire the kind of nerve and timing that distinguished the outstanding defenders? Was Ferguson going to start growing impatient in the new season of 2003/2004? Only time would tell.

As Johnny Giles also pointed out, 'Ferguson has worked on sharpening Ferdinand's game. No doubt he has pointed out that looking good on the ball is fine but it will always remain of secondary importance to someone who should have the top priority of defending properly. For the moment the jury will need a lot more evidence before reaching a verdict on the most expensive defender in the history of football.

'Ferdinand's worry now must be that his boss, who has made clear his priority of winning another European Cup, has seen enough to add another name to his shopping list. A name like Terry, a player who long ago proved he didn't need to be told that the main role of a defender is to defend. Ferdinand needs to grasp that truth as a matter of urgency. His United career will, sooner rather than later, depend on it.'

Rio's activities off the pitch also continued to hit the headlines. In June 2003, he was 'exposed' by the *News of the World* when two hotel workers alleged he attacked and humiliated them during the England team's 'training break' prior to a crucial Euro 2004 qualifying game against Slovakia. The incident took place at the luxurious Hyatt Regency hotel in southern Spain's La Manga holiday complex. Chelsea's John Terry was also alleged to have been present during the incident.

According to the newspaper, despite orders to abide by a bedtime curfew of 1am, Ferdinand and Terry called staff at 3.30am to fix a jammed pool table. The entire team had been under orders to get to bed by 1am at the latest. The pool table had been specially set up for the England squad in the hotel's ballroom. Rio was then alleged to have grabbed a hotel maintenance worker who in turn called his boss on his walkie-talkie. A fracas occurred. According to hotel staff, Rio tried to offer the maintenance man a tip. He refused and the two players then disappeared to their rooms. Minutes later England security chief Ray Whitworth was called out of bed to placate the hotel staff. He marched Rio back to the Grand Ballroom and made him apologise to the men he supposedly attacked.

Neither of the alleged 'victims' would talk about the incident afterwards but one other worker at the hotel later told reporters: 'It was the talk of the hotel. The England team tried to hush it up and hotel managers ordered us not to talk about it to anyone, but by then it was too late.'

Significantly, England boss Sven-Goran Eriksson talked to both Rio and John Terry about the incident later that same day but Eriksson was quickly satisfied and decided to take no further action against the two players.

A day later, Rio faced reporters when he turned up in Monaco to watch the Grand Prix. He said: 'It's all been taken out of proportion.' When asked if the story had ruined his trip to the south of France, he added: 'Not really, I'm still having a great time. It's amazing to see the cars close up and watch how the drivers like Michael Schumacher focus. I aim to come here every year now.'

Rio then used his lucrative column deal with the Sun to air his opinions about what happened at the hotel in Spain. In a piece headlined 'I only wanted a game of pool', Rio explained: 'We were playing pool and challenged two of the hotel staff to a game. We said, "Let's have a match, England v Spain." But they did not seem to understand what we were talking about. When we asked them again, they called in these other blokes. It's all been blown up out of proportion. There were no hard feelings between us. I can hold my head up high, as I know the truth of it.'

As it turned out, Rio then had to have an exploratory operation on a knee injury, which meant he would now miss England's European Championship qualifier against Slovakia on 11 June, which England won 2-1 thanks to two goals by Michael Owen. Rio admitted: 'It can be quite depressing. We have the best surgeons, but you're still on tenterhooks before an operation as to how it'll turn out. It's best to get away if you can.' Rio added: 'I've had a few injury problems and never felt able to get into a proper rhythm. I'm really disappointed I won't be able to play at the moment but I will be rooting for the boys and I'm sure they will do the business.'

In the early autumn of 2003, problems on the personal front emerged yet again for Rio. The *Daily Mail* headline summed it up: 'Party animal on the brink of ruin at 24.' It may have sounded a tad overdramatic but the tabloids had Rio in their sights and Rio wasn't helping things by refusing to curtail his own busy 'social life'.

This time he became embroiled by association – despite not being involved – in the latest scandal to hit the Premiership which happened when a gang-rape allegedly occurred in the exclusive Grosvenor House Hotel, in London's Park Lane. The room where the supposed attack took place had reportedly been booked in the name of England star Kieron Dyer, but the Newcastle player was not present at the time of the alleged incident.

When it was revealed that Dyer spent much of the day with Ferdinand following the alleged attack, Rio found himself once again tainted by association. But there was much worse to come. Rio was about to find himself at the centre of the biggest crisis of his headline-hitting career...

Chapter 20

Testing Times

O n 6 October 2003 it was publicly revealed that Rio had failed to take a routine drugs test at Manchester United's training ground two weeks earlier. Rio was immediately dropped from England's crucial match against Turkey and his international boss Sven-Goran Eriksson was said to be 'disappointed'. England needed to win or draw the Turkey game in order to qualify for the following summer's European Championships in Portugal and Rio had established himself as a valuable member of the team. He would be missed in defence.

Rio insisted to FA investigators that he was so preoccupied with moving house that he simply forgot to be make himself available for the test, although he did provide a clear sample 36 hours later. However, his failure to attend when required remained a technical breach of the sport's strict anti-drugs code.

Newspapers immediately pointed out that the delay in taking the test would have allowed some drugs, including recreational substances, to have passed through Rio's body and become undetectable.

However, Manchester United insisted they would stand by their record signing and the club immediately issued a statement: 'The player has not been charged with any offence, but has been asked to attend a personal interview to explain the reasons behind his non-attendance.' Rio undoubtedly faced an anxious wait until then.

Rio's agent and father-figure Pini Zahavi reportedly said the FA would be 'shooting themselves in the foot' if they banned him from playing in the Turkey game.

Meanwhile the whole of British sport, not to mention the Government, was watching carefully to see how football's governing body would handle the delicate situation.

The public and many newspapers were outraged at Rio's alleged 'forgetfulness' and Fleet Street let fly in typical fashion. On 9 October 2003, the *Daily Mail* headline read: 'Treachery – pampered playboys betrayed our trust.' The paper's respected sports journalist Jeff Powell wasn't just referring to Rio but other England players who had stunned the FA by threatening to strike over Rio's 'suspension' from the game against Turkey. Rio was already seen as guilty even though his 'drugs test problem' hadn't yet been dealt with by the FA. Jeff Powell said: 'Our man, Rio, they object, has been let down. So has our £30 million centre half, squealed his mighty club. So has our Mr Ferdinand, protests their shop-steward-in-chief (Gary Neville), the highest paid shop-steward-in-chief, the highest paid trade union leader in the land. And yes, Master Ferdinand has been let down. By himself.'

In reality, Gary Neville's attempt to rally the England

players in protest against what they saw as kangaroo court justice against Rio was well intentioned, but the problem was that it actually highlighted the details behind the drugs test incident, which sparked even more questions about Rio's motivations.

In the end, the England players' protest ran out of steam but Rio, the man at the centre of all the controversy, continued to insist he was nothing more than an innocent man. Streetwise Rio knew the rules of the game and as far as he was concerned he had done nothing wrong.

But if Rio was hoping the scandal would calm down after a few days of tabloid outrage, he was to be bitterly disappointed. By the following weekend, the Sunday papers had also joined in and they'd uncovered some fascinating background information. The *Sunday Telegraph* revealed that at the previous World Cup in Korea and Japan, Rio had willingly provided a urine sample for a drugs test in a FIFA television broadcast aimed at educating the public about the importance of doping control.

His willingness to co-operate with the film made Rio's failure to do the same at Manchester United's training ground all the more bewildering. It also proved that he was far from naïve when it came to providing samples to drug testers. Unfortunately for Rio, this particular story did nothing to help convince the world of his innocence.

At the *Sunday Times*, journalists provided their readers with a day-by-day, blow-by-blow account of the 'drugs test fiasco' as it was now being referred to. It emerged that Rio was told he had one hour to report for the drugs test after a three-man testing team arrived at United's Carrington training ground at 11.15 am on Tuesday, 23 September. Several players including Rio, Nicky Butt and Ryan Giggs were amongst those to be tested.

United doctor Mike Stone even sent a reminder down to Rio while he was still getting changed. United later insisted that by the time Stone realised Rio had forgotten to attend the drugs test, he had already left the ground. Meanwhile the testers continued waiting for Rio.

It was only after the testers left the training ground that United realised there really was 'a problem'. The club then sent a number of text messages and voicemail messages to Rio's mobile phone but were unable to contact him. A club official claimed that Rio kept his phone switched off much of the time because of hate messages from Leeds fans. By the time Rio finally got the messages it was early evening and he returned to Carrington to find the drug testers were long gone. At around 4pm that same afternoon, Rio was spotted out shopping at department store Harvey Nichols, in Manchester's city centre. He, meanwhile, still insisted he was preoccupied with moving house.

There were many unanswered questions surrounding Rio's drug testing problems but the fact remained that he was in yet another hot spot. It often seemed that wherever Rio went controversy was sure to follow.

Back on the field, Rio continued playing for Manchester United while awaiting a hearing on his case and, despite having plenty on his mind, produced some fine performances, much to the relief of his team boss Sir Alex Ferguson. Rio admitted in the Sun: 'I know how important it is that I concentrate on my football despite everything that's been going on. This is a different time to what I've been used to in my career but you just have to deal with it. If I had let things get to me and hadn't been doing the business on the pitch I'm sure the manager would have dropped me. I wouldn't have expected anything else. When you are at a club like United, there is no room for passengers.'

Rio could not directly discuss the drugs test case because of the FA hearing but being able to play in the meantime had proved the ideal therapy. 'I haven't sensed any extra pressure while I've been playing. In fact, it is where I have felt most comfortable. I have a job to do for my club. I'm getting on with it and focusing 100 per cent,' added Rio.

But United's mediocre form following Rio's 'exposure' for failing to attend that drugs test did little to convince Old Trafford's diehard fans that his behaviour had not had a knock-on effect upon the team.

Rio's two-day disciplinary hearing over the missed drugs test was eventually held in late December 2003. A three-man FA commission of chairman Barry Bright and his colleagues Frank Pattison and Peter Herd aimed to find out why one of England's most respected and talented footballers drove away from the Carrington training ground that day without being turned back to attend the drugs test.

Rio attended proceedings held at Bolton's Reebok Stadium each day dressed in a dark, sombre suit and tie and accompanied by his counsel Robert Thwaites, QC. The commission heard evidence from the UK Sport testing team as they sought to piece together the chain of events which led to Rio contravening the drugs regulations.

On day two of the tribunal, United's manager Alex Ferguson gave the impression that Rio would be found innocent and breezed in and out of the Reebok Stadium, saying nothing to waiting press but looking extremely pleased with himself. Later that day he made a point of telling journalists that Rio was definitely in the United team to play Tottenham at White Hart Lane the following day.

Through his lawyer, Rio continued to insist that

although he did forget to take the original test, he had in fact returned within two hours – but by then the testing team had departed. In a corridor near the hearings, Rio's agent Pini Zahavi was chewing on one of his favourite cigars. He insisted Rio was very relaxed about the proceedings. 'We have said from the start that Rio didn't do anything wrong and that is still what we believe,' explained Zahavi. 'Rio is okay. Obviously he would rather be somewhere else other than here, but he is handling things well. He is just looking forward to getting this over with and returning to his football.'

But the FA were convinced Rio had contravened the rules and he was found guilty of misconduct. He was handed an eight-month suspension and fined £50,000 for missing the drugs test. The suspension was due to start on 12 January and effectively ruled Rio out of the second half of United's Premiership campaign, as well as missing Euro 2004 in Portugal with England. Rio was also ordered to pay all the FA's legal costs, estimated to be in the region of £100,000. Taking his own costs into account, Rio was facing a bill of at least £250,000.

The sentence produced a gasp from the assembled media at the Reebok Stadium, especially as many were predicting a ban of no more than three months. Rio was given 48 hours to ask for a written judgement and then another fourteen days to appeal. In fact, United lodged an immediate appeal following the FA's decision, issuing only a brief statement – through an obviously angered club director and solicitor Maurice Watkins – when the verdict was announced.

Rio's lengthy suspension left his boss Sir Alex Ferguson's team potentially very weak in defence. The outspoken Scotsman was typically frank about his dilemma: 'I would say we are still a bit light in defensive areas. Only time will tell if we have enough flexibility to cope.'

However, Ferguson remained impressively loyal to Rio and even talked about taking legal action against the FA. He told reporters: 'We'll need to assess the situation. It may not end with the FA – we may have to go to court and he's got a right to go to court to protect his reputation. The club would certainly support him.'

Later Ferguson added: 'We were never going to say anything in immediate response to whatever the FA's verdict was because that would be unwise. We would just take stock of the situation and see where we're going from there.'

The United manager contended that Rio was 'a condemned man' from the moment the FA banned him from international duty when news of the missing drugs test was made public. 'Right from the word go, he was bound to get charged because they left him out of the English team. That condemned him right away. He has had to carry that burden from that minute when they banned him from playing for England.'

But would taking legal action against the FA endanger Rio's England career? Ferguson responded: 'I don't know about that. Whether he ever plays for his country again, or whether he ever wants to play for them, he has been condemned. No matter what people say, it will still be there, that he was refused permission to play for his country because of a drugs situation.'

Meanwhile, Rio wrote about his feelings on the situation in his column in the *Sun*: 'I was shocked and devastated when I heard the verdict. It hit me like a thunderbolt.' And Rio's United and England team-mate Gary Neville said that Rio had been dealt with very harshly in light of a £2,000 fine handed to Manchester City's Christian Negouai for missing a drugs test the previous season. Neville said: 'You can't start making one rule for one and another for another. It's as simple as that. Perhaps the pressure from outside has gone against Rio.'

Others were not as sympathetic towards Rio. On hearing of the sentence, Dick Pound of the World Anti-Doping Agency said: 'I don't know what the disciplinary board heard that caused them to give a penalty that is only a third of the maximum. But it is clear they have rejected any suggestion that Ferdinand accidentally failed to take the test.'

Ironically, just before Rio's suspension took effect on 20 January 2004, he played one of his finest games for United in their 2-1 win at Tottenham, which took them to the top of the Premiership. Team-mate Mikael Silvestre was full of praise for Rio after the game: 'We knew Rio had a hard day and hard night after the hearing and he probably didn't get much sleep either but he was fantastic at Tottenham. That shows his character to come through and carry on playing. It's been a release for him. Playing is the best way to get away from his problems.'

Boss Alex Ferguson made a point of defending his decision to play Rio. 'I was very pleased with him. It was probably the best thing for him, to get everything out of his mind and concentrate on playing football. He acquitted himself very well in the circumstances. His performances merit his place in the team. Since all this happened he has got better and better. He has great maturity and a great partnership with Silvestre so why should I leave him out?'

But Rio's alleged plans to sue the FA were effectively blocked by outspoken FIFA president Sepp Blatter, who insisted that under the laws of the game Rio could not take his case to a civil court. 'According to the statutes of FIFA and its member associations, in this case, no recourse may be made to civil courts' said Blatter, who denied earlier reports that he had threatened United with expulsion from the game should Rio take the civil action option. Blatter also 'noted with satisfaction that this case has finally been dealt with and a decision passed.'

However, Rio was assured that he would still retain the support of his sponsors and the players' union and there were many in the legal profession who believed the whole affair would not stand up to any real scrutiny. John Hewison, a senior partner with Manchester-based sports law firm George Davies, said: 'If it had been a criminal case, it would have been thrown out because there was no way Rio was ever going to get a fair trial.'

In January 2004, Rio's kid brother Anton had just broken into the West Ham senior side when he made a public appeal in the aftermath of Rio's playing ban. 'I'm there on the other end of a phone when Rio needs me. It will always be like that. Being the younger brother of a big star can be an advantage and the opposite.'

It was even pointed out that now Rio was sidelined, he'd have a lot more time to watch his kid brother play for the Hammers. 'It would be good if he comes to watch me sometimes but he does his own thing and I respect him for that,' added Anton.

The big question on everyone's lips in football was what on earth would Rio do with all his spare time now he'd been suspended from the game for eight months? Rio was preparing to appeal against the length of his playing ban as well as fronting an anti-drugs campaign in Manchester and his native south London. Then the tabloids spotted him out in a brand new £110,000 silver Bentley Continental GT sports coupe he'd just added to his collection – which already included a £36,000 BMW, a £168,000 Aston Martin, a £52,000 Lincoln Navigator and numerous other vehicles. Rio's latest toy had a 6-litre turbocharged 12-cylinder engine to help propel it from 0 to 60mph in just 4.7 seconds. There was even a built-in massager in the seats to help ease Rio's stress-ridden life.

On 18 March 2004, Rio withdrew his appeal against his suspension. The reasons for his about-turn were never fully explained, but it looked as if Rio was now going to have to swallow his punishment and hope he could revive his career when he was allowed to play again the following September.

United's European campaign came to a halt when they lost at home to Jose Mourinho's FC Porto in the second round of the Champions League. Many of the English club's fans believed that Rio's absence had considerably weakened the side. In the Premiership, results were not going United's way either and yet more fingers were being pointed at Rio's absence.

As if Rio's playing ban hadn't sparked enough bad publicity, he then had to endure yet more exposure of his personal life in the tabloids. On 21 March 2004, *The People* revealed how Rio had filmed himself having sex with two women – and then showed the video to his mates.

Both girls told the newspaper they were impressed with Rio's prowess between the sheets but felt humiliated by the way he showed the video of their orgy to pals. *The People* pointed out: 'News of Ferdinand's antics will also come as another blow to his long suffering live-in lover Rebecca Ellison.'

The incident happened after Rio met the two women while he was on holiday in his favourite holiday resort of Ayia Napa, where he'd earlier filmed another sex romp with some England pals. One girl told *The People*: 'It was wild sex. He was good in bed and well endowed. He could go on for hours. We'd stop and he would be ready to go again in no time.'

A spokesman for Rio would only say to the newspaper: 'We have no comment.' The girl insisted: 'He tries to pretend he is charming and the perfect gent. But it was demeaning the way he treated me. It left me feeling dirty and used.'

Manchester United's dismal showing in the run up to the Premiership title race sparked a surprising article from suspended Rio in the *Sun*. He told the paper there were no excuses for the club's disappointing dip in form which saw them have to qualify for the following season's Champions League after they finished third, behind Arsenal and Chelsea.

Rio insisted his playing ban should not have affected the club's form. He said: 'This club has enough good footballers to be able to cover for the absence of one individual. Of course I wanted to be out there doing my bit and helping the team. It has hurt not to be part of it. But I'm not someone who thinks if I'd been playing we'd have won the Premiership and the Champions League.'

Rio also missed out on a FA Cup winner's medal, thanks to his suspension, when his United teammates lifted the trophy after beating Millwall in the final at Cardiff's Millennium Stadium. The FA triumph was the eleventh time United had won the competition. A dazzling display by Ronaldo and a brace from Ruud van Nistelrooy helped them take the famous trophy back to Old Trafford. Rio insisted he was doing constructive things during his suspension, including working for the charity Sport Relief. He visited a special football programme for children from a range of ethnic backgrounds in Ashton-under-Lyne, near Manchester, and enjoyed a kick around with some of those involved. Rio explained: 'I'd like to think I've been using my spare time wisely. I've been training all the time with the rest of the lads but with not being involved in games I have also focused on other things.'

But an increasing number of Manchester United fans were wondering whether Rio's 'forgetfulness' in failing to do that drugs test had cost their team any chance of the two titles that really mattered – the Premiership and the Champions League. Although it must be said that Chelsea, who finished second, had been bolstered by a £100 million outlay on top-class players funded by billionaire new owner Roman Abramovich. United's attack seemed as strong as ever with free-scoring Ruud van Nistelrooy but the midfield had been weakened by David Beckham's departure to Real Madrid and the defence had sorely missed Rio.

Sometimes it seemed as if Rio's main preoccupation while suspended from the game was to write articles for the *Sun*, sister paper of the *News of the World*, which had exposed Rio's antics off the pitch numerous times. When, in May 2004, Manchester United bought fiery Leeds striker Alan Smith, Rio pitched in with words of praise for Smith, whose loyalty to relegated Leeds had seen him more than a little reluctant to switch clubs. Rio explained: 'People should understand Alan is doing what is right for him. He deserves a break. He has given everything for Leeds. He is not letting anyone down. He could not have done more to try and keep them in the Premiership.'

Rio's response to the Smith transfer was heartfelt because

in many ways this was exactly how he felt about leaving the Yorkshire club two years earlier. Rio added: 'Alan will love it at Old Trafford. I never regretted the move for a moment – and I am sure he won't either.'

On the eve of the European Championships in Portugal in the summer of 2004 it was publicly revealed for the first time that Rio – still serving his eight-month ban – had made 'up to twenty' phone calls to FA chief Mark Palios before his hearing, saying he was prepared to face a long club ban if he could play for England in Portugal.

The rest of Europe was amazed at the treatment of Rio. Most other football associations usually only banned players in such circumstances for four or five months. It even emerged that the FA had been pushing for Rio to be banned for twelve months, instead of eight. Rio's agent Pini Zahavi commented: 'Rio should be playing in the European Championships and his ban would not happen in any other country than England.'

Just before the European Championships kicked off, Rio made a special journey to visit the England squad at their Manchester hotel to wish them luck. His old friend Frank Lampard explained: 'Rio came to have dinner with us. Everyone knows how good a player Rio is and we will miss him. It must be hard for him at the moment. I know from talking to him that the closer we get to the matches the more frustrated he is feeling.'

In the middle of June 2004 – which should by all accounts have been a football-obsessed month – Rio's colourful personal life once again hit the headlines thanks to his 'old friends' at the *News of the World*. This time a pretty brunette called Holly McGuire told the paper that she had been Rio's secret lover for four years. That meant he had been juggling two long-term mistresses in addition to live-in partner Rebecca Ellison, because an air hostess had earlier told the paper about her three-year affair with Rio.

A friend of Holly's told the *News of the World*: 'Rio's family live in London so he'd tell Rebecca he was seeing them. He was very careful that no one found out about their affair – least of all Rebecca – but Holly was like a drug to him. He couldn't resist her.' The affair had only ended earlier that year. Holly's friend added: 'She doesn't want to see or speak to him again. She's wasted a lot of time on someone who is not free. She deserves her own man now.'

Yet again, one of Rio's friends spoke up for him with a quote to the *News of the World*: 'Rebecca is the love of his life, his rock. She'll be devastated but Rio won't want to lose her – she is the one.'

Two months later, another brunette came out of the woodwork and told *The People* newspaper that she'd enjoyed hours of lovemaking with Rio in a Tokyo hotel during the 2002 World Cup campaign. Aussie-born Coralie Robinson said that Rio's lovemaking skills had 'turned me into an animal in bed.'

Hours after waving goodbye to Coralie, Rio found his long-term partner Rebecca turning up unexpectedly in Tokyo. As one of Rio's pals later explained: 'She'd decided to surprise Rio because she knows what he's like.' Rio's penchant for slipping out of trouble seemed to know no boundaries.

When Rio returned to pre-season training at Manchester United, he amazed team-mates by showing up sporting a big afro hairstyle after growing it throughout the summer. One local barber even offered to pay £10,000 to charity if Rio would allow him to give him a trim. Rio came up with his own solution, though, by tying his hair in braids

instead of going for a short back and sides and it is a style he has stuck with ever since.

Even when it came to hairstyles, Rio seemed capable of sparking newspaper headlines across the world...

Chapter 21

Rio Grand

Rio's personal life had already been blasted across enough front pages when Channel 4 screened a documentary featuring video footage of Rio's sex romp in Ayia Napa, 'co-starring' England stars Frank Lampard and Kieron Dyer a few years earlier. The programme – 'Sex, Footballers and Videotape' – pulled in an estimated 5 million viewers and sparked furious responses from all of the players. Lampard's agent told one tabloid that the England midfielder was intending to sue Channel 4.

Channel 4 claimed the real-life footage illustrated a 'culture of group sex' that the producers claimed was rife amongst top footballers. The drama was based on documentary research and interviews with managers, agents, current and former Premiership players as well as women who'd slept with stars.

Meanwhile, at Manchester United, new signings Wayne

Rooney and Cristiano Ronaldo were grabbing all the headlines while Rio remained suspended until September. And defensive recruit Argentinian Gabriel Heinze had quickly won over the Old Trafford faithful with a number of superb performances for the club.

On 20 September 2004, Rio made his first appearance since his suspension ended, in United's clash with old rivals Liverpool. It was now 363 days since that fateful day when he'd missed the drugs test sparking his suspension. Rio was welcomed back like the prodigal son by the diehards of the Stretford End, who have always known when to throw a protective arm around their own, particularly those – Eric Cantona, David Beckham and Roy Keane – whom they perceive to be have been victimised because they play for United.

Rio's United boss Alex Ferguson made a point of telling a packed press conference before the Liverpool clash: 'I've never had more admiration for a lad than I have for Rio for the way he handled his suspension. He has been absolutely terrific.'

Many at the club shared Ferguson's opinion on how Rio dealt with his suspension, training wholeheartedly all week and then sitting in frustrated silence as his team-mates struggled without him. On the other hand, observers from outside the hierarchy believed that Rio's training, charity duties and habit of popping up at regular intervals to remind everyone of his sense of injustice in the *Sun* showed a cynical disregard for the rules of the game.

Rio's importance to the team had assumed almost legendary proportions during his absence, although some hardcore fans remained sceptical about Rio when he talked openly about a 'debt of honour' to Ferguson and the club for backing him so wholeheartedly.

Team-mate Gary Neville – who'd led the England players' protests before Euro 2004 – had even more praise for Rio: 'He certainly surprised me because I never believed anybody could show that degree of professionalism during those eight months. The way he came to training every day, the way he kept his focus. I half expected him to disappear on holiday until the following pre-season.'

Neville even pushed for Rio to get a rapid-fire return to the England team for their World Cup qualifying campaign match against Wales in early October. 'I know what Rio brings to Manchester United and England. In 2002 he and Sol Campbell were the best central defensive pairing in the World Cup, and Rio has a case for being considered one of the best in the world.'

Rio himself seemed to know that he owed both Ferguson and England boss Eriksson 'big time' – or at least that's what he told journalists. Within weeks of his return to Manchester United's team, Eriksson hailed Rio as the best centre-half he had ever seen. So, when Rio found himself back in the England team to face Wales, few were surprised. Rio explained: 'For your managers to be showing that sort of confidence in putting you straight back into two great teams breeds confidence in yourself.'

'Hopefully I will be able to keep repaying those two managers who have done that for me. In terms of having someone who shows loyalty towards me, Mr Eriksson has been great. He put his name to a statement supporting me and spoke to me a few times on the phone and having those sort of touches was a great help to me during the ban.'

Eriksson was positively glowing in his praise of Rio: 'He has been incredible since his return to the game – in many ways his performances have been impeccable. It has surprised me that Ferdinand is at this level already after having been out of football for so long. He must have worked very hard.'

But all that praise on the back pages didn't last long, for soon he was back on the front pages. At the end of October 2004, Rio was 'exposed' for being out clubbing hours after being given leave to miss a United game for his grandmother's funeral. Some were wondering if – not when – Rio would ever learn to keep his head down. Rio had missed United's Champions League away match against Sparta Prague. It's not known how Ferguson reacted to Rio's antics. But one observer seemed to sum up the player's character when he explained: 'Rio is Rio. He seems to be a law unto himself. I doubt if even this will persuade him to watch his back. He seems to believe he is above any real punishment. It's almost as if he's saying "catch me if you can" and laughing at everyone in the process. Only time will tell if his career can keep surviving the onslaught of stories about his off-the-field behaviour.'

Once again it was left to the *Daily Mail* to sum up Rio's current predicament: 'Whether he knows it or not, Ferdinand still has some repair work to do to his reputation at United. He may be a fine player but many supporters remain unconvinced of his commitment and, if he has any sense of responsibility at all, he should have felt more than a little embarrassed when he rejoined his team-mates for training at their Carrington headquarters two days after his latest nightclub appearance.'

Already eleven points behind Arsenal in the race for the title, United needed to keep winning to prevent their bitter rivals from North London reaching a milestone of fifty Premiership games unbeaten and claw back lost ground at the top of the table. It was rumoured that some of United's most senior players were unhappy with Rio's behaviour, but for the moment his place in the team remained unquestionable.

On the European front, United only got as far as the second round where they were knocked out by AC Milan after suffering 1-0 defeats at home and away. The Manchester United winning machine seemed to be faltering somewhat.

In April 2005, Rio's loyalty was put to probably its most severe test when he was spotted in two London restaurants with Chelsea chief executive Peter Kenyon. In one photograph, former United executive Kenyon appeared to be dining with Rio and his agent Pini Zahavi. Alex Ferguson was reported in one newspaper to be 'incandescent' with rage after seeing the pictures. Ferguson had already accused Kenyon of treating his former club United with contempt.

Many were asking how a man as experienced and shrewd as Zahavi could invite his most valuable client (Rio) to a London restaurant in which Kenyon was eating on a Saturday night without realising the publicity it would create. For the moment, that question would have to remain unanswered or simply a matter of coincidence. As usual Rio brushed off the rumours that he might be off to Chelsea. It seemed that nothing ever stuck on Rio. He had an amazing ability to sail close to the wind.

United ended the 2004/2005 season a disappointing third in the Premiership behind Arsenal and newly crowned champions Chelsea. Many were starting to wonder if the club's incredible run of success was grinding to a halt.

In May 2005, Rio was reported to have been head-butted by a gangster in Stockholm, Sweden, at the city's Café Opera club after security guards were said to have intervened to stop punches being thrown when the pair bumped into each other. A few hours later Rio was alleged to have 'caused chaos' in a hotel back in the UK during the pre-wedding celebrations for his old Leeds colleague Jody Morris. One guest at the hotel, near Watford, told a *Sun* journalist that Rio was amongst a group of guests 'knocking on doors, then squirting people with the fire extinguisher. I complained to the hotel. I was there with my young family. It was a horrible experience.'

Then it emerged that Ferdinand and Zahavi were involved in some protracted talks with United over Rio's contract. He was demanding £120,000 a week. Significantly, Ferguson fed the press a ringing endorsement of Rio, saying: 'I do not blame him. He wants to stay with us.' Ferguson also refused to criticise Zahavi, who later said: 'Of course he didn't say anything. Alex and I are friends and he trusts me.'

But the controversy surrounding Rio's 'encounters' with Kenyon had already highlighted the close relationship which now existed between Zahavi and United rivals Chelsea. The Israeli super agent's world had turned around since he first delivered Roman Abramovich to Chelsea in the summer of 2003. Having subsequently played a part in bringing in Kenyon and coach Jose Mourinho to Stamford Bridge, Zahavi was now more than just an advisor to the West London club, who'd just won their first championship in fifty years.

However, the ever-canny Zahavi continued to insist: 'Rio loves it at Manchester United and wants to stay there, but it depends on United, not on him, whether that happens. Everybody has to give a little. It's called negotiation. Rio deserves to earn, if not more than the other top central defenders in the world, then at least the same.' Zahavi added: 'Rio cannot see himself playing for another club and I can assure everyone that Chelsea is not on the agenda.'

But by late June 2005 Rio and agent Zahavi had still failed to agree a new contract with United. The club's fans were astounded that he would dare hold out for £130,000 a week considering the loyalty shown to Rio during his drug test 'problems'.

On 4 July, Rio was even booed by supporters during a 5-1 friendly win at Clyde. Many called him 'greedy', but United assistant manager Carlos Queiroz brushed off the abuse, saying: 'It's not a concern. Just a reaction from a few fans and it won't bother him.'

However, a few days later the *Mail on Sunday* reported that Alex Ferguson was furious with Rio for refusing to sign an improved contract offer of £110,000 a week and was intending to demand that the England defender make a public pledge of loyalty to the club. Rio was now holding out for £120,000 a week but United were refusing to go that high. Ferguson told the paper: 'He says he wants to stay so he should say that now. That would take away any lingering suspicions and doubts.'

Rio's old Leeds pal and new United team-mate Alan Smith insisted: 'Rio's fine. Rio's a player who will make his own mind up when he wants to sign a new contract. That's got nowt to do with me or the rest of the players. That's up to Rio. He's said he wants to stay with us. I'm sure he'll do that.'

In the middle of all the Manchester United controversy was the Glazer family of American multi-millionaires, who'd just completed a highly contentious takeover at Old Trafford. During United's Asia tour – which was marred by low attendances and questions about the absence of skipper Roy Keane – there were face-to-face clashes between supporters and members of the Glazer family. Fans stormed a VIP area in Beijing to vent their anger at Bryan Glazer, who was travelling with the official club party. Two men broke through a security cordon but had a reasonably civil conversation with Glazer, whose family were part of a takeover that had left United with debts of almost £100 million.

Then, agent Pini Zahavi threw the whole wages negotiations saga into confusion by telling the *Independent*: 'No-one is having talks. There is no need to speak. He has two years. There was at some stage an idea for a new contract but we could not reach an agreement.' However Zahavi then added: 'But he is loyal to Manchester United and I am sure at the end of the day he will stay.'

United chief executive David Gill tried to calm the situation down by telling the media: 'We want him to stay, he wants to stay and in my experience when that situation prevails, invariably the player stays.'

At the beginning of August 2005, Manchester United suddenly announced they had won the wages stand-off with Rio when he agreed to sign a new four-year deal worth around £5million a year, which effectively ended months of uncertainty over his future. It is believed that Rio settled for a weekly wage just in excess of £100,000. Rio privately told friends and associate he hoped that the settlement would mark the end of his summer of abuse from fans.

Rio and his England team-mates received one hell of a setback when they were thrashed 4-1 in a friendly by Denmark during the summer of 2005 and then beaten 1-0 by Northern Ireland in a World Cup qualifying game in September. The tabloids turned up the pressure on coach Sven-Goran Eriksson to drop Rio because England's place in the 2006 World Cup Finals in Germany appeared to be under threat and his performances in both games were poor.

Rio was pragmatic about his own form, which had noticeably dipped. He accepted that his own displays were not up to scratch and explained: 'If any player has a bad game it's there in the back of your mind in the next game. There's always a hangover. When you put in a good performance it puts it to rest a bit, although it doesn't completely disappear. After a bad defeat the sense of urgency always rises. It is like a wounded animal in a way, as you want to get out there as quick as possible and rectify it.'

After the Denmark defeat, coach Eriksson even insisted the England squad sat through a painful re-run of the game with their mistakes highlighted to learn from. 'We all agreed it was unacceptable,' explained Rio. 'I set my standards very high and that was nowhere near the standard. It was a case of it finally hitting home and showing us first-hand exactly what he wasn't happy with. We were disappointed and embarrassed as players.'

But it was the 1-0 defeat by Northern Ireland that turned up the pressure even more on Eriksson to drop Rio for the next World Cup qualifying game against Austria at Old Trafford at the beginning of October. 'Humiliation' was the most popular word used on the sports pages and it summed up the public's reaction to the shock defeat. Henry Winter in the *Daily Telegraph* wrote: 'England slumped to their most embarrassing defeat since the 1981 reverse to Norway. Bereft of thought and fight, strangled by a system they clearly did not enjoy, England's players lost their first qualifier under Sven-Goran Eriksson, who faces an autumn of deepening discontent. "Sack the Swede" chanted England's fans.'

A few weeks later, Rio rushed to the defence of under-fire teenager Wayne Rooney whose red card in United's opening UEFA Champions League Group D Game at Villarreal CF sparked even more criticism of the 19-year-old's temperament. 'Wayne has worked very hard on his discipline and improved it no end since coming to United,' explained a very fatherly Rio. 'He plays on the edge and that is important to his impact on a game, but Wayne is already being booked less regularly for United than he was at Everton.'

On the domestic front, Manchester United's opening to the 2005/2006 campaign seemed to be heading in a healthy direction with three straight wins but two draws and a defeat at home to Blackburn Rovers on 24 September were a mighty blow to United's attempt to keep up with all-conquering Chelsea, who started the season with nine wins on the trot and were already seven points clear of the rest of the pack by mid-October. And Rio couldn't put a foot right, or so it seemed. When United travelled to Fulham and won 3-2, Rio was heavily criticised for being at fault for both of Fulham's goals.

With speculation rife that he might be dropped from the England team, Rio once again admitted his own form had fallen below his own high standards. Rio said: 'You have to show the strength of character to come through the difficult times. I know I have got that and I know my team-mates have it as well.' Rio insisted that the embarrassing defeat in Northern Ireland would motivate the England team. He explained: 'Nobody wants to be associated with failing to qualify for the World Cup finals. I cannot imagine the shame of it. There is a huge responsibility on all of us to get England through. It would be one of the biggest disasters in sports history if we blew it and we must make sure it does not happen.'

Others, like former England defensive stalwart Terry Butcher, pointed out that Rio's place in the team was under threat. 'Chelsea's John Terry must be an automatic selection and Sol Campbell has been outstanding for Arsenal since returning from injury,' said Butcher. Rio certainly had his fair share of problems to sort out.

Eriksson remained typically pragmatic and even indicated that for the moment Rio's place in the England team was still safe. He said: 'I know he was criticised because of the two goals against Fulham, but I have seen him in many games this season and I think he is playing well.'

However, by the time of England's crucial World Cup qualifier against Austria on 8 October, coach Eriksson bowed to pressure from all directions and dropped Rio from the heart of his defence. There was a growing feeling that he had been under-performing for both club and country on at least the previous half a dozen games. Fans across the country applauded Eriksson's courage in dropping Rio. One of many soccer fansites on the internet summed up the reaction: 'The call for bold leadership was only a few hours old when Eriksson responded by dropping Rio Ferdinand. Although the Manchester United defender's poor form demanded discussion, few had expected that Eriksson would axe such an established member of his England team. Yet the centre half has shown such slackness since the 2002 World Cup finals and besides the eight-month drug test ban there have been dozens of misadventures, mostly self-inflicted.'

Chelsea skipper John Terry and Arsenal veteran Sol Campbell were paired for the Old Trafford clash with Austria but, as has so often been the case for Rio, he had a lucky break when Campbell was injured early in the second half and he came on as substitute.

England scraped through 1-0. That evening Holland defeated the Czechs, effectively handing England automatic qualification for the World Cup with the best runners-up record. The media once more lambasted Eriksson for a poor performance but from the players' point of view, the only thing that mattered was that they had booked their trip to Germany 2006.

Four days later, England faced group leaders Poland at Old Trafford with Rio restored to the side. This time England took control from the start and Rio never put a foot wrong as his side upped the tempo of the game and ended up comfortable 2-1 winners with a greatly improved performance and went to the top of their group above the Poles.

And in November 2005 England secured a gripping 3-2 triumph over long-standing rivals Argentina, with Rio, earning a place in the starting line-up, having to be on his mettle from the outset against the spirited South Americans.

Now the World Cup in Germany was beckoning and Rio was going to have to fight for his place in the England side. Many saw it as healthy competition and Rio had a habit of reacting well to this sort of pressure so, unless he had injury problems, Rio was on the verge of re-establishing himself on the world stage.

Chapter 23

EPILOGUE

It is with some justification that Rio has been regularly compared to Bobby Moore. There is something of Moore's air of detachment in the way Rio commands the turf. He appears to be able to handle huge responsibility without crumbling under pressure. It's obviously impossible to say what will happen to Rio in the future, but there seems little or no doubt that – providing no major injuries occur – he will be on the international stage for at least the next 10 years.

Rio catches the eye of every supporter of skilful football with hope for the future. His unflustered air, his extraordinary appreciation of positioning throughout a game. How he stepped up from youth-team football to the Premiership without any trouble. His serene, untroubled performances of the last couple of years and the way he virtually strolls around the park. These qualities also spur comparisons with players like Franz Beckenbauer. No one who appreciates the art of football can watch Rio without purring.

His calm assurance on the ball has set him apart from other English centre-backs, and his ability to bring the ball out of defence and initiate counter-attacks led Hammers manager Harry Redknapp to brand him the next Bobby Moore in the first place. Over the past couple of years that title has proved more of a hindrance than a help as it encouraged pundits across the nation to analyse Rio's every move in a football shirt, leading to pointed questions about his all-round game. But, typically, Rio has taken it all in his stride and will continue to improve his game at an impressive rate.

As his first-ever mentor, Dave Goodwin, explains: 'Rio trains hard, always wants to do some more, and even now when he goes home he puts on football videos to learn. I've never heard anyone say a bad word about him or against him.'

There ain't no stopping him now ...

Meanwhile, back in Peckham, the building that currently bears the name of the Friary Estate's most famous resident after Rio is already daubed in graffiti. The Damilola Taylor Centre was originally seen as a symbol of hope in a ravaged inner-city ghetto. But, despite all the efforts of local people, including Rio, little has changed on one of the most dangerous housing estates in Europe.

The tell-tale signs of urban unrest are still everywhere to be seen: abandoned shop fronts protected by metal bars, perimeter walls lined with razor wire, police in stab-proof flak jackets, crack dealers plying their trade just yards from a police station, groups of hooded youths on virtually every street corner.

Less than 50 feet from the spot where Damilola bled to death, the terrible legacy of violence and intimidation has meant a line of shops have remained closed down except for Mohammed's grocery, which still opens despite more than 20 assaults, burglaries and robberies over the past couple of years.

There are new buildings being constructed everywhere in a bid to regenerate the area, but will it work? As Camila Batmanghelidjh, who runs the Kids Company charity, which helps the troubled children in the area, explained: 'It is not just a question of buildings. What these youngsters need is human contact and resilient people who are going to stand by them and work with them.'

On the same street corners where Damilola and Rio spent their childhoods, bored youngsters continue to congregate, sometimes menacingly. The cancer that took hold of the Friary Estate many, many years ago will take more than the murder of one brave boy and the phenomenal success of another to cure it. Rio's adventures at this year's World Cup in Germany couldn't be more of a contrast.

But at least his story gives hope to the kids and proves there is a pathway out of there.

ACKNOWLEDGEMENTS

I owe my deepest thanks to many individuals who have helped me make this book possible. But without my son Fergus Clarkson's skill and knowledge, it could never have been completed.

Also, my heartfelt gratitude to everyone in the warm and welcoming area of Peckham, south-east London, whose help and guidance while I was investigating Rio Ferdinand's extraordinary rise to soccer stardom was unwavering. Top of the list is my good friend Jimmy McShane, whose knowledge of that particular 'manor' led me to numerous new angles and leads. Others I must thank include Rio's old pals Leon Simms, Steve Higgott and Yung Chu, plus Bob Duffield, Mark Woodham, Terry Burnside, John Blake, Heather Cartright, Billy Goodall and Frankie Taylor.